'Fifteen Rounds a Minute'

'Fifteen Rounds a Minute'

The Grenadiers at War

August to December 1914

Edited from the Diaries and Letters of
Major 'Ma' Jeffreys and Others

by
J. M. CRASTER

Pen & Sword
MILITARY

First published in Great Britain in 1976 by
MACMILLAN LONDON LTD

Reprinted in this format in 2012 by
Pen & Sword Military
an imprint of
Pen & Sword Books Ltd
47 Church Street
Barnsley
South Yorkshire
S70 2AS

ISBN 978 1 84884 685 2

Printed and bound by CPI Group (UK) Ltd,
Croydon, CR0 4YY

Pen & Sword Books Ltd incorporates the imprints of
Pen & Sword Aviation, Pen & Sword Family History, Pen & Sword Maritime,
Pen & Sword Military, Pen & Sword Discovery, Wharncliffe Local History,
Wharncliffe True Crime, Wharncliffe Transport, Pen & Sword Select,
Pen & Sword Military Classics, Leo Cooper, Remember When,
The Praetorian Press, Seaforth Publishing and Frontline Publishing

For a complete list of Pen & Sword titles please contact
PEN & SWORD BOOKS LIMITED
47 Church Street, Barnsley, South Yorkshire, S70 2AS, England
E-mail: enquiries@pen-and-sword.co.uk
Website: www.pen-and-sword.co.uk

For Fiona, with all my love –
second time lucky.

Contents

List of Illustrations

The editor and publishers are grateful to The Lord Jeffreys for plates 1, 2, 6, 13; to the Grenadier Guards for plates 4, 5, 7, 8, 9, 10, 11, 12, 14; and to the Imperial War Museum for plate 3.

MAPS

Reproduced from maps drawn by Emery Walker for
The Grenadier Guards in the Great War 1914–1918 Volume I
by Lieutenant-Colonel The Right Hon. Sir Frederick Ponsonby
(Macmillan, 1920)

Acknowledgements

This book would not have been possible without the enormous amount of help and kindness that has been forthcoming from all directions during its preparation. In particular I would like to thank Mr Patrick Forbes for his part in the genesis of the idea, and Mr Alistair Horne for his encouragement, his advice and my publisher.

I am most grateful to the present Lord Jeffreys for permission to use his grandfather's diary as the framework on which the rest of the story could be built and for providing many of the illustrations from his family albums, and my thanks are also due to the following: The Regimental Lieutenant-Colonel (Colonel N. Hales Pakenham Mahon) and the successive Regimental Adjutants of the Grenadier Guards who allowed me to research in and retain parts of the Regimental archives; Mr Ralph Abel Smith for permission to quote from the letters and diaries of his father, Lieutenant-Colonel Wilfrid R. A. Smith; Lady Gweneth Cavendish for permission to quote from the papers of her husband Colonel R. H. V. Cavendish; The Dowager Lady Hardinge of Penshurst, for permission to quote the letter from Lady Edward Cecil (later Viscountess Milner); Lord Killanin, for permission to include the account written by his uncle, then Lord Killanin, of the search for the graves of those killed at Villers-Cotterets; Lieutenant-General Sir George Gordon-Lennox, for permission to use the diary of his father, Major Lord Bernard Gordon-Lennox; Lord Ridley, for permission to quote from the diary of his cousin, Colonel E. D. Ridley; Sir Oliver Welby, for permission to quote from the diary of his brother, Lieutenant Richard Welby; The Marchioness of Zetland, for permission to use the letters of her father Colonel E. J. L. Pike.

Mr Harold Macmillan, Major-General Sir Allan Adair and

Acknowledgements

Colonel R. S. Lambert were all good enough to set aside some time to give me their personal recollections of the personalities involved.

Mr Antony Brett-James and Mr John Keegan of the Department of War Studies at R.M.A. Sandhurst were both kind enough to read the manuscript either in whole or in part, and to offer advice and guidance where needed. To Mr Ken White of the Staff College Library and his assistants I am indebted for their patience and help during the period of production.

Finally, I would like to thank Miss Caroline Hobhouse of Macmillan for the patience and good humour with which she has guided yet another complete novice through the complicated process of literary gestation; Mr Keith Simpson of the Department of War Studies at Sandhurst for undertaking the monumental task of compiling the biographical index; and Mrs Vanessa Leicester Thackeray for the production of an excellent, workable typescript from a chaotic manuscript.

J. M. Craster

Addendum

On the reissue of this book being first proposed I was delighted when, in reply to my plea, Richard Holmes responded with typical insouciance "Grim Reaper permitting, I would be happy to do a foreword for the admirable *15 rpm*." Alas that permission was not granted, and the loss of course was felt far wider than this modest sphere. But without Richard's quiet and continuing support this would not be happening. My thanks to Michael Orr, who picked up the ball and ran it over the line, and to Jamie Glover Wilson who has coaxed yet another idle author to the point of publication

I am supremely grateful to Major-General Sir Evelyn Webb-Carter KCVO, OBE, DL for his Foreword, and to the descendants of those who gave permission for the extracts from their forebears' letters and diaries to be used. Every effort has been made to contact them, but if this volume comes as a surprise to some I can only apologise!

Michael Craster
February 2012

Foreword

Richard Holmes, the well-known military historian, was going to write this Foreword but sadly for us all he died before he could do so. Although I am hardly worthy to take his place, it gives me great pleasure to write this foreword for an old friend, Michael Craster, with whom I served in the Grenadiers.

I remember vividly when "Fifteen Rounds a Minute" was first published, in 1976. It was well received then as a book of great interest to historians, but particularly so to Grenadiers interested in their forbears. Men such as "Ma" Jeffreys, Wilfred Smith and Lord Bernard Gordon Lennox were bywords for the Regimental standards which Colonel Craster summarises as "discipline, smartness and professionalism" – to read their hitherto unpublished accounts of those desperate days of 1914 was illuminating. Michael did particularly well to find so many linked contemporary accounts to reinforce those of Jeffreys' diaries, because they capture the mood and add huge depth to the story of a battalion engaged in those first few months of the Great War.

Like many of his brother officers, "Ma" was born in the Victorian era and had fought in colonial wars in South Africa, Egypt, and the Sudan; his Brigade Commander in 1914, Scott-Kerr, had fought in the Zulu War in 1879! Their age, now documented in sepia, was one dominated by the influence of the Queen Empress, the Church of England and a sharp sense of duty. These values were to be tested to the limit in the years following 1914, but in the diaries and accounts of these great men their relevance was clear and unequivocal. 1914 however was very different from those earlier skirmishes. If Michael and I can draw a parallel, the wars of the Victorian period, while sharp and unpleasant, were mostly 'small' in scope, like the operations in Northern Ireland in which he and I were involved, but they were followed by much more extensive and costly fighting, as the British Army and their allies have experienced in Afghanistan these last five years. 1914 heralded a war on an entirely different scale. "Ma" Jeffreys responded well to the challenges of commanding men under fire: by 1918 he was commanding a Division.

Richard Holmes and I rode the route of Retreat from Mons in 1992, and passed several of the places mentioned in this book. We stood by the spot where the 2nd Battalion of the Grenadiers withdrew from their position at Mons, which led to the Commanding Officer being removed from command, most unreasonably in our view. We went on to Landrecies where 4th Guards Brigade was surprised, and Jeffreys was caught stark naked in his bath and subsequently acquired a charger which survived the war with him. The Germans weren't supposed to traverse the great Foret de Mormal, which was incorrectly thought to be impassable. One of our most evocative days, however, was riding through that part known as the Foret de Retz to Villers Cotterets, and eating a picnic at the Rond de la Reine where the 2nd Battalion Grenadier Guards had a particularly bloody time. Richard, with his astonishing memory, recited to us parts of Jeffreys' diary for that day which brought the story to life, and revealed the tragedy of the futile search for the body of George Cecil, a popular subaltern and scion of the Salisbury family, killed aged 18.

Richard was to use these accounts extensively in his book "Riding the Retreat" and in "Tommy" which he wrote later. He placed great value on these diaries because they tell the story as witnesses saw it. "Fifteen Rounds a Minute" is not just of interest to Guardsmen, however. Most of the battalions of the 1914 British Expeditionary Force, who marched to war with very little heavy artillery and few machine guns per battalion, and with no helmets or hand grenades, shared similar experiences – and losses. While the battalions and regiments engaged (until late-October 1914) were all Regular Army, many of the soldiers in their ranks were reservists, hurriedly recalled to the Colours and breaking in new ammunition boots the hard way. Whatever their cap badge, the leadership and training of these battalions and regiments, which the diaries describe so well, and their remarkable shooting, guaranteed an enviable level of effectiveness, as German casualty rolls for that time testify. What better way to gain an understanding of those early days of Great War manoeuvre, confusion, courage – and simply "hanging on" and doing one's duty against huge odds – than to read this excellent book so well edited by my old friend.

Evelyn Webb-Carter
2012

Introduction

In the course of preparing the script for a battlefield tour of the Battle of the Marne 1914, run by the 1st Battalion Grenadier Guards in 1973, I found among the archives of the Regiment in Birdcage Walk an astonishingly rich collection of contemporary records. Even the 2nd Battalion War Diary, in general a sober account of daily happenings compiled by one author only, was made up of extracts from letters and diaries which gave it a life and colour not normally associated with these habitually dour volumes. The whole story of the battalion in those five months of war was there, told from every angle; from the hastily written operation orders by the Brigadier, through the vivid accounts by the officers of the engagements in which they had taken part, to the letters written by those of their families who had gone out to France afterwards to find the unmarked graves of the fallen.

The story was well told by all of them, but one narrative was outstanding; that of Major 'Ma' Jeffreys. He, alone of all except one of the combatant officers in the battalion, was present at, and survived, all the fighting of that summer and autumn, going with the battalion from Mons to the Marne, back to the Aisne, and finally to Ypres.

The style in which Jeffreys wrote, the grasp which he displayed of his subject, and the detail which he included, made his narrative utterly absorbing. Others wrote well also, but were unable to cover the whole sequence either because, like Bernard Gordon-Lennox, they were killed, or because, like Wilfrid Smith, they arrived later. My first idea, therefore, was that the Jeffreys diary should be published on its own, for it seemed wrong that such a tale should remain hidden in the archives. In the end, however, so much of the other material available cried out for inclusion that the project grew, and became a history of the 2nd Battalion in 1914, told in the words of those who took part.

So often is the First World War spoken of in terms of the trenches, the static warfare that dominated the Western Front from 1915 to 1918, that it is sometimes forgotten that this was not the manner in which it was expected that the war would be fought, nor was it the way in which the armies were engaged in 1914. The troops of both sides were trained to fight a war of movement, in which defensive positions, if occupied, would be held only for limited periods prior to the next advance or withdrawal. It was to be a war much in the tradition of the European wars that had preceded it, with the difference that this time the armies involved would be much larger. The picture painted by the letters and diaries is, therefore, quite unlike that portrayed in the contemporary accounts of a year or two later. It has the spice and variety of movement and change. There is room for the totally unexpected, and for a humour that is less macabre than that displayed by subsequent writers. The countryside, although suffering the effects, was not yet blasted by the war, and there was still time and scope for the visiting troops to note and comment on the peculiarities of their hosts. Indeed one of the interesting features of this collection is the gradual transition from the enthusiasm and optimism of the early days to the dogged pessimism of the latter days at Ypres, when this colour and diversity disappeared in a Flanders winter.

Inevitably the view of the regimental soldier will be a limited one, confined more or less to the actions on his own immediate front. The limitation must be accepted in an account such as this, but the deficiency is more than made up for by the immediacy and vigour with which the tale is told. As it unfolds it gives an intimate and personal view of a Battalion of the old Regular Army at war; and it gives also an insight into the people involved, both officers and men, their characters and their attitudes.

This was not quite an ordinary battalion of course. The Brigade of Guards, the modern Household Division, did not have a monopoly of discipline, smartness and professionalism in the B.E.F., but as an élite they did believe in the highest standards in all three, believe in them, demand them and maintain them, whatever the circumstances and whatever the cost. They might be matched, but never beaten. This attitude, the product of long traditions and much success, is well reflected in the writings of its officers. Approbation was not given lightly, either within or without the Brigade, but when given it was well merited. Those who served in 1914 were nearly all regular officers, but the memoirs of wartime officers such as Harold Macmillan and Oliver Lyttelton give a vivid picture of the way in which the standards were maintained throughout the war. The experience left a deep impression on all of them, and they carried many of its lessons into their later lives; summed up by Harold Macmillan's comment, 'I owe a great deal to what I learnt in the Brigade of Guards'.

The Grenadiers are the Senior Regiment of Foot Guards. Their friendly rivalry with the Coldstream goes back to the time of the Restoration of King Charles II, and many signs of it will be found in the pages that follow. The Irish Guards were still very new in 1914. Founded in 1900 by special order of Queen Victoria in recognition of the services of her Irish troops in the South African War, they had not yet seen action. But whatever their cap badge, all men of the Brigade were bound together in their sense of belonging to what was, in effect, a large family. Guardsmen should not be commanded by non-guardsmen, but on the other hand they would respond to the orders of any officer of the Brigade. In return they were heirs to a tradition of care for their welfare that was by no means always common at the time. Their officers were brought up to think always of their men first, of their own personal comfort and requirements later.

The guardsmen themselves were drawn from a wide variety of backgrounds. No longer the sweepings of society that had gone to make up the junior ranks in earlier wars, they yet provided a wide cross-section of the lower classes of the country. Although there is a strong Northern element in the Grenadiers, the strength of the branches of the Regimental Association through - out the Midlands, East Anglia and the South-West is a measure of the attraction of the Regiment's title and its reputation. Their size (due to the minimum height restriction) and their tremendous discipline made them indeed formidable opponents.

But it was not these factors alone that built the legend. There was a pride in themselves, in their regiment and in their conduct which would brook no comparisons, and which could not have been achieved by discipline alone. The days of the old long service soldier were passed, and a man no longer committed himself for most of his useful life when he took the Queen's shilling. He could now serve for 3 years, before leaving the service with only a commitment of 9 years on the Reserve. Many took advantage of these terms, and it was their ready response to mobilisation that made it possible for the battalions to be made up to their war establishment strengths so quickly in August 1914. In particular those who had left after the South Africa War, and now returned to the Colours – often in the most physically demanding roles, despite their ages – were a most valuable addition to units in which, at the junior levels at least, there was a shortage of experience of active service. But the backbone of the Regiment, then as now, was the nucleus of men, mostly non-commissioned officers but with a few privates, who had devoted their lives to the Regiment, to whom it was home and family, and whose customs, manners and traditions meant sometimes more than life itself. Despite continuing improvements in pay and conditions it was still a hard and tough life. However, at a time when life elsewhere was also hard it was perhaps less objectionable than might appear today.

In his *Origins and History of the First Grenadier Guards*, published in 1874, Lieutenant-General Sir Frederick Hamilton wrote:

Education and military information are the most absolute necessities for all officers, and thorough scientific studies quite indispensable for those who would rise to the top of their profession; but the strength of an army in the field, and its power to overcome its enemies in the day of battle, depend, after having once secured officers who can place their troops to the best advantage before the enemy, as much upon the spirit with which each officer and soldier is imbued, as upon the knowledge those officers may have acquired of their profession; and we may rest assured that the soldier in the hour of need and danger will ever be more ready to follow the officer and gentleman whom education, position in life, and accident of birth, point out to be his natural leader (as in the feudal times of old), than the man who, by dint of study and brainwork, has raised himself (much to his own credit, certainly) from the plough or the anvil, to rule without discrimination, and with a rod of iron, those who were born to be his superiors. In no profession should the feeling of *noblesse oblige* be more recognised than in the army, and we should be careful how, in enforcing the necessary amount of education for officers, we do not lose that high and independent spirit that is so essential. . . .

It is from such imperial echoes as these that the popular image of the Guards officer is often drawn. Leaving aside the ever contentious point – that leaders are born and not made – the public has preferred to believe in the search for amusement, the neglect of professional studies, the officers who capitalise on their membership of an exclusive club to make the most of all that Society has to offer, while leaving the work to their non-commissioned officers and guardsmen. It is a view which will hardly bear scrutiny today, and which even in 1914 was difficult to reconcile with the performance of the Regiments of the Brigade of Guards in war, and with the number of Guards officers to rise to positions of high command within the Army. There were, inevitably, those who having joined for a brief period only, were less concerned with the job than the opportunities for enjoyment. But there was a larger number who, without always aiming for high position, were nevertheless determined to produce the highest standard at their own particular level. 'A sense that, if a thing is done at all it ought to be well done', is for all Guardsmen, whatever their terms of service, an article of faith.

The result of this can be seen in the pages that follow. It was a very close, tight-knit community that took the Guards Battalions to war in 1914. They all knew each other well; many, like Lord Bernard Gordon-Lennox, had married the sister of a brother officer (in this case Lord Loch); and many, like George Cecil, had succeeded their fathers in the Regiment or, like Eben Pike and Bernard Gordon-Lennox again, were succeeded by their sons and grandsons. To them, as much as to their soldiers, the Regiment was a way of life, a family to which they belonged and which commanded their ultimate loyalty.

The picture of the Grenadiers that emerges from the diaries is of a thoroughly professional battalion, commanded by experienced officers all of whom, down to below Company Commander level, had already seen active service in South Africa. They went to war with high spirits, confident in their ability to defeat anything that the enemy could send against them. They entirely justified that self-confidence, although at a terrible cost to themselves. They held values and displayed virtues that are today often considered unfashionable but are not contemptible. Courage was not the least of them, and was the one that they shared in common with the rest of the B.E.F., but perhaps their most striking characteristic was their self-discipline, because from this all the others spring. Nowhere can this be seen better than in the work and writing of Jeffreys.

George Darell Jeffreys was the son of the Rt. Hon. Arthur Frederick Jeffreys, a Privy Councillor and the Member of Parliament for North Hampshire. Educated at Eton and the R.M.C. Sandhurst, he joined the Grenadiers in 1897 where he quickly acquired the nickname 'Ma' because, as Oliver Lyttelton explained '. . . It so happened that a well-known *maison de rendezvous* had been kept by a Mrs Jeffreys, known as Ma, and the subalterns were quick to transfer the sobriquet to their brother officer'.

He took part in the Nile Expedition in 1898, and the Battle of Khartoum, and served throughout the South African war with the Regiment. At the outbreak of war he was commanding the Guards Depot at Caterham. Almost immediately he was sent out to France as Second-in-Command of the 2nd Battalion, and he spent the remainder of the war on the Western Front, except for a period in 1916 when he was severely wounded. He rose steadily in rank, commanding the 1st Guards Brigade in 1917, and by the end of the war was commanding the 19th Division, having been mentioned in despatches nine times, and been made C.M.G. and C.B. He subsequently became the General Officer Commanding London District, and G.O.C.-in-C. Southern Command in India. After being A.D.C. to the King from 1936–38 he finally retired, and subsequently became Conservative Member of Parliament for Petersfield until 1951. He was created a baron in 1952, the same year in which he was appointed Colonel of the Grenadiers, thus breaking a succession of Royal Colonels of the Regiment that stretched back over a hundred years. He died in 1960 aged eighty-two.

A descendant of the seventeenth-century Lord Chancellor, notorious for his severity at the so-called Bloody Assizes after the Monmouth rebellion, Jeffreys had married in 1905 Dorothy, Viscountess Cantelupe, the widow of the heir to the seventh Earl De La Warr. A lady of strong character, she insisted on retaining her title despite her remarriage, which was the source of much gossip and speculation at the time among the less well-informed. In 1906 Jeffreys inherited from his father the house at Burkham, near Alton in Hampshire. Although they were to travel much over the years, and live in many different places, Burkham remained their home. Here the family lived during the 1914–18 War, and it was to Burkham that Jeffreys retired, after leaving the army, to follow his father's example and play a leading part in the life of the county. They had one son, Christopher, who joined the Grenadiers in his turn, and who, by 1939–40, had become the personal assistant to Gort, the C.-in-C. of the British Expeditionary Force. Christopher Jeffreys was killed in action at Dunkirk in May 1940, leaving two sons. To those who knew him and who served under him 'Ma' Jeffreys came to be something of a legend. Major-General Sir Allan Adair, who succeeded him as Colonel of the Regiment, wrote, 'He was the perfect Guardsman, absolutely straight and fair, quite ready to state his mind when he objected to anything – a great leader of men, always setting a high standard by his own example. No wonder we Grenadiers all respected and, perhaps I may say, loved him.' Although he subsequently rose to high rank he was at his best as a regimental officer. No one knew more about the workings of every aspect of a battalion's life. Harold Macmillan has described him as one of the greatest of Commanding Officers. The stories about him are innumerable; perhaps two may be quoted, both told by outsiders to the Brigade, to round out the self-portrait that emerges from his diary.

The first concerns Winston Churchill, who was attached to the 2nd Battalion Grenadiers at the end of 1915 to gain some experience of trench warfare before taking up a command of his own. He described his reception in 'Thoughts and Adventures':

Having packed what I thought was a very modest kit, I repaired to the Headquarters of the Guards Division and was most kindly welcomed by its gallant Commander. As soon as a frugal lunch was over, the General took me himself in his car to the Grenadier battalion I was to join as a Major under instruction. . . . The Companies had already begun their march to the trenches and the Colonel, the Adjutant and the Battalion Staff were on the point of setting out. There were salutes and smiles and clickings of heels. A few friendly commonplaces were exchanged between the Divisional General and the Battalion officers; and then His Lordship got into his car and drove off, leaving me very like a new boy at school in charge of the Headmaster, the Monitors and the Senior Scholars. We were to ride on and overtake the Battalion a mile or so ahead of us. My new host had considerately provided a pony; and jogging along we soon caught up the marching troops and reined our horses into a walk among them. It was a dull November afternoon, and an icy drizzle fell over the darkening plain. As we approached the line, the red flashes of the guns stabbed the sombre landscape on either side of the road, to the sound of an intermittent cannonade. We paced onwards for about half an hour without a word being spoken on either side.

Then the Colonel: 'I think I ought to tell you that we were not at all consulted in the matter of your coming to join us'.

I replied respectfully that I had had no idea myself which Battalion I was to be sent to, but that I dared say it would be all right. Anyhow we must make the best of it.

There was another prolonged silence.

Then the Adjutant: 'I am afraid we have had to cut down your kit rather, Major. There are no communication trenches here. We are doing all our reliefs over the top. The men have little more than what they stand up in. We have found a servant for you, who is carrying a spare pair of socks and your shaving gear. We have had to leave the rest behind.'

I said that was quite all right and that I was sure I should be very comfortable.

We continued to progress in the same sombre silence. . . .

It should perhaps be added that despite this somewhat inauspicious beginning Churchill very quickly established himself in the battalion, and a life-long friendship developed between himself and Jeffreys.

The second story is taken from an account in the Household Division Magazine of Spring 1975. It is an anecdote by Major J. Deverell, formerly Royal Artillery, who was acting as Forward Observation Officer in a part of the front line recently taken over by the 4th Guards Brigade at about the same time as the Churchill incident:

> On the night I remember . . . the 6th Division had been pulled out for a brief rest. To my alarm I found that I was now covering the Guards Brigade. . . . At dusk I paddled down the communication trench and in fear and trembling, presented myself to the Colonel of the Grenadier Guards. I was, of course, welcomed with the greatest charm, was given a magnificent plate of stew and a glass, not a tin mug, of whisky, and full of good cheer made my way to my bedroom. This was a shallow shelf, dug out of the wall of the communication trench, roofed with a sheet of corrugated iron to keep the rain off except through the numerous shell splinter holes, and almost three feet above the level of the water in the trench.
>
> Sleeping as only an eighteen-year-old can, I was awakened by a shake of the shoulder. Peering out into the near black darkness, I made out a huge figure scratching his ear and saying, 'Beg leave to speak, Sir.' I grunted, and he continued, 'Colonel's compliments, Sir, there is a gas attack. You, Sir, being a Gunner officer, have probably forgotten your gas mask. Here is one.'

Jeffreys wrote his account in a series of small pocket diaries. There were, inevitably, occasions when the pressure of events prevented him from writing up each day as it passed, but he always took the earliest opportunity subsequently of making up the deficiency. The picture drawn by this austere man, with his dry sense of humour and his eagle eye for detail, is a very complete one. I have however attempted to supplement it with extracts from the diaries and letters of some of his brother officers, and others, to cast extra light on some of the incidents that he describes. In particular I have drawn heavily on the diary of Major Lord Bernard Gordon-Lennox, one of the Company

Commanders of the Battalion, and on the letters and diaries of Lieutenant-Colonel Wilfrid Abel Smith, who commanded the Battalion from the middle of September 1914. Additional material has come from the diaries of Captain E. D. Ridley, Captain the Hon. E. M. Colston, and Lieutenant R. W. G. Welby, from the letters of Captain E. J. L. Pike, and from an account of the Battle of Ypres by Captain R. H. V. Cavendish.

My aim has been to allow those who took part to tell their own story. The gloss that has been provided is therefore not extensive. I have tried to sketch in the background against which the history of the battalion in these five months of 1914 unfolded, and to amplify those references which the participants made to events outside their own immediate milieu – nothing more. The extracts are presented as they appear in the documents from which they are taken complete with the sometimes rather hazy command of place-names, except for the occasional correction of a word wrongly transcribed, or the alteration of punctuation to allow the narrative to flow more easily. Unless otherwise stated in the text, extracts are from the Jeffreys diaries.

Addendum – January 2012

In the 36 years since the book was first published, much more has come into the public domain about those years of the Great War, and the detailed lives of the men who fought it. The experiences of Jeffreys and his comrades-in-arms have perhaps most recently been summarised in the chapter dealing with the conflict in Simon Ball's excellent "The Guardsmen", in which Jeffreys makes a number of appearances drawn from the accounts of those (generally junior) officers who had dealings with him. It is clear that he inspired awe and respect, not least for his supreme professionalism, but rarely affection, something that ran on perhaps into his family life. Only in the diaries does one find the occasional chink in this apparently complete armour.

But the book is about more than one man – it is about a battalion at war, and General Evelyn is absolutely right to draw the parallel between then and now. This was a battalion that had been hurled from peacetime soldiering into a war of an intensity the like of which had never before been seen. In the 50-odd years of peace that followed the end of the Korean War we have forgotten the reality of that type of conflict, and now the soldiers of today are relearning it – witness "The Junior Officers' Reading Club". Today's Grenadiers draw on the same qualities of self-discipline, comradeship and professionalism to enable them to do their duty.

I

'To take our part in the War'

WAR came to Britain on 4 August 1914. France and Germany
had mobilised on 1 August, but it was not until Germany invaded Belgium that Britain finally accepted the inevitable and
set in motion the plans to send the Expeditionary Force to take
up its position on the left of the French Armies. They were to
be the first British troops to fight on the Continent of Europe
for a hundred years, and their official historian described them
in a famous passage as 'in every respect . . . incomparably the
best trained, best organised and best equipped British Army
which ever went forth to war'.

Their committal was the result not of a formal treaty, but
of informal staff talks held between the French and British staffs
in the years succeeding the *Entente Cordiale*. A scheme was
worked out in detail by the staffs after 1911 for the landing of
the Expeditionary Force, and for its concentration in the area
of Maubeuge–le Cateau-Hirson. It was in accordance with this
scheme that the Force was deployed to take its place on the very
left of the Allied line.

Mobilisation had been planned in the greatest detail and had
been practised regularly. As a result the whole operation went
with remarkable smoothness and efficiency. The Reservists,
needed to bring the units up to war strength and summoned
by letter or by telegram, came pouring into the depots, where
they were issued with new equipment. In the time that remained
before embarkation some training was undertaken, particularly
route marches, to harden them in preparation for what lay
ahead. Movement orders were issued – with the ports of embarkation left un-named – and advance parties left on 7

August. In the event the main bodies crossed between 12 and 17 August, the troops sailing from Southampton and the stores and equipment from other ports around the country. The ports of disembarkation were Boulogne, Le Havre and Rouen, and from the camps here the troops moved up in a steady stream to the concentration area, where the B.E.F. was virtually complete in position by 20 August.

By this time the French had put into action their Plan XVII. The 'Battle of the Frontiers' with which this opened had met with some initial success in the attempt to regain the territories of Alsace and Lorraine, but the enthusiasm and confidence expended in the *offensive à l'outrance* had come to nothing. Defeated at Sarrebourg and Morhange, the French First and Second Armies were falling back. The Third and Fourth Armies were about to advance into the Ardennes with the aim of taking in the flank the German forces that were known to be massing there, before they could deploy and attack south. The French belief in 'the attack', the basis of all their military thinking and planning, had already been put severely to the test, and its cost to the country in lives – in particular the lives of officers and N.C.O.s that could ill be afforded – had been heavy. It was about to be shaken still further.

The French plan failed because the Staff did not appreciate the magnitude of the threat that faced them. Convinced that the Germans would not employ their reserve formations at the outset, the French Intelligence, in the days when the rival armies were concentrating and moving forward, estimated the enemy strength at only a little over half of the real figure. Such a miscalculation meant that the full significance of the German presence in Belgium was not understood until it was almost too late.

The success of German operations up to this time had been complete. Despite the check imposed by the gallant resistance of the fortress of Liège, the prosecution of the war had gone almost exactly according to their time-table. The Schlieffen Plan, which provided for holding operations in the east while sending a massive force pivoting on the fortified area of Metz-Thionville, wheeling through Belgium into Northern France, had been admirably executed. The employment of the Reserves in the front line from the beginning had given the three armies of the German right wing (on the right the First under Von Kluck, then the Second under Von Bülow, and on the left the Third under Von Hausen) a totally unexpected numerical superiority with which they threatened to overwhelm the Allied left wing, comprising the French Fifth Army under Lanrezac and Sir John French's British Expeditionary Force. Thus the Germans mustered seventeen Corps (thirty-four Divisions) of which seven Corps (fourteen Divisions) were Reserve formations, while opposing them were the five Corps (ten Divisions), five Reserve Divisions and the Cavalry Division of Lanrezac, and the two Corps (four Divisions) and the Cavalry Division of the British.

Little of this was known to the men of the B.E.F. as they set off on 21 August to take their part in the general advance ordered the night before by General Joffre, the French Commander.

The British Expeditionary Force that landed in France in August 1914 consisted initially of four of the six Infantry Divisions of the Regular Army at that time serving in England, with the addition of the Cavalry Division and five Battalions of Lines of Communication Troops, of whom four were subsequently formed into the 19th Infantry Brigade. It was divided into two Corps, I Corps commanded by Lieutenant-General Sir Douglas Haig, containing the 1st and 2nd Divisions, and II Corps commanded by General Sir Horace Smith-Dorrien (his predecessor, Lieutenant-General Sir James Grierson, having died in the train on his way to the front) containing the 3rd and 5th Divisions. III Corps was formed under the command of Major-General William Pulteney at the end of August and included the 4th Division which landed in France on 22/23 August, and the 6th Division which embarked for France on 8/9 September. The Cavalry Division was commanded by Major-General Edmund Allenby. Further reinforcements were received in time for the Battle of Ypres in the form of the 7th Division commanded by Major-General Thompson Capper and the 8th Division under Major-General Francis Davies, grouped together in IV Corps under Lieutenant-General Sir Henry Rawlinson; the 3rd Cavalry Division which joined the newly formed Cavalry Corps; and the Indian Corps under Lieutenant-General Sir James Willcocks.

The 4th Guards Brigade, to which the 2nd Battalion Grenadier Guards belonged, was one of the three Brigades of the 2nd Division under Major-General Monro. The others were the 5th and 6th Infantry Brigades. Commanded by an ex-Grenadier, Brigadier-General Scott-Kerr, who was wounded at Villers-Cotterets on 1 September and was succeeded by another ex-Grenadier, Brigadier-General the Earl of Cavan, the 4th Guards Brigade was made up of four Guards Battalions: the 2nd Battalion Grenadier Guards, the 2nd and 3rd Battalions Coldstream Guards and the 1st Battalion Irish Guards. For the last named it was a momentous occasion, as this was to be the Regiment's first experience of active service.

The Grenadiers landed in France with twenty-nine officers and some thousand men. Brought up to its War Establishment, the Battalion was made up of a small Headquarters and four Companies. The Headquarters consisted of the Commanding Officer, Lieutenant-Colonel N. A. L. Corry D.S.O., his Senior Major (or Second-in-Command), Brevet Lieutenant-Colonel Lord Loch D.S.O., M.V.O. and the Adjutant, Lieutenant I. McDougall. The four Companies each had a Company Commander (sometimes referred to as 'the Captain'), a Company Second-in-Command, and four Platoon officers. No. 1 Company was commanded by Major G. C. Hamilton, No. 2 by Major Lord B. C. Gordon-Lennox, No. 3 by Captain D. C. L. Stephen, and No. 4 by Captain the Hon. E. M. Colston. In addition the Battalion had a machine gun section of two guns, under a machine gun officer, a small signalling section, the Quartermaster's Platoon, responsible for the provision of all stores and rations, and its transport (all horse-drawn), under the Transport Officer. Wearing khaki service dress and the khaki cap, they were armed with the Lee Enfield .303 rifle with which the British army as a whole had developed a standard of shooting that was unrivalled among the other armies of the world. It was the ability to produce a firing rate of fifteen aimed rounds a minute (the so-called 'mad minute') that did so much to break up the massed German attacks that autumn, and to convince the enemy that they were facing a force with an immense superiority in machine-guns.

The British were accustomed to fighting the small wars inherent in the process of Imperial expansion. Its experience of active service around the world brought to the Army a pro-fessionalism in the field, especially in the lower echelons, that was not always available to its Continental contemporaries. A study of the Army list shows that many of its officers of the rank of Captain and higher are described as having 'seen war service', often in South Africa. On the other hand the colonial war, fought against an enemy usually inferior in equipment if not in numbers, was a quite different matter to the conflict on which the Army was now embarking. In particular a European war required an experience in the commanding and controlling of large formations which was not always available to the Staff of the B.E.F., whereas constant practice had perfected it in the French, and in particular, the German armies.

British tactics in 1914 had also evolved from the experience of the South African War. The fundamental principle on which all else was based was that of 'fire and movement', one part of a unit or formation moving, while covered by the fire of the other part, until a suitable firing line was reached from which an assault could be made. Emphasis was laid on the spacing of troops, leaving a suitable distance between individuals to mini-mise the effect of enemy artillery fire. Artillery support for an attack was provided by the Royal Field Artillery (R.F.A.), of which three batteries of 18 pounders were available to the Brigade, while a further three batteries of 4.5 in. howitzers were in support to the Division. Control however was a very diffi-cult problem without modern means of communication, and artillery support for the infantry had not yet been perfected to the degree attained later in the War.

British methods, as befitted an all-Regular army, laid stress on the initiative of the individual. French and German tactics, however, dealing with enormous conscript armies, made much more of mass attacks, almost in the tradition of the wars of a century earlier. The French in particular, fired with the spirit of *l'attaque*, persisted in this costly expedient in the face of over-whelming defensive machine gun and artillery fire, and paid an extreme penalty in loss of life. All too often they failed to make the best use of their '75', the best quick-firing field gun on the Western Front, to support their assaults. The Germans on the other hand learned quickly, and by the start of the Battle of Ypres their more experienced formations had learned to copy the British. The one great advantage that the Germans possessed was their artillery, which was plentiful and very good, and which was always used to soften up the objective before any attack. Nonetheless, even at Ypres many of their units continued to advance to the assault in close formation, and suffered annihilation in consequence.

Ypres saw the end of the tactics of open warfare. With the armies fighting from static positions, amid all the amenities of a long-prepared defence, the principles of fire and movement remained in abeyance until revived and re-taught for use in 1918.

On 21 August the first units of the B.E.F. moved off from their concentration area to take their place on the left of the Allied armies. On their right was the French Fifth Army. On their left there was nothing between them and the sea except a few scattered cavalry patrols, and some French Territorial troops. Their advance coincided with the advance of the French Third and Fourth Armies into the Ardennes. On the 22nd the first contact was made with the Germans, and by that night the two British Corps had closed up on Mons. I Corps was on the right, facing north-east, and II Corps on the left, facing north. From these positions the next day they fought the Battle of Mons.

In this battle, during which the British engaged and halted Von Kluck's First Army, the 4th Guards Brigade played a small part. Placed in reserve, it sent two Battalions, the Grenadiers and the Irish, to the support of the 3rd Division where they remained behind the Royal Irish Rifles on Hill 93, without being engaged, for the rest of the day.

Although the British held their own that day the French on their right were less successful. Their Third and Fourth Armies had met with disaster in the Ardennes. The Fourth Army was retreating and Lanrezac, shaken by the attacks of Von Bülow's Second Army and finding his own right wing now exposed, had decided to withdraw also, leaving the British with little option but to conform. Thus began the Retreat from Mons, in which the B.E.F. covered some hundred and ninety miles in fourteen days under the most trying circumstances. The Allies were pushed back with bitter fighting. On the left II Corps, which had borne the brunt of the Battle of Ypres, made its historic stand at Le Cateau on 26 August and finally managed to break contact, although at a heavy cost. I Corps, under less pressure, fell back steadily behind a series of rearguard actions. In the meantime Joffre spent the last days of August preparing his counter-stroke, the key to which was the new French Sixth Army, under General Maunoury, created from the Army of Paris and positioned to take the German right wing in the flank.

The Retreat involved the 4th Guards Brigade in much weary marching, and, even more exhausting, the digging of interminable trenches which were no sooner dug than they were abandoned. Only twice were there serious engagements, the first of which was at Landrecies on 25 August, when the Brigade was surprised in billets by the advanced guard of the German 7th Division who had marched on the town with the intention of billeting there themselves. In a sharp night engagement the 3rd Battalion Coldstream Guards drove them off with a loss of 127 casualties. The second engagement, on 1 September at Villers-Cotterets, was more serious. While acting as the rearguard to the Division in the forest north of the town, the Brigade was attacked by elements of the German III Corps. In the subsequent sharp fighting in thickly wooded country the Germans lost over three hundred officers and men. The Retreat continued uneventfully thereafter, and by 6 September the Brigade was at Fontenay, south of the River Marne.

The opening shots of the Battle of the Marne, Joffre's counter-stroke against the German right wing, were fired on 4 September. On 6 September a general advance was ordered, and was greeted with immense enthusiasm throughout the B.E.F. who, in the best insular manner of British troops, had never understood the need to withdraw in the face of an enemy whom they considered to be in no way their superior. The fighting was heavy. The Germans were not prepared to renounce their great successes easily. On 9 September, however, with the widening of the gap between their First and Second Armies, into which the British were advancing, the German Supreme Command ordered 'preparations for occupying a rearward defensive position to be made at once'. In the days that followed their forces were pushed back to the line of the River Aisne.

In the early stages of the advance from the Marne the 4th Guards Brigade formed the vanguard of the 2nd Division.

Although they suffered some shelling and took many prisoners
they were not held up until 8 September when the Germans
fought a delaying action on the line of the Petit Morin, a small
stream south of the River Marne. In a brisk, if confused, little
engagement the Brigade – now under the command of Lieutenant-Colonel Fielding, Coldstream Guards, Brigadier-General
Scott-Kerr having been badly wounded at Villers-Cotterets –
eventually forced the crossing by outflanking the enemy. (It is
worth noting that throughout this fight both the Divisional
and the Corps Commanders were at the scene, having come up
to discover for themselves the reason for the delay, which would
account for the agitation displayed by the Brigade Commander
and noted in the entry for 8 September.) Thereafter the Brigade
remained in reserve, and it was not called upon again until 13
September.

By the night of 12 September the B.E.F. had closed up to the
south bank of the River Aisne. On their left General Maunoury's Sixth Army had also come up to the river while on their
right the Fifth Army, although over the River Vesle and in
contact with the British, was not so far north. The next day
crossings of the Aisne were effected in several places, and were
consolidated on the 14th, by which time, except for a salient
around Condé, the B.E.F. had established positions north of the
river along the whole of its front, and was supported by the
French who had come up on either flank. On the night of 14th
the position was still precarious. There was no permanent bridge
over the Aisne available to the British, and the nature of the
terrain (steep, heavily wooded slopes, rising straight up from
the river banks) made it very difficult for their artillery to deploy effectively in support of the infantry. The Corps were extended over a very wide front, with practically every battalion
in the firing line, and the strength of the enemy in front was
still uncertain, although it was plain that a determined stand
was being made. On the 15th the Germans attacked along the
whole line, and by that night it was clear that the Allied advance had been halted. In these positions therefore the line
stabilised, and on 16 September orders were given for it to be
strongly entrenched. In the event these positions were to remain virtually unchanged until 1918.

On 13 September the 2nd Battalion Coldstream Guards forced

the passage of the river, and advanced to the top of the ridge on the other side. The crossings remained under enemy fire, however, and that night the Divisional Commander ordered the withdrawal of the Battalion back across the river. The 5th Brigade however remained on the north bank, and it was one of the Battalions of this Brigade (the 2nd Battalion the Connaught Rangers) that the Grenadiers found in occupation when they crossed the following morning. The fighting on the 14th was heavy and progress was limited. The whole Brigade was committed and by that night they had established themselves on the ridge above Soupir but could go no further. Here they stayed, except for a slight adjustment that resulted in a movement a mile or so to their left, until 13 October.

With the situation deadlocked on the Aisne, and with the success of the French defence in Lorraine, both sides now looked to the western flank for further progress. Here, and here alone, there still existed the chance to continue the enveloping movements which could bring decisive success. During the next three weeks, therefore, there took place that extension of the battle-line northwards which came to be known as 'the race to the sea'. It was a race between the French and the Germans, the moves of each being blocked by further offensive moves of the other. British involvement came with the despatch of the Naval Division and the 7th Division to help in the defence of Antwerp. While planning for this move was being carried out Sir John French suggested to General Joffre that the British forces should be transferred to their former place on the left of the line. This would allow the new arrivals to be brought under command, and would give a great advantage in shortening the lines of communication. This proposal was agreed, and the move began on the night of the 1/2 October, II Corps being the first to go. I Corps were the last, handing their trenches over to the French on the night of 12/13 October.

In his initial deployment Sir John French aimed to continue the enveloping movement of the German right flank. The true strength of the opposition was not appreciated at this stage. II and III Corps therefore pushed forward to the Aubers Ridge south-west of Lille, with II Corps on the right and III Corps continuing the line northward. By 19 October the line ran from La Bassée in the south where II Corps were in touch with the

French, to the Ypres–Commines Canal, where the Cavalry on
the left of III Corps were in touch with the right of the 7th
Division around Zandvoorde and Zonnebeke, south-west of
Ypres. On the left of the 7th Division were the French Cavalry,
linking in with the Belgians. In accordance with the policy of
trying to find the German flank, I Corps was committed to the
north of the 7th Division.

In the days that followed powerful German attacks forced II
and III Corps, and the Cavalry on their left, to give ground. In
the north I Corps met with some initial success, but by 28
October it also had been thrown on to the defensive, finding
itself opposed by considerably superior forces. From the 29th
onwards it became apparent that the main thrust of the
German attack was being made north of the River Lys, in the
area held by the Cavalry and I Corps, culminating on 31
October in an all-out drive to break through to reach the Channel ports. The line of the 1st Division was broken at Gheluvelt
and the Divisional Commander killed when his headquarters
was shelled. The situation was saved by the gallant counter-
attack of the 2nd Battalion the Worcestershire Regiment that
retook Gheluvelt. On 1 November the Cavalry were finally dislodged from the Messines Ridge, but by this time French reinforcements were coming up, and took over the line between
the left of the Cavalry and the right of the 7th Division (which
had now been absorbed into I Corps). Although the pressure
continued it did not reach the same intensity until 11 November,
when the great attack by the Prussian Guard again broke
through the line of the 1st Division and penetrated to Nonne-
Bosschen wood, where it was checked and finally dislodged by a
counter-attack by the 52nd Oxfordshire Light Infantry. This
was the last major German attack, and on 15 November the
French began to take over the positions in the Ypres salient,
allowing the exhausted remnants of I Corps to withdraw.

'First Ypres' cost Britain the best of her fighting men; but it
was a magnificent exit. As Liddell Hart wrote, 'They attained
their end – in both senses. Ypres saw the supreme vindication
and the final sacrifice of the old Regular Army. After the battle
was over, little survived, save the memory of its spirit.'

The 4th Guards Brigade was committed to the battle on 20
October. Their first operations took place along the Zonnebeke–

Langemarck road, followed by an attack further south on Reutel. On 30 October the units of the Brigade became split up, as mounting casualties throughout the Corps made it necessary for battalions and even companies to be detached and sent to wherever the need of the moment was most urgent. The Brigade Commander, Lord Cavan, was ordered to take his two reserve Battalions, the Grenadiers and the Irish Guards, to support the right flank of 2nd Brigade in the area of Klein Zillebeke. The detachment remained here for three days, and on being relieved by the French moved to the support of the Northamptonshire Regiment in Zillebeke wood. After nine very trying days in this position the Grenadiers went into Corps Reserve for four days, during which time they took part in the abortive counter-attack at Polygone Wood on the night of 11/12 November. On returning to Lord Cavan's command on 15 November the Battalion found itself back on the Zillebeke road, but this time split into two halves on either side of the Cavalry Brigade. Here they were subjected to their last engagement during the battle, the attack on 17 November.

On 19 November the Battalion was finally relieved in the trenches, and on the 20th they moved off to rest and refit at Meteren. It was from here, a reconstituted Battalion with only a few survivors of the original unit of August, that they moved down to Festubert on 22 December to take their place once again in the line.

2

'A date that is easily remembered'

WHEN the Grenadiers sailed for France Major Jeffreys was still serving at the Depot at Caterham. It was not until after their arrival that Lord Loch, the Senior Major or Second-in-Command, was posted to the Staff and that Jeffreys was sent across at short notice to replace him. The following account of the Battalion's arrival in France is drawn from the diary of Major Lord Bernard Gordon-Lennox, commanding No. 2 Company.

12 August 1914

A date that is easily remembered and the more so in this special case as we left Chelsea Barracks to embark for an unknown destination to take our part in the War and to help the brave Frenchmen and Belgians. Queen Alexandra, Princess Victoria and Princess Henry came to see us off from Barracks and we were all presented to the former before leaving. We had a hot but uneventful journey down to Southampton Docks, where we embarked on board the Cawdor Castle: we found the 3rd Battn. Coldstream Guards already half on board. Shipping the horses and waggons and carts was a long job and we were not finished until 7 p.m. Dig's horse and mine provided the most trouble and for some time resisted all efforts to be boxed. We were packed pretty tight on board and it was a good quarter of an hour's work to pick one's way along the deck over the recumbent forms from one end of the ship to the other. The Brigadier and Staff were also on board, and various small etceteras, such as Signalling Company and R.E. To show with what secrecy our destination had been kept, the Captain of the ship did not know where we were bound for till actually under weigh. Eventually we left about 8 p.m. and it was a lovely night, with not a ripple on the water, which was just as well, as it would have been remarkably unpleasant with so many men on board had it been rough. The night passed quietly enough but once soon after starting, we had to go full speed astern to avoid running down a tug. Just before going to bed, we were told our destination, which was to be Havre. This had been my 'one horse snip' all along. We sauntered quietly across the Channel, which was like a mill-pond and awoke next morning to find a lovely morning and out of sight of land.

13 August 1914

We kept on slowly and as we neared the French coast we went close by several fishing boats and trawlers, the crews of which waved frantically at us and cheered us to the echo. We responded by singing the Marseillaise, which caused a continual "eep 'eep 'ooray' in return. I have no doubt that we shall hear several more ' 'eep 'eeps'. Every boat that we passed got its quota of cheering and song (?) including the pilot boat. We went very slowly into Havre – the tide not being right – but we eventually fetched up alongside our quay about 11 a.m. after having passed through endless docks and basins, the shores of which were lined with little groups who emitted the now usual ' 'eep 'eep 'ooray' intermixed with cries of Vive l'Angleterre and Vive les Anglais. These French people are certainly enthusiastic beyond British comprehension and it would do old England a world of good to see the unbounded patriotism and bon camaraderie displayed on all sides. It was fearfully hot in the docks, a blazing sun and no wind. We (2nd Battn. Grenadier Guards) disembarked first and formed up in an enormous hangar alongside the quay, and awaited the disembarkation of our transport. This was carried out much more expeditiously than the embarkation, and the horses were walked down a gangway in a continual stream. At Southampton on the previous day there were not enough appliances, and the horses had to be boxed and hoisted into the hold one by one. We then started off on our march to the Rest Camp and never shall I forget that march to my dying day: it was the hottest march I have ever done and hope ever shall. Our rest camp was about five miles off and our way led us through numerous docks into the town. Here we had an even more enthusiastic welcome than ever, the inhabitants crowding round us and throwing flowers at us with the usual cries. With the sun on our backs and no air, everyone felt the heat very much, and the men started falling out, a few at first and then more. The inhabitants in their kindness were responsible for a good lot of this, as they persisted in giving the men drinks, among which was a very acrid form of cider, which had dire results. I have never seen march discipline so lax before, and I hope I never shall again. At our first halt the kind ladies ran up and down pouring out water, and such was the heat that we all just allowed it to be poured over our heads and let it run down inside our clothes – we couldn't be wetter and we might be cooler – for a short time. After our first halt we started climbing up a long and steep hill and the men fell out by tens at a time: they simply dropped down in the roadway face downwards, and I had to pull several out of the way of the rest of the column bodily, just leaving them at the side in any bit of shade there was, where they were attended to by the inhabitants – it was impossible to look after them all individually. At length we reached the top and had a long halt just short of camp in the shade, there being no shade in camp. We then went into camp and arrived there about 4 p.m. and were glad to get there. We all undressed as much as possible and let our clothes dry on us. Our baggage turned up during the evening and we were real glad to get a change. George Powell our Mess President, and the indefatigable O.R.Q.M.S. [Orderly Room Quartermaster Sergeant – Chief Clerk] Martin had meantime gone off on a foray and returned with numerous good things for our consumption. We had a good, if modest dinner, and were glad to get to bed in a tent. The men had already begun fraternising with the French soldiers and it was most amusing to see the sort of dumb crambo show going on between them. The Frenchmen were all oldish sort of men, & territorials – called out to garrison Havre and do fatigues etc. as there is going to be a permanent camp there – the rest, bar a few *chasseurs*, being all up at the front.

14 August was spent in the camp at Le Havre. That night the Battalion moved off for the Front. This description is also taken from Major Gordon-Lennox's diary.

15 August

We entrained about 2 a.m. and were soon off: the accommodation was bad and the men very crowded. We got bumped about throughout our journey in a most ruthless fashion: there were no brakes such as we know in England on a passenger train, as there were trucks in which our horses & waggons were: the consequence was whenever the train wanted to stop, there was a succession of the most awful bumps imaginable. Before we got to our destination we got quite clever at anticipating them, and made everything fast till it was over. Our first stop was Rouen, where we arrived about 6 a.m. and were expecting to halt for an hour – we had been told so – an *arrêt pour repas* – which was to consist of hot coffee etc. We only stopped there ¼ of an hour and the coffee might possibly have been hot yesterday. Then we bumped along to Amiens. Each little wayside station through which we passed and all bridges and approaches to the line were thronged with people who cheered us. On arrival at Arras about 3.30 a large crowd of people assembled around the door of the carriage in which Noel [Corry], Douglas [Loch] and self were sitting, and the former was presented with three enormous bouquets, the biggest I have ever seen – by the Mayor and the Mayoress, and the Prefect of the Town Councillors. It was most amusing. Noel came up to the scratch well and in a few well-chosen and felicitous phrases tendered the thanks of the Officers and the Army in general. As we were all more or less in a state of *déshabillé*, it must have been a funny sight. The carriage was already littered with accoutrements, boots, puttees and the remains of several meals, so after we were safely out of sight the bouquets were, I am afraid, relegated to a much less dignified position in the carriage. The Station Staff Officer, a Frenchman, told us that he was passing through complete trains at the rate of one every 10 to 15 minutes, so it doesn't look as if we shall be long concentrating. We next stopped at Cambrai and the nearer we got to the Belgian frontier the greater was the enthusiasm and fervour shown by the inhabitants. From there we struck southwards to Busigny which we were told was our destination, but on arrival there at 6 p.m. were told that we were to go on to the next station at Vaux. We finally arrived there at about 7.15 in the pouring rain. It had been raining off and on most of the day, but our arrival seemed to be the signal for it to put in its best efforts in that

Route of the Second Battalion 1914

English Miles
0 10 20 30 40 50

FLANDERS

Calais

Ypres   BELGIUM

Hazebrouck   Tournai

Étaples   Mons

Condé

Arras   La Longueville

Cambrai   Binche
Maubeuge

Busigny   Landrecies
Grougis
Vadencourt   Flavigny

Amiens

La Fère

Havre

R. Oise

Rouen   Pont-Arcy
R. Aisne

Beauvais   Fismes
Soissons
Villers-Cotterets
Dulchy
Betz   Neuilly
R. Marne
Meaux   Charly

PARIS   Coulommiers

Route to Mons:—
by train ......
by road ....
Retreat from Mons & advance to the Aisne...
Route from the Aisne to Flanders...

to Arras

Condé   Mons
St. Symphorien
Spiennes
Genly   Binche
Harveng
Blaregnies   Quevy-le-Petit
Quevy-le-Grand
Malplaquet

La Longueville
R. Sambre
Maubeuge

Pont-sur-Sambre

Cambrai   Leval
Caudry   Noyelles
Landrecies   Maroilles
le Cateau

Busigny   Vaux-Andigny   Le Nouvion
Oisy
Wassigny   Etreux
Vénérolles   **The Mons Area**
Grougis   Tupigny   **1914**
Vadencourt
Flavigny   English Miles
0   5   10

way. My company, being in waiting, had to unload the waggons, horses etc. and this turned out to be rather a long job, as there were not enough ramps to go anywhere near round the trucks, and what there were, weren't strong enough to bear our G.S. waggons, which are much heavier than those used by the French. However we had finished off the unloading by about 9.30 and then proceeded to the village to find our billets – the Battn. having gone ahead. My Coy's billets were rather scattered, and it took me a good long time to get them settled up for the night. The billeting system here is an excellent one, and I only wish it was adopted at home, but I don't think our nature would allow it to become the success it is here. No trouble was too much for those who had to supply billets – clean straw was all ready, water etc. all prepared. I reported myself to Headquarters at 11.30 p.m. and then went in search of my own billet. Here I found three young Officers comfortably ensconced already, and the better for an excellent meal provided by the lady of the house. The lady in question was a charming lady, the wife of a French Army Doctor already at the front and of whom she had heard nothing for the last ten days. Madame Dupré, as I afterwards found out her name to be, was kindness itself: she cooked me an excellent meal and a delicious omelette and sat up looking after our needs till long past midnight. We implored her to go to bed and leave us, but she refused, saying she was quite accustomed to this sort of thing and only too glad to do anything for us etc. She already had French troops billeted on her. We got to bed about 12.30 and I much enjoyed clean sheets. I forgot to mention that at Amiens my company suffered its first casualties in the shape of four Officers: George Powell, Drino, Des Voeux and Miller, all going off in search of food at the buffet (*pro bono publico*) and got left behind, but they came on by a later train and joined us some time during the night.

On 16 August the Battalion marched to Grougis, where they were to stay for four days while the B.E.F. completed its concentration. They carried out a certain amount of Company training, which helped to harden the Reservists, and the Commanding Officer took the opportunity to have the Battalion inoculated against typhoid. The same day Major Jeffreys started his journey to France:

Sunday, 16 August

Left Caterham by motor. Depot lined the drive and cheered as I went away. Lunched at Burkham and said 'Goodbye', and went on to Tatchbury for the night.

Monday, 17 August

After luncheon motored to Southampton. Stopped the car and said 'Goodbye' to Dorothy, as we couldn't face parting at the Docks, and she walked back. Went to Embarkation office, where I saw amongst others, Billy Darell and Lionel Knight, who have gone on the Embarkation Staff, and found that my servant, Hill, and my horse (the black hunter I bought from Harold Grenfell) and groom (Grice) had arrived. Embarked on board *Canada*, which was full of Artillery, and about 10 p.m. we sailed. No one was about, except a solitary man with a cornet, who played *Auld Lang Syne* as the ship moved out. A lovely night and very calm. No cabins were allotted, but the Captain, who was very kind, gave me leave to lie down in his cabin, which I did, after sitting some time on deck with some other Artillery officers and a Chaplain, a very good fellow called Fleming, who had come from the R.M.A. Woolwich. We talked of the possibilities of the War, and the Gunners were very emphatic that, whatever else might happen, we should have a better gun and better shell than the Germans. We had an escort of 2 destroyers.

Tuesday, 18 August

After an uneventful crossing we got in to Havre soon after 5 a.m. A few French soldiers, (rather elderly, and untidy in long blue coats and red trousers) were on the breakwater, and shouted Vive l'Angleterre. A man in the forecastle shouted 'Are we down-'earted'? and was answered with a mighty shout of 'No'. Otherwise no demonstration or enthusiasm of any kind. As soon as we got alongside the disembarkation officers came on board and were so busy with orders for the R.A. etc., that they hadn't much time for details such as me, a horse, and 2 servants. However, after a great deal of bothering and refusing to be put off I got my orders and ticket for Wassigny, and we left Havre at 5 p.m. on an ordinary civilian train. We arrived at Rouen at 9.30 p.m. and there I found we had to change. It was lucky I could speak French or I think my horse box and groom might never have come off that train. We waited at Rouen till 12.30 a.m., when we got into another train. On the platform at Rouen were Cis Bingham and the staff of his Cavalry Brigade – also changing. Carne Rasch was his Staff Captain, and they told me of Godfrey H. having got into trouble for stowing away with the Carabineers and appearing when they landed at Havre. I gather that he is to be sent home.

Wednesday, 19 August

Reached Amiens 5.30 a.m. and again changed. A long wait, and feeling very stuffy and dusty I went to a Café outside the Station and had a *Café Complet*. The horse box was shunted into a siding. We went on again about 9 in a very slow train, very crowded to Tergnier, near La Fère, where we were once more turned out. A good deal of trouble here over my horse box, which they made difficulties over putting on the next train. However I eventually squared them and said that it was of the utmost military importance that we should get on. A long wait here and I got some sandwiches at the Buffet. On the whitewashed wall in the Station yard was an enormous drawing of the Kaiser with the face of a pig, a helmet on his head, and an iron cross. Very cleverly done and very hideous.

Great interest was manifested in me, so much so as to be rather embarrassing. They wanted to know my nationality, my rank, my branch of the service, what my badge meant etc. etc., and they were full of anxiety to know how many of us had come, or were coming to the War. Some of them were in uniform, and these looked anything but soldierly, to our notions. On again at last after $2\frac{1}{2}$ hours wait. The country we passed through was a mass of corn fields, some standing and some cut, and we jogged along very slowly by St Quentin (no change!!) to Busigny, where we again changed. A British R.T.O. [Railway Transport Officer] here, so no difficulties, and after a short wait we went on to Wassigny, Headquarters I Corps and also Headquarters 2nd Division. Here we detrained and I went in search of orders. Eventually I found Bertie Hudd, who passed me on to Headquarters, 2nd Division, which had only arrived that same morning. General Monro most kind and ordered me one of his cars to take me to the 2nd Battalion at Grougis. I had my horse saddled, and rode him; put my kit and 2 servants in the car (a W. and G. taxi with yellow and green body) and set off. A very hot evening, and the horse, having only just been got up and being soft, sweated pretty freely, as did I. We got to Grougis about 7 p.m. and found the Battalion at once, meeting the C.O. (Noel Corry) and Douglas Loch, (whose place as 2nd in Command I take) in the street. Douglas goes off to the Staff at G.H.Q. Officers and men just recovering from the effect of inoculation for enteric. I was billeted in a small house, quite clean, and was glad of a wash and change. We dined all together in a biggish room with borrowed plates, knives, etc. No one seems to have made any arrangements for the Officers' Messing, and I gather that once we get going we split up into 1 Headquarter and 4 Company Messes and live as best we can. I was thankful for a good night's sleep in a clean bed.

The country around Grougis was well cultivated, and the guardsmen entered into the life of the community on which they were billeted, as this extract from the diary of Captain the Hon. E. M. Colston, dated 19 August, shows:

Light training without packs. Fire direction. Evening cleared 5 acres of corn. Carried by hand as horses had gone to the war. Mayor said it was taking bread out of the mouths of local labourers. Transpired that Mayor received percentage of labour hired!

The concentration of the B.E.F. was now complete, and the period of rest was over. Jeffreys continues the story:

Thursday, 20 August

No one knows anything about the general situation but the impression is that our concentration is nearly complete. The 2nd Bn. Coldstream are also billeted in Grougis. They have told their men that now they are on Active Service they need not salute – a very bad beginning by slackening discipline, we think – and have told our men to be extra particular to salute Coldstream Officers. In the middle of the morning came sudden orders to move in the afternoon, and at 1 p.m. we marched off. It was very hot, but the Battalion marched well in spite of some men not being quite fit after inoculation. I rode most of the way in rear of the Battalion with the transport officer, A. Cunninghame, a son of Smith-Cunninghame, late 2nd Life Guards. The other boys call him 'Flash Alf', but he is very much all there and has got the transport in great order. We passed John Ponsonby's 1st Bn. Coldstream going in the opposite direction – route marching, so the 1st Division has evidently not started yet. We marched northward about nine miles and billeted in Oisy – good billets.

Friday, 21 August

Marched at 9 a.m. about 10 miles to Maroilles and billeted. Again very hot. This time we put out outposts for the night. Officers' messing arrangements primitive. Each Company has a fitted Canteen with plate, knives, etc., but otherwise no mess equipment. We got stew out of the cookers for lunch. The Orderly Room Q.M. Sergeant Martin, who really ought to have been left at the Base, and who has no very arduous duties, is going to run the Mess.

We have a two-wheeled mess cart, which was brought out in two sections and to which we are not entitled. It is painted the same green as the rest of the transport and has not been spotted. It ought to be useful as we can get plenty of things for the mess in the country.

Billeting was not always a simple process. The following account, taken from Colston's diary dated 21 August, gives a glimpse of some of the problems:

Marched 5.40 a.m. Difficult to get men out of billets. Tiring dusty march, half road *pavé*. Billeted at Maroilles, No. 4 Coy in the town, remainder along the road. One householder troublesome about billets. Put in lock-up, much to the satisfaction of the Mayor, who suspected the man of being a spy. Inhabitants less hospitable, probably more Flemish blood.

The advance to Mons had now begun.

Saturday 22 August

Marched at 5 a.m. by Pont sur Sambre to La Longueville, where we billeted. About 12 miles and again very hot. The Battalion marched well, but some of the reservists are not really fit and find their heavy packs very trying in the heat.

Also their new boots are not properly broken in and there are some sore feet. A lot of these roads are *pavés*, and these are particularly trying to march on. There are some French Infantry billeted in the western outskirts of the village: they are the first body of French troops we have met. They belong to a Territorial Division – *Tous Territoriaux* they said they were – and are not impressive to look at, being mostly getting towards middle age and clothed in rather ill-fitting and shabby long blue coats and red baggy trousers, but they are very intelligent to talk to, having very definite ideas as to the situation, about which we know nothing, and about the strategy, which according to them is to be offensive. This afternoon we could hear gunfire in the far distance, and the general impression is that the Germans have come on a good deal faster than was anticipated. Battalion Headquarters are in a biggish house of the farm-house type – quite comfortable and civil people.

3

'A very sweating march'

BY 10 p.m. on the night of 22 August it had become clear to
Sir John French, as a result of the reports of the Flying Corps
and the news from Lanrezac's Fifth Army on his right, that
the offensive planned for the next day could not take place.
Unable to accede to Lanrezac's request that he should attack
in the flank the German columns pushing back the Fifth Army,
Sir John nevertheless agreed to remain in his present positions for
twenty-four hours. In the Battle of Mons that followed the
Grenadiers played only a minor part, as reinforcements to the
battalions of the 3rd Division holding Hill 93. The story of
their withdrawal is an instructive illustration of the problems
created by the absence of good, quick communications, espe dally
between formation Headquarters.

Despite the successes of 23 August, it was clear that the
B.E.F., faced with an enemy greatly superior in number, and
with both its flanks unprotected, must withdraw. The Retreat
from Mons that started that night was one of the hardest tests
the Army could have been called upon to undergo, for it was
not a manoeuvre in which the troops were practised, nor did
they understand the reason for it. In carrying it out, however,
they created the conditions which made possible 'The Miracle
of the Marne'.

Sunday, 23 August

Overnight we had orders to be prepared to move at 3 a.m.
Fresh orders in the very early morning to march 3.30 a.m. to
Mons. Guards Brigade was leading Brigade of Division. About
2¹/₂ miles along the road we crossed the field of Malplaquet
and were ordered to fix bayonets – why we didn't quite
gather – a mile or so further along we crossed the Belgian

frontier. The drums are not allowed to play, which is rather
ridiculous, as they are a tremendous help on the march, and
it is absurd to think that they give away the march of such
columns as ours, which must be evident enough, even if
there were no such things as aeroplanes. The drummers are
acting as orderlies, and the drums are on the transport. To
the west of the road approaching Mons the country is a mass
of mining villages and there are a lot of slag-heaps and pit-
heads: also a lot of light railways. After marching about 11
miles we halted in what appeared to be the southern outskirts of Mons. Here we had a long halt by the roadside. We
got no information but could hear firing in front and could
see shells bursting over what we were told was Mons station.
On the march up we had a report of the Cavalry (4th D.G.s)
having had a successful brush with the Germans yesterday.
[This was the action at Soignies, in which C. Squadron of
the 4th Dragoon Guards, under Major Bridges, was engaged
in the first encounter of the war between British and German
troops.] The inhabitants seem to be taking things very
quietly so far. We (officers) went into a Café by the roadside
where we got some coffee and a local newspaper, which had
an account of British troops entering Lille. After a long halt
we got orders about 11 a.m. to move southwards by the bye-
road to Quevy le Petit, a little over 4 miles, and we got there
about 1.30, and went into billets, Battalion Headquarters
Officers in a very clean, fair-sized house, with a very civil
man and woman, who were very anxious to make us comfortable.

There were a lot of rumours about the brutality of the
Germans, and amongst others, one that they had burnt
Peronne. This seemed to frighten our hostess very much. We
had luncheon laid out, but before we had time to do more
than swallow a very little, we were ordered to move to
Harveng, a village about 3 miles to the north-east. We packed
up and moved on again about 3.30 p.m. along a very bad un-
metalled track, and when approaching Harveng, we and the
Irish Guards were ordered to move forward to a prominent
hill just north of Harmignies, to be in support of the right
Brigade of the 3rd Division. The two Coldstream Battalions
were to entrench a position just east of Harveng. As we
came through Harveng we could see the hill about 1½ miles
to the north-east with enemy shrapnel bursting round the
top of it. Several of our batteries were in action west and
north-west of Harmignies, and the C.O. sent me forward to

reconnoitre and get in touch with the troops holding the hill and to find out if they wanted any help. The Battalion shook out into artillery formation to cross the open ground west of Harmignies, and I went ahead. A railway runs roughly east and west past the southern foot of our hill, and the Mons–Givry road runs up its southern slope, taking a very sharp jerk eastwards through a bit of cutting, and then another jerk northwards along the forward slope. I went up the cutting, hugging the left-hand bank, as there was a machine gun firing in bursts straight along the road. When I got to the second jerk I found the reserves of the Irish Rifles sheltering in the cutting and apparently quite alright. Their forward companies were entrenched a little way down the forward (eastward) slope. I saw a Major (2nd in command), who said they were holding their own without difficulty; that they had had some casualties, but not many; and that they were glad to have us close by, but they didn't want any help. I went back and met the C.O. and we closed up the Battalion on the western (reserve) slopes of the big chalk hill, where we lay for some two hours until it began to get dark. The Germans were bursting shrapnel over the top of the hill, but the contents went whistling down into the valley below, and did us no harm. The Irish Guards were to our right on the lower ground. As it began to get dark the firing died down in front, and I suggested to Noel that we should get the Battalion disposed so that we could defend ourselves or advance if necessary, and that we should put a post on the railway. This we did. Just before dark a railwayman walked down the line lighting signal lamps. We shouted to him that the Germans were not far ahead, but he went on. Afterwards we wondered if he was a spy. As it got dark it also got cold. We had all sweated with the long march in the heat and were now cold, stiff and tired. Luckily we had had a hurried meal at Quevy; otherwise nothing since 3 a.m. Most of the men dropped off into an uneasy sleep. Noel Corry and I sat and talked and were joined by George Morris (C.O. of Irish Guards). We had no information as to the situation beyond that the II Corps on our left had had hard fighting. There was some desultory rifle fire from the Germans at intervals, and a certain number of bullets came over us. It was pitch dark and about 10.30 p.m. a voice from the darkness said, 'Is the C.O. of the Grenadiers here?'

Porky [Noel Corry] said 'Yes', and a figure came up and said, 'I am the C.O. of the Irish Rifles and I thought I had

better let you know we are going to withdraw.' Porky said
'Withdraw: Where to? and who is going to take your place?'
He said, 'We don't know where we are going, nor why, but
so far as we know our whole Division is to withdraw, and no
one is to take our place. I thought you ought to know as
you'll have no one in front of you nor on your left flank.'
He also said they were to withdraw at midnight. The telephone
wire to Brigade Headquarters had been cut, and Porky decided to go back to Brigade Headquarters and ask for in-
structions. When he got there he found that the Brigadier
had gone to Div. Headquarters, but Gerry Ruthven (Brigade
Major) got on to Div. Headquarters on the telephone and
was told that nothing was known of any withdrawal and we
were to stay where we were. Porky said that he told Gerry
that there was no doubt about the withdrawal and pointed
out that our two Battalions would be in a very dangerous
position, to which Gerry said he must do as he thought best.
After what seemed a very long time Porky got back to us,
and he, George Morris and I talked things over. Porky said
he thought we ought to withdraw as he was sure Brigade
and Division didn't realise the situation. George Morris said,
"Well! it would be a damned stupid thing to stay here,' and
this, I think, decided Porky, who said he would withdraw.
Soon after this the line was got through again, and he telephoned and said what he was going to do.

Monday, 24 August

About 12.30 we closed the Battalion and started to march
down the hill. The Irish Rifles had already gone. Everyone
very stiff, tired and cold, and the night inky dark. When we
had got to the bottom and had got some hundreds of yards
over the low ground towards Harveng, an orderly met us
with a message from the Brigadier ordering the C.O. not to
quit the position. He thereupon turned the Battalion about
and we started back again. At the foot of the hill we met
the Irish Guards coming away and George Morris again urged
that it would be folly to go back there. Porky then said that
he would disregard the order and that he would justify himself by the para. of F.S.R. [Field Service Regulations] which
lays down that an officer is justified in disobeying an order
if he is satisfied that the issuer does not know the conditions
on the spot. Thereupon he once more turned the weary
Battalion about and withdrew to Harveng, where we lay down

in the street. I selected a doorstep because it was cleaner than the rest of the street and slept on it for about an hour. I never imagined that anything could be so hard. Soon after daylight we marched to Quevy-le-Grand, in front of which we entrenched a position. The last we saw of our hill it was wreathed in enemy shrapnel bursts. The withdrawal became general about 5 a.m., and the 6th Bde. and the Artillery withdrew through our Brigade, some Cavalry remaining out in front. From our position we could see the line of the Mons–Maubeuge road and the Cavalry withdrawing on to it. The enemy came on very slowly and eventually shelled the line of the Mons–Maubeuge road, which had no one on it, except one or two Cavalry patrols, very heavily. It was not until about 2.30 that he began to look for our real position and he then scattered a few shells about the fields north of Quevy where our forward companies were entrenched, but never really found them. Our Bn. H.Q. was in the slightly sunken road just north-west of Quevy-le-Grand, where we had scraped into the bank, but he never actually shelled us, although there were several of our batteries in action just behind us and firing over our heads.

About 4.30 p.m. we got orders to retire, and had a long and trying march back to Malgarni (close to La Longueville) in great heat and over very bad and dusty roads. The men very tired and rather puzzled as to what we are at. The 2nd Bn. Coldstream were in front of us and their march discipline very bad. A lot of men fell out and no real effort was made to keep them in the ranks. Some of our very tired men seeing them sitting by the roadside tried to fall out too, but we kept them all going, and let no man fall out. I marched behind the Battalion and kept them in the ranks, putting packs and rifles of some of the most beat on the transport. Battalion bivouacked in the open: the officers in a barn with plenty of clean hay, in which we slept like logs.

This was the start of the Retreat from Mons. Major Gordon-Lennox saw it this way at the time.

24 August

Off again at daybreak and saw the Germans simply pounding the ridge we had evacuated. As their infantry would probably shortly be up there, and find out we had left, and

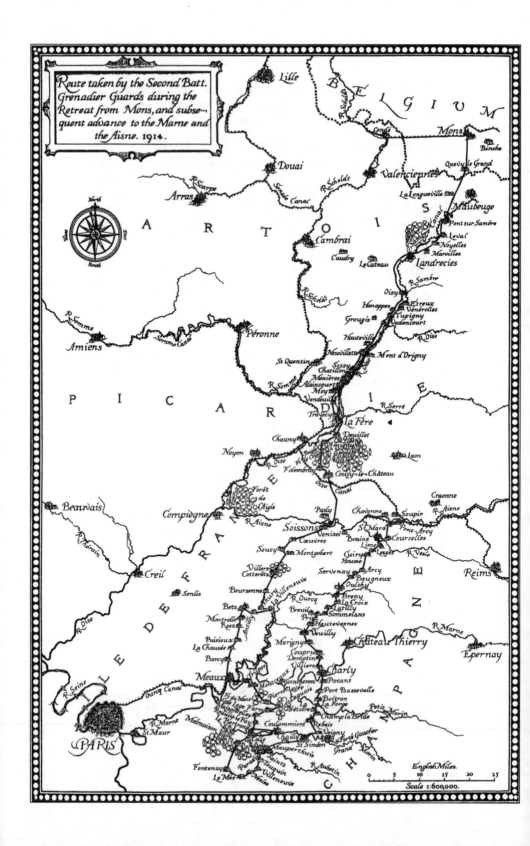

send word and as we were in full view of the ridge and massed, we lost no time in getting out of our unenviable position. This began our long and tiring retirement, beginning at Mons and finishing up near Paris, and I don't think any of us wish to go through such a trying time again. Also the British Army is not accustomed to retiring. To revert. We retired about 2 miles to Quevy-le-Grand where we reached about 6 a.m. and received orders to dig ourselves in, and fight a rearguard action. We had hardly arrived there, when the German shells began dropping on the last place we had evacuated. We afterwards heard they turned 15 batteries on it and pounded it up to mincemeat for 3 hours, so it was lucky we left. We could see the shells bursting just ahead of us. Gunning was going on all round, and it looked as if our flanks were being turned. Owing to the absolute secrecy which pervaded everything, no one knew what was going on anywhere: this has been maintained up to date and is most disheartening. No one knows what one is driving at, where anyone is, what we have got against us, or anything at all, and what is told us generally turns out to be entirely wrong.

The events of 25 August were described laconically by Lieutenant Richard Welby in his diary:

Very sweating march to Landrecies. Night attack. I on outpost.

The full story as told by Jeffreys was considerably more dramatic:

Tuesday, 25 August

Marched off 5 a.m. and marched by Pont sur Sambre to Landrecies, about 14½ miles. A very hot day again and a very trying march, owing to constant blocks and delays. Many refugees now on the roads, causing blocks and confusion. They were a pitiable sight – all ages and sexes, some in carts, many on foot. Some of the latter pushing barrows and handcarts, piled up with bedding and belongings: a good many with little carts pulled by dogs. Another cause of blocks and delays is 'double-banking', i.e. troops coming up alongside those in front of them, so that two columns are abreast. This generally means that no one can move either way. The

Artillery constantly did this, and no one stopped them. We
have no information, but every kind of rumour is afoot – of
Germans advancing in quite unexpected numbers; of units
being surprised in billets etc. etc. Generally believed that the
II Corps repulsed the Germans with loss and that the cause of
the retreat is that the French on our right retired without
letting us know. The railway sidings at Pont sur Sambre were
crowded with trains and rolling stock, including hospital
trains. We wondered if they would all get away. We marched
into Landrecies about 3.30 p.m. As we marched in I saw G.
Ruthven standing at a street corner and asked him, 'What
about outposts?' He said there were to be no outposts, as we
were covered by other bodies of troops, and by the great
Forêt de Mormal, through which there were no roads that
could be used by troops. Landrecies a considerable town and
Sir D. Haig's (I Corps) Headquarters were in it. We went into
some quite good billets, Battalion H.Q. officers being in a lawyer's house. We had only been a short time in billets
when the Alarm blew, and we all turned out and stood
to arms. A lot of men of the Irish Horse (Corps Cavalry
Regt.) were rushing down the street shouting 'The Germans
are on us', and the French inhabitants were in a great state
of excitement. After standing by for some time we were
told we could dismiss. It appeared that a German Cavalry
patrol had ridden unopposed into Landrecies and had caused
all the excitement. Finding the place full of British troops
they had not unnaturally gone out of it as quick as possible. However as a result of this the 3rd Coldstream (very
luckily as it turned out) were ordered to take up an outpost
position beyond the Sambre on the western outskirts of the
town. We turned in again and I was stark naked having a
bath about 6 p.m. when very heavy firing broke out and
some shells came over into the town. The Alarm sounded
once more and we tumbled out and were shortly ordered
forward to support the Coldstream, who, as they came up to
the rising ground they were to hold beyond the railway, met
the Germans coming from the opposite direction. A German
Officer called out, 'Don't fire: We are French', and an N.C.O.
of the Coldstream covering party, not knowing one foreigner
from another, hesitated, but Charlie Monck who was close
by ordered them to fire, and in a moment they were fighting
at close range. The Sambre (broad and deep) runs through
the north-western side of Landrecies and a railway runs nearly
parallel to the river, and a few hundred yards beyond it. The

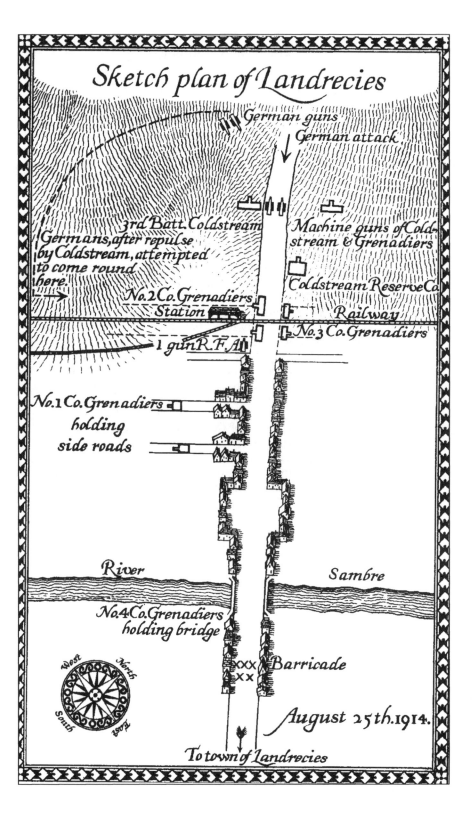

Sketch plan of Landrecies

German guns

German attack

3rd Batt. Coldstream

Machine guns of Coldstream & Grenadiers

Germans, after repulse by Coldstream, attempted to come round here.

No.2 Co. Grenadiers Station

Coldstream Reserve Co.

Railway

1 gun R.F.A.

No.3 Co. Grenadiers

No.1 Co. Grenadiers holding side roads

River   Sambre

No.4 Co. Grenadiers holding bridge

XXX Barricade
XX

West North
South East

August 25th. 1914.

To town of Landrecies

main street of Landrecies crosses the river by a bridge (the
only one), and the railway by a level crossing close to the
station. Beyond the railway the town really ends though
there are houses on both sides of the road for several hundred
yards. The street between the river and the railway is very
wide and at the level crossing it widens out into a sort of
little square. We left No. 4 Coy to hold the bridge; dropped
No. 1 to watch side streets, and went with Nos. 2 and 3 to the
level crossing. There was heavy firing in front and a good
many bullets ('overs' no doubt) came skimming down the
road, which was also being intermittently shelled. A message
came from the Coldstream asking if we could send our
machine guns to help them, and we sent them up under Lt.
Cecil. We got Nos. 2 and 3 Coys into shelter behind walls
and in houses, with posts to watch the railway each way.
The enemy Artillery, besides shelling the Coldstream, was
searching backwards and forwards up the road and shelling
the bridge, and bullets (though they didn't do much damage) made the level crossing a very unpleasant spot. Just after
dusk Geoffrey Feilding (Commanding 3rd Bn. Coldstream)
came back to us and told us that they were alright and had
definitely held up the enemy; also that our machine guns
had come just when they were wanted and had helped them
tremendously. There was now a lull in the fighting and the
rifle fire only desultory. Noel Corry now told me to go back
and report the situation to Scott-Kerr (Brigadier). I went
back; saw Ted Colston and No. 4 at the bridge (where they
had pulled up paving stones and made shelters), and found
awful confusion in the town, where men (I think Corps and
Brigade H.Q. personnel) were making barricades across the
street with waggons and wire. I found Brigade H.Q. established in the house which had been Corps H.Q., the Corps
Commander and staff having evacuated it pretty hastily when
the attack started, and one of the first shells hit the house. I
described the situation to the Brigadier, and was just going
to start back when a Coldstream Sergeant came in and said
he had got a spy dressed as a French Officer and should he
bring him in? The Brigadier said 'Yes' and a very smartly
dressed little man in blue tunic and red trousers was marched
in between two large men with fixed bayonets. The Sergeant
said 'This man was handed over by an Officer of Corps Headquarters before they went away. He said he was a spy. Hadn't
we better shoot him at once, Sir?' The Frenchman's face was
a study at this! The Brigadier said 'No, but you can search

him.' Whereupon the Sergeant tore open his jacket, turned out his pockets and with no undue gentleness searched him pretty thoroughly and found nothing. Then the Brigadier asked him what he had to say, and in good English he protested indignantly and volubly at his treatment: said he was a French officer attached to Sir D. Haig's Staff; that he was no spy etc. etc. At this moment a Colonel on the Corps Staff came in and the little man appealed to him as to whether he did not know him. The Colonel said 'Oh Yes: I've seen you with Corps H.Q.' The Brigadier asked why he was under arrest, and the Colonel said he didn't know, but thought it was the orders of the B.G.G.S. [Brigadier-General General Staff]! Whereupon the Brigadier ordered him to be taken away and kept under arrest. I felt sorry for the poor little man! The Colonel said he thought he had been 'panicky' and had made himself a nuisance when the attack started, but didn't believe he was a spy. I then went back and had a nasty journey up the street beyond the bridge. They were shelling the street with salvoes of shrapnel, and I dodged into side streets to shelter from them and got back safely to the level-crossing. By this time a Field Howitzer had been got up to the crossing (manhandled the last two or three hundred yards) and was answering the German artillery fire. They seemed to have got some guns very far up, and our guns appeared to make such good practice that their fire slackened quite appreciably. About 11 o'clock the Germans began to try to work round our left flank. We could see shadowy figures crossing the [railway] line and at the same time there was an increase in the firing in front. However, No. 2 opened fire straight down the line and not many got across. After this there was no further actual attack, though there were occasional bursts of firing for the next two hours or so up to 2 a.m.

Wednesday, 26 August

We sent a patrol along the river to our right to a place where a lock and possible crossing is shown on the map, in case they should try to come round that way, but they reported all clear. About 3 a.m. the Irish Guards came up through us, having apparently been sent up to make a counter-attack, but this (if intended) never developed and all remained quiet. About 4 a.m. we got orders to retire at day-break, the 3rd Bn. Coldstream and Irish Guards to be with-

drawn through us and we to cover the withdrawal. They
came through us in the half-light and it was just getting light
as we started to withdraw, platoons getting into single file
and hugging the walls of the houses on each side of the
straight street. We never thought they would let us get
across the bridge without molestation, and Porky said to me
before we moved off, 'Well in case we don't get out of this,
Goodbye.' However, not a shot was fired and it was daylight
by the time the last of us got across. The town was like a
city of the dead. All other troops had evacuated it and the
inhabitants had taken refuge in the cellars. The only living
thing we saw in the town as we marched through was a
very frightened man of the Irish Horse holding a nice-looking
bay horse. A. Gosselin said to him. 'What are you doing there
with that horse?' The man said, 'I – I don't know Sir. Captain
——— told me to wait here for him. I've been waiting for
the last six hours. I don't know what's happened to the Captain: I don't know what to do!' Goose said, 'I'll tell you
what to do. You look after yourself: I'll look after the horse!'
The man said, 'Oh thank you Sir,' and was off as fast as he
could go, leaving the horse with Goose, who got onto him.
[The horse subsequently came into Jeffreys' possession and
survived the war]. We withdrew up on to the rising ground
south-east of Landrecies, where the Irish Guards and 2nd
Coldstream were in position to cover the withdrawal, and
we then marched south along the main road about 8 miles
to just north of Oisy, where we halted. The enemy did not
interfere with our withdrawal, which was as well, as we were
deadly sleepy, and I like most others kept falling asleep as I
marched along. As the sun got up it got hot and the road
was very dusty. I saw last night's alleged spy being marched
along in escort, looking very wretched. He had patent leather
boots on and they must have been agony to march in. On
reaching Oisy, we (Grenadiers) were ordered to send two companies to take up a position astride the road and dig in about
800 yards north of Oisy. It was only then that we discovered
that we had lost our heavy entrenching tools, the tool-carts
having been taken by some zealous Staff Officer to make barricades in Landrecies. However, they dug wonderfully well
with their light entrenching tools, and made quite good
trenches in the stubble fields. The rest of the Brigade bivouacked in fields just north of Oisy. A good many of us
(officers) of the different regiments got into a small empty
house by the roadside, where we washed and shaved (badly

wanted), wrote letters and diaries, compared notes and slept. Someone had a *Times* with an account of the German entry into Brussels, which must have been very impressive. I found that my kit had also been left in Landrecies, Hill having put it on a waggon which was taken to make a barricade, so I had nothing but what I stood up in, except my washing and shaving things, waterproof and spare socks, which were in the wallets on my saddle. The 3rd Coldstream did very well last night, but had over 100 casualties, Hawarden and Clive killed; Bobby Whitbread, Rupert Keppel and Dick Rowley wounded. Torquhil Matheson appears to have been wonderful, controlling the fire by all the latest Hythe methods. We had Vereker killed, W. Cecil slightly wounded (at duty) and about six other casualties. The Irish Guards and 2nd Coldstream were not engaged. Our machine guns did very good service with the Coldstream. One of them was blown over by a shell which pitched almost on it, but was remounted and worked very gallantly by Private Rule. In the dark and confusion at Landrecies a good many men lost their kits. Very heavy firing has been going on all day – apparently about 5 or 6 miles in the direction of Le Cateau.* We all thought that we should be bound to have to do something about it, but hour succeeded hour and we got no orders. In the evening Philip Chetwode's V Cavalry Brigade, which had been put out as a screen to the northward in the direction of Landrecies, came back through us. I saw a good many friends in the Greys, XII Lancers and 20th Hussars. They said they hadn't seen a German all day. The only German we saw was a German airplane which flew low over our bivouacs. I don't think anyone recognised it as German until it dropped a bomb, apparently about the size of a field-gun shell right in the middle of the bivouac. It went off with a bang and a puff of smoke, but touched no one. However every man seized his rifle and shot at it, and it was obviously hit and flew wobbling away and came down about a couple of miles off, when we hear its two occupants were captured by a Cavalry patrol. We still know nothing of the general course of the War. The 6th Brigade also were attacked last night at Maroilles,† where the Berkshires lost heavily. The air is full

---

* This was the stand of Smith-Dorrien's II Corps.

† 6 Bde. in billets at Maroilles were attacked by German patrols which withdrew to the bridge over the Sambre when they found the town held in strength. The Berkshires had sixty casualties, trying unsuccessfully to rush the bridge.

of rumours and stories of units being 'cut-up'; also of spies.
A quiet night and a good sleep in spite of rain.

Gordon-Lennox's diary describes the fight at company level....

25 August, 1914

Off back again about 5 a.m., a long and very hot march
with continual gunning going on in our rear. They seem
pushing devils these Germans. We reached Landrecies about
4 p.m. and went into billets. Shortly after our arrival a French
Cavalryman rode into the town in a wild state of excitement
and said the Germans were coming. We all turned out but
treated him more as a harmless lunatic and nothing came of
it. The Coldstream Guards put out an outpost line, & we all
turned in to wash and eat. No. 2 Company's Officers found a
nice house, which we invaded, the rightful owner having
fled, and made friends with the caretaker, who was to cook
our dinner. We were in the middle of our dinner about 8.30
when the alarm went and we rushed out to hear heavy
firing – musketry – going on just outside our end of the town.
Everyone fell in hurriedly and there was a good deal of scurry
but no disorder when the word came down that the Coldstream Guards outposts were being driven back: the remainder of the Battalion was sent up to where the firing
was going on, in support. Nobody seemed to know anything
definite and it was pitch dark. The Grenadier Guards were
sent up to look after other entrances. No. 2 went right on
and lined up by a railway line and across two roads. No.
3 just behind them. Two houses were rapidly put in a state
of defence by being broken open, the windows smashed, loopholes made and manned. Firing was now increasing and the
machine-guns came into play. The Germans brought up a
couple of guns and shells were soon being poured over our
heads at almost blank range into the town. They also fired
case shot at 150 yards down the road on the Coldstream.
The various fronts were very narrow and consisted only of
the width of the road or open space – the Germans wouldn't
have it, and the two forces were only a very short distance
from one another and packed tight. The moment the Dutchmen [a corruption of Deutscher, or Deutscherman] tried to
advance a deadly rapid fire was poured into them. They
charged pluckily three or four times, but each time they

were mown down. Then we got word that they were getting round towards us. We waited quietly, and saw a couple of dull red glows which were no doubt the lamps of the leading Officers. We opened a salvo of rapid fire and one of the lights disappeared to be followed shortly after by the other one. Bullets began to whisk past us and it was just about this time that poor young Vereker was shot dead through the head. I also had two corporals wounded at the same time. We were all lying within a yard of each other. We brought up two guns and they fired at the Germans, but it was chance work in the dark; as it happened they did knock out with their last shot the German gun. So the night wore on with bursts of rapid fire at intervals, one of the longest nights I have ever spent. About 2 a.m. I lay down and had ½ an hour's sleep, but woke up so cold I had to run about to get warm. Just before daylight the order came that we were to withdraw gradually out of the town: this we did, the Grenadiers covering the retirement of the Coldstream who had been at it all night and were pretty well mauled. The streets had been barricaded through the night with every conceivable sort of thing, carts, waggons, and faggots and all available paraphernalia. Unfortunately we had no time to get our kits, the men having turned out in such a hurry, and they had to be left behind. Daybreak found us at the far end of the town retiring, and we marched on and finally reached Étreux about 11 a.m. We were all done to a turn and I have never felt such difficulty in keeping my eyes open while marching.

The Brigade Commander, Brigadier-General Scott-Kerr, sent the following account of the Landrecies fight to the Major-General Commanding London District, on 29 August:

29/8/14

My dear General,

As you know I must not give details, but, in addition to a good deal of fighting of a desultory character, we have had a little night affair, which with any troops but the Brigade would probably not have ended as well as it did – a night scare, inhabitants rushing through in panic. I reinforced the exposed half company with half a Battalion. Soon after, a crowd of French Soldiers and Civilians came up to our Post, calling out Vive l'Angleterre, singing French Patriotic Songs, etc. Getting close to our men they made a rush and tried to seize our rifles. They were closely followed by a column of enemy. When we realised the game, we bayoneted the front lot, and then got to work on the column, which opened fire with two guns, at a hundred yards, as well as rifle fire. I brought up two howitzers (to shoot at 50 yards range). O.C. 3 Coldstream too splendid for words. He walked out in front to see where our shells went and directed their fire – the most wonderful piece of bravery I think I ever heard of, considering he was under a very hot fire of guns and rifles at under 100 yards.

800 dead Germans were collected next day belonging to the Jager Guard Regt.

There have been difficulties about our casualty returns, which I need not explain, but in case it may be thought I am careless in the matter, please say that as we are situated it is impossible to do more than has been done in that respect.

The Brigade has behaved as usual. One can't say more.

Please let my Missus see this. There is very little time to write.

Yours ever,
R.S. K.

In the morning the march resumed:

Thursday, 27 August

We were under arms early, but did not move off till 8 a.m., when we marched back through Étreux*, and then by a good but rather winding road through Venerolles and Hauteville to Pont d'Origny, where we went over the river and up on to the high ground about a mile along the St Quentin road. The people of Étreux, who had been so friendly as we went forward, were quite the reverse as we went back. A long and dusty march, about 10 miles, with many checks due to double-banking. A German aeroplane flew right along the column whilst we were halted on the march and was given rapid fire all along the Brigade, though with no apparent result. I think it was out of range. Our men marched well,

---

* The scene, that night, of the annihilation of 2nd Battalion Munster Fusiliers, cut off and surrounded by at least six German Battalions, after a resistance lasting for twelve hours.

but were tired at the end. We had no sooner got on to the high ground than we were told to entrench a position facing west, and were told that the Germans were advancing towards us from St Quentin. We dug hard and were well entrenched by about 11 p.m., when a column appeared from the direction of St Quentin. We stood to, but on being challenged it turned out to be a column of British lorries from St Quentin, where they said there were no Germans – at any rate when they left! After that excitement we got two or three hours sleep, though it was very chilly on top of our hill. Again many rumours, including one that we were surrounded on three sides by the Germans.

Friday, 28 August

Under arms 3 a.m. and moved off shortly after. Just as we were starting I saw Rollie Charrington with a few men of the 12th Lancers. We cut across country to Regny and thence marched southwards by the road running on the west bank of the Oise to outskirts of La Fère and on to Devillet, about three miles south of La Fère, where we crossed the Oise. Here we bivouacked after a long march (about 19 miles) in great heat. All very tired, but not one Grenadier fell out. As much could not be said for the Coldstream. We saw and heard nothing of the enemy, but there were rumours of the Cavalry having a successful encounter with German Cavalry. A quiet night when we slept like logs.

Saturday, 29 August

We entrenched a position about Devillet, facing north, but otherwise did not move during the day, and everyone got a chance, much appreciated, of washing, resting and writing letters. A strange message received from the C.-in-C., expressing appreciation of our work, and saying that he hoped shortly to withdraw us to 'rest and refit'.

What will the Germans do meanwhile? I took the Mess Cart and went into La Fère, where there are quite good shops, and got food for the Mess. In the grocer's shop I met Sgt. Osborne, Yorks & Lancs Regiment, and late Corporal in the Grenadiers, whom we sent to them as a Drill Instructor. He told me rather harrowing stories of the losses of his Regiment. The French on our right are said to be attacking today*, but the rumour in the evening was that they had had little success. Late at night we got orders to resume the retirement at 3 a.m. and that the bridges over the Oise were to be destroyed.

Sunday, 30 August

Marched off 3 a.m. through the Forêt de St Gobain. When the sun got up it became frightfully hot. We went on through the Forêt de Coucy and passed Coucy le Château, which looked a wonderful old place. At one place in the forest a lot of pheasants were being reared in rows of coops. At a halt I had a talk with George Morris. He was very gloomy: said it was the old story of Allies failing to get on together and that everything was going wrong. He finished up by saying that we should be re-embarking for England in a fortnight! We halted in the middle of the day for dinner. The 1st Brigade were halted on a road a little to the east of us, and we saw some of the Scots Guards, Willie Wickham, Stephen etc., for a few minutes. Then we marched on and bivouacked about 6 p.m. on a high down-like hill west of Pasly and overlooking the valley of the Aisne and Soissons, which was about 3 miles to the south-east of us. This was a very trying march in great heat and about 23 miles. The men marched well and in spite of the heat we didn't have a man fall out, though some were very done. There are some catacombs near our bivouac, but we were too tired to explore them.

Monday, 31 August

Marched off 7.15 and crossed the Aisne by the bridge at Pommiers. At the junction just beyond the bridge with the main Soissons road a crowd of people stood watching us go by, including a very pretty *ambulancière*, when unluckily one of our men fell down in a kind of faint. The nurse was at him in a moment sprinkling water on his forehead and making a fuss of him, and our Doctor, Howell, was also quickly there making a fuss of the man and the nurse! I didn't feel I could drive them both off and hoist the man on to a limber as I should like to have done, and so we had to

---

* The Battle of Guise, in which Lanrezac's 5th Army on the right of the B.E.F.'s I Corps checked the advance of Von Bülow's 2nd Army, and drove it back 5 kms, before resuming its own withdrawal.

leave him, the only man we have so far left behind on the
march. Followed another very trying march in blazing heat
about 11 miles to Soucy. Some of the roads between Permant
and Coeuvres were little better than sandy tracks and the
dust was stifling. The men were very tired and it was a job
to keep some of them in the ranks, but we didn't lose another
man out and bivouacked about 4 p.m. on some high ground
above a steep wooded slope just north of Soucy. At the foot
of the slope a deep valley with a stream at the bottom of it
runs nearly due north and south. I saw Gerry Ruthven in
the evening and asked him why his orders never gave us any
information about our own troops or the enemy. He said,
'Because we haven't any information to give. We don't get
any ourselves.' We slept under trees at the top of the slope.

Gordon-Lennox commented sardonically the same day:

31 August – Marched at 7 a.m. another long and hot march
to Soucy, finishing up with a very steep climb up: a lot of
gunning going on just in rear. We now know that as soon as
a gun is heard – be it five miles off or 25 miles – we shall be
shortly inundated with orders to march, to be followed shortly
with counter orders.

*The Germans had been pressing hard, but hitherto the Grena-
diers had not been heavily engaged. This state of affairs was
about to change.*

Tuesday, 1 September

A very still night, and during the night we could hear the
rumbling of wheels of masses of transport to the northward.
The C.O. was dead beat, and was sleeping like a log when
orders came in soon after midnight. I shook him but couldn't
wake him properly, and when I said 'Orders' he said, 'You
deal with them' and slept again. The orders were to take up
and entrench a rear-guard position on the line Mont Gobert-
Soucy, spur north of Viviers (1st position): Grenadiers to be
on the right, 3rd Bn. Coldstream on the left. The 5th and 6th
Brigades were to pass through us. 5th Brigade went through
about 2 a.m. and 6th Brigade about an hour later. We
(Grenadiers) were to detach one company on to the high
ground north of Mont Gobert (i.e. east of the valley and

stream) to protect our right flank. The Irish Guards and 2nd
Bn. Coldstream were to take up a second position along the
northern edge of the forest of Villers-Cotterets between
Puisieux and Viviers. Reveille was 3 a.m. and the men got
breakfasts. At 4 a.m. we started to take up our positions and
as soon as it got light started to dig. I was sent to take the
detached company (No. 4) under Colston, and post it on the
high ground north of Mont Gobert, and before marching
off I was told that a Brigade of Belgian Cavalry was believed
to be in that direction, but their exact whereabouts was unknown. There was a thick mist when we crossed the stream at
Mont Gobert and pushed up on to the plateau above. We
could see the imposing gates of a large château, but we could
neither see nor hear anything of any other troops, whether
friendly or hostile, and eventually I posted the Company,
giving them orders to keep the closest possible touch with
the Battalion (they had two signallers and a lamp for use, if
the fog lifted), and when we withdrew to withdraw also, and
to rejoin us on the road running east and west through
Rond de la Reine (the junction of a number of rides in the
forest). I left them rather wondering if I should ever see them
again, for they seemed very much in the air, and rejoined
Battalion Headquarters a little before 6 a.m. I found them dug
in, and shortly afterwards the fog lifted. About 6.30 a.m. some
German Cavalry patrols appeared in front of us and we at
once opened fire at about 1000 yards range. This caused them
to gallop back, and almost at once we got orders to withdraw through the second position on to the Rond de la Reine
position. Just as we were moving a German battery came into
action and fired a few shells, which did no harm, whilst some
infantry (or dismounted Cavalry) began to deploy. We withdrew without any casualties (I don't think the 3rd Bn. Coldstream had any either), and passed through the Irish Guards
and 2nd Bn. Coldstream on the edge of the forest, where they
seemed pretty strongly posted. The forest was thick but had
a good many rides running through it, mostly from north to
south; down some of these we fell back on to a ride running
roughly east and west through Rond de la Reine, which was
a kind of ring with rides converging on it. West of the ring
the forest was quite thick right up to the ride on both sides:
east of the ring the ground rose slightly away from the ride
to the southward and was more open for about 100 yards to
the south of it.

Very shortly after we got back on to this line, No. 4

Company rejoined us, which was a great relief. We then took up a position, Battalion Headquarters at Rond de la Reine, Nos 1 & 2 Companies on the rising ground about 100 yards south of the main ride east of Rond de la Reine; No. 4 Company along the ride west of Rond de la Reine. The 3rd Bn. Coldstream prolonged the line to the left of No. 4 Company along the same ride. We (Grenadiers) left standing patrols out down each of the rides on our front towards the northern edge of the Forest. Shortly after getting back on to this position we heard with some astonishment that we were to hold on to this position till 1 p.m. *in order to enable the rest of the Divisions to halt and have dinners* [Jeffreys's italics] in and about Villers-Cotterets! We had not long been in position when there came quickly down the main ride from the eastward the Greys and XII Lancers of Chetwode's 5th Cavalry Brigade. They halted with the head of the Column (which was in half-sections) at Rond de la Reine, and dismounted, and as we all had a good many friends amongst the officers, we stood talking together for quite a considerable time, a risky proceeding considering how vulnerable they and their horses were, and that they were masking our fire, if the Germans should come on. As it was it was very pleasant coffee-housing in the shady ride for all the world like a big field hunting in the New Forest on a spring day. Eventually they mounted and rode slowly along the ride across our front, saying they were going to help us by operating on our left. It was that Brigade (not a Belgian one) which had been out beyond Mont Gobert. They knew as little of our whereabouts as we did of theirs, and they had come over on hearing the firing. The C.O. had put me in charge of Nos. 1 & 2 Companies on the east side of the Rond de la Reine, and I went back to them when the Cavalry moved off. Ours was the strongest flank of the position as we had a low ridge to shelter us and a field of fire (through scattered trees) of about 100 yards. West of Rond de la Reine there was no field of fire beyond the breadth of the ride. Owing to the trees one could see very little beyond one's immediate neighbourhood which made co-operation difficult. Very shortly after the Cavalry had moved off we heard a good deal of firing from the direction of the northern edge of the forest, and after a bit a herd of deer appeared opposite my two Companies. They looked extraordinarily pretty and at first didn't spot us as we lay quite still, but when they did spot us they galloped off to our right. It was hard to believe it was War!

The firing increased to our left front, and suddenly about 11 a.m. there was a tremendous outburst of firing about Rond de la Reine, and west of it. We could see nothing of what was going on there, but opposite our two Companies there did not seem to be many Germans, or at any rate they did not face our bit of more open ground, but kept among the thick trees. A good many bullets began to come over from our left which showed that the enemy must, to some extent, have got round that flank. I heard later that there had been some misunderstanding about the withdrawal of the 2nd Coldstream and that they had been withdrawn before the Irish Guards, who had become involved in a running fight and had eventually withdrawn with the Germans right on top of them in the thick wood. In this way they had come back on to our left and the 3rd Coldstream, so that there was very confused fighting at point blank range. Part of our No. 4 Company made a counter-attack, charging with the bayonet, and I fear lost very heavily, Buddy Needham, John Manners and George Cecil being all wounded and missing, and most of their men missing as well. At the time I got no information and the first I heard of what was happening to my left was when Gerry Ruthven appeared leading a horse on which was the Brigadier badly wounded and obviously in great pain. He shouted to me that the enemy was held but that we should shortly have to withdraw, and disappeared to the rear in the Forest. Then I saw Stephen Burton (3rd Coldstream) also badly wounded and staggering back. He said, 'For God's sake help me get out of this or I shall be captured: I can't get much further.' By some lucky chance one of our ammunition pack horses was coming along and I and the transport man hoisted Stephen on to him with some difficulty and he was got away. Shortly after this an orderly from Battalion Headquarters came to me with a verbal message that we were going to withdraw, and as I knew, from seeing the Brigadier taken away wounded, that Noel Corry must be taking command of the Brigade, I concluded that I must be in command of the Battalion, and I told him to tell the Adjutant (I didn't then know that he was missing and almost certainly killed) that the rest of the Battalion was to retire keeping touch with the Coldstream and that we would hang on till they were back a little way. In order to get back to what appeared to be the only bridge over the Villers-Cotterets–Corcy railway, troops at Rond de la Reine and west of it had to fall back diagonally behind the position of our two Companies, and

Engagement at
Villers-Cotterêts
September 1.1914
Scale 1:120,000

in doing so, they were covered by our slight ridge. I threw back a platoon of No. 2 Coy to protect our left flank and withdrew No. 3, putting out posts to watch the northern outlets of the rides. I left posts on the ridge, and gradually withdrew Nos. 1 & 2 behind No. 3's posts, the posts on the ridge keeping up a brisk fire meanwhile. Then, when so far as I could see all the Battalion had got back, I withdrew the position on the ridge, and under cover of No. 3's posts, withdrew the whole Battalion first back down the rides through the thick forest and eventually over the railway bridge. The Germans did not press us at all. They had evidently not only lost heavily but got very mixed up in the thick forest, and we could hear them shouting orders and blowing little horns apparently to rally their men.

As we got back towards the railway bridge (I had some qualms as to whether I had read the map right with its maze of rides, but luckily I was alright), we began to meet parties of the 3rd Coldstream also making for it, and we let them cross first, as most of their Battalion was already on ahead. I saw 'Cakes' Banbury on a horse and rather rattled. He said, 'For God's sake get on out of this, or you'll be cut off.' I assured him we were not delaying and we rode on. Once over the bridge I assembled the Battalion (except for No. 1, who were first across and had formed up and marched off), and we then marched off down the road and through Villers-Cotterets. We had no orders. The Brigade organisation had, I suppose, been upset by the Brigade Major escorting the wounded Brigadier out of action. Our C.O. had gone off with what remained of Brigade Headquarters, and so we just followed the rest of the Brigade. We passed through the town, of which the streets were quite empty, and emerged on to open ground south-west of the town. We could see what appeared to be enemy on the edge of some woods to the northward and I extended the Battalion, but we were not fired on, and passed through the 6th Brigade who were lining the edge of the Forest, and 2 batteries of Artillery who were in action in the open just outside the edge of the Forest. When we got into the Forest, on the road to Boursonne, and were clear of the 6th Brigade, I halted the Battalion and formed it up. No. 1 was still on ahead with Brigade Headquarters, but the 2nd Bn. Coldstream were also formed up in the road. The other two Battalions were on ahead. We had no orders of any kind and having formed up we marched off along the road to Boursonne, followed by the 2nd Coldstream just as some

German shrapnel began to burst over the Forest, and we could hear considerable firing from the 6th Brigade and our guns. We had only gone a short way when Lt. Colonel Pereira (Commanding 2nd Coldstream) sent me a message to say that he had been ordered back to support the 6th Brigade. About ½ mile further on Gen. Monro himself rode up to me and ordered me also to turn about and go back to support 6th Brigade. We had only gone a few hundred yards when he again came up to me and ordered me to go back to Boursonne and take up a position there to cover the withdrawal of the troops in front. Accordingly back we went to Boursonne, which is a straggling village with a number of gardens and enclosures surrounded by walls. We loopholed these and made such trenches as we could with our light entrenching tools, and after 2 hours work had a reasonably strong position. From the firing we had gathered that the 6th Brigade had had stiff fighting and at about 6 p.m. Gen. Monro came back to us and told us that the guns had been in a tight place and that there had been difficulty in getting them back, but that the Germans were definitely held up. He stood (or rather sat on his horse) with us just on the northern outskirts of Boursonne where Stephen's (No. 3) Company was astride the road, when out of the Forest about 500 yards or 600 yards away to our left front appeared some Cavalry riding quickly along and apparently going to pass our left flank. General Monro said, 'They've got their Cavalry round! Quick! Get these men to change front and open fire!' I was almost certain they were British but I ordered the platoon to change front, but not to open fire, and got my glasses on to them when I at once saw the grey horses of the Scots Greys. I said, 'But it's the Scots Greys Sir,' to which the General said, 'Thank God! Thank God!' I think he was tired and overwrought. The time dragged on and gradually the 6th Brigade dribbled back through us, and last of all the 2nd Coldstream came back through us. I then collected the Battalion and followed the Coldstream, who followed the 6th Brigade. We had no orders and appeared to have been forgotten by our own Brigade Headquarters. After marching for about two hours, partly by cross country tracks, and going very slowly, for the men were dead tired, we came to a place called Thury, where were Divisional Headquarters. It was 10.30 p.m. and we found that our Brigade was at Betz, some four miles to the westward of us, and with them our supplies and transport. The men were dead beat and starving, as apart from fighting and digging, we had covered some fourteen miles since 3 a.m. All available accommodation was taken up by Divisional Headquarters and 6th Brigade, and I asked Cecil Pereira what he was going to do. He said, 'Lie down in the streets and push off very early to Betz.' I said, 'I'm going to have a try to get some food.' He said, 'Its no good: our supplies are all at Betz.' I went to Divisional Headquarters and found some rather tired A.S.C. [Army Service Corps] clerks establishing themselves and I said I wanted rations for a Battalion. The Head Clerk said it was impossible to get any, so I said I wanted to see the A.Q.M.G. [Assistant Quarter-Master General], one Conway-Gordon. He was not over civil; said we ought to be at Betz; and what did I mean by coming and bothering him at that time of night. I said I wanted to see the Divisional Commander, to which C.G. replied that the General was very tired, that it was no good my bothering him, and that he wouldn't do anything for me. I said, 'Anyhow I want to see him.' He then took me in to where General Monro was just sitting down to dinner, and the dear old man said, 'Hullo Jeffreys, what do you want? Have something to eat.' I told him I'd got a starving Battalion outside and told him what had happened, and that I wanted rations. The General said to Conway-Gordon, 'Haven't you got a ration dump?' C.G. said he had one about a mile down the road towards Villeneuve. The General said to me, 'Will you wait while we send waggons for rations, or will you walk there?' I said it would take time to get the waggons ready and we could manage another mile. He said, 'All right. You go with them, Conway-Gordon, and see they get their rations!' Conway-Gordon's face was a study! The General then gave me a whisky and soda and a bit of chicken, and off we went. I fell the weary Battalion in; told them they were going to walk a mile to food, and we set off in pitch darkness.

Conway-Gordon was not exactly companionable, but he took us to the rations and said we could take what we liked. I wasn't going to have a scramble, so had a good ration of bully, biscuit and jam issued. Then the Battalion just lay down by the road and slept. There was a farm-house close by and (having issued orders that we would march at 2 a.m. to join the Brigade, who were to march from Betz at 4 a.m.) I and Stephen went in and groped our way into a pitch dark room full of sleeping humanity of sorts; however we found a vacant corner on the floor and we two slept.

The casualties suffered by all battalions in the Brigade in this engagement were heavy. The Grenadiers lost four officers and 160 men. Two platoons under Lieutenants Manners and Needham never received the order to retire and were cut off. All were killed or wounded. Lieutenant Cecil was killed while leading a bayonet charge, sword in hand. For the Irish Guards it was an historic moment, because it was their first serious action; but it was sad that they should lose their Commanding Officer, Colonel George Morris.

For the next four days the Brigade continued to withdraw and despite various alarms remained out of contact with the enemy.

Wednesday, 2 September

Up at 1.30 and found room full of peasants, soldiers and ourselves also waking up. Atmosphere awful. In next room found Eustace Crawley and Rollie Charrington, 12th Lancers, who gave us some welcome hot coffee. Marched off at 2 a.m. back through Thury to Betz. As we moved off the 12th Lancers were setting fire to the ration dump, which had to be abandoned. Joined the Brigade at Betz and picked up No. 1 and some of No. 4 who had gone on ahead of us after we left the Forest. Marched off from Betz 4 a.m. southwards. We now were off the maps issued to us, but Gosselin had a *Guide Taride* map [maps issued by a French cycling club], which he gave me and which was better than nothing, as it showed the roads. We halted at 9.30 at Puisieux and had breakfast, which did us good. Then on again after an hour's halt, southwards to Meaux, where we went right through the town and out about 2 miles on the south side of it and bivouacked near Rolentier about 4.30 p.m. The hottest and hardest march so far – about 22 miles – but thanks to those rations the Battalion marched wonderfully, in spite of being tired and desperately short of sleep. No man fell out, but a great number of the 2nd Coldstream did. We bivouacked close to a stream and the men bathed. I was just going to go in when I saw a lot of animal guts come floating down, and hot and dirty though I was, I couldn't face that. After rejoining the Brigade we were able to realise our losses. Poor 'Lunga' McDougall was taking a message from the C.O. to me and apparently was in front of our line on his horse, when he was shot and is almost certainly dead. No. 4 Company lost heavily and Buddy Needham, John Manners and George Cecil are all wounded and missing. George Morris (C.O.) and Hubert Crichton (2nd in command) of Irish Guards are both killed; also Tisdall who was with me at the Depot, and Geoffrey Lambton, 3rd Bn. Coldstream. I took Pike to act as Adjutant, as he had been Adjutant before, and was also 2nd Captain of a Company [Company Second-in-Command]. A quiet night and quite a good sleep.

Thursday, 3 September

Marched 7 a.m. back through Meaux, (where we commandeered some bicycles from a shop, and gave receipts for them), then through Trilport and thence south-eastwards to Pierre-Levée. The bridges over the Marne were blown up, and there was a report that the bridge at Trilport went up just as some German Staff Officers in a car came on to it. A quiet night in bivouac. About a 12 mile march.

Friday, 4 September

Marched off 9.30 a.m. and took up a rearguard position about Les Laquais. After entrenching we did nothing further till dusk when we withdrew through Maisoncelies to Le Bertrand, where we bivouacked. March was about four miles. Officers slept in a clean and warm haystack. Late that night (about 11.45 p.m.) the first reinforcement (90 N.C.O.s and men under E. D. Ridley) joined us. Bernard Lennox had met them at Coulommiers and brought them up. A very hot day.

Saturday, 5 September

Marched at 5 a.m. southwards about twelve miles to Fontenay, where we halted and eventually bivouacked. Uneventful march. A quiet afternoon and an opportunity to wash and clean up. In the evening N. Corry returned and resumed command of the Battalion. He is still under a cloud owing to our withdrawal at Mons. G. Feilding (3rd Coldstream) has taken over temporary command of the Brigade. Various rumours in the evening that we may be going to advance.

An interesting footnote to the engagement at Villers-Cotterets
is provided by the following two letters written later in the
same year. The exact fate of those missing as a result of the
fight was not known at the time, and great efforts were made
by the families of those concerned to try to clarify the situation.
The first letter is from Lady Edward Cecil, the mother of George
Cecil, who went out to France, and visited the battlefield in
September 1914 to try and find some trace of her son. Dated 1
October 1914, and written from Sussex to Colonel R. G. Gordon
Gilmour, who was temporarily in command of the regiment at
the beginning of the war, it runs:

I think you would like some account of my visit to Villers
Cotterets last Saturday as I was looking not only for my own
boy but for other officers in his regiment.

I had such difficulty in getting out. Villers Cotterets and
Vivières lie only a few miles behind the line held by the
French Western Army – I suppose 15 miles to the rear and it
is not easy to get permission to go there. But for the kindness of the American Ambassador in placing his car at my
disposal and one of his military attachés I doubt whether I
could have reached the scene of activities even when I had my
military passes in good order.

I got to Villers Cotterets at 2.30. The Mayor had had in-
structions to facilitate my search. I found many relics picked
up on the battlefield, some of them men's pocket books,
and among them some signed by my boy. These will be for-
warded via the French authorities to England in course of
time.

The French doctor of Villers Cotterets had stayed in his
hospital all through the German occupation – and a register
had been kept of patients. There was no sign of any of
our 3. Colonel Hogg had died there and had been interred as
Colonel Morris, this entry was corrected by Mrs Hogg a few
days before I went to Villers Cotterets.

I ought to say that Lord Robert Cecil had made a previous
visit to Villers Cotterets, had cleared the ground there, and
had already been to Vivières. . . . To Vivières Church Mr
Needham and his men were carried – you will have heard his
story and the story of the private, Mr Needham's servant,
who believes that he saw George dead.

At Vivières we were unlucky. In a previous visit Ld Robert
Cecil had seen a woman, the village schoolmistress, who told

him that among the prisoners marched off by the Germans was a very young, very big and fair officer speaking excellent French. My brother in law is certain he had not described George to anyone as yet in Vivières, and certainly not mentioned his excellent French scholarship, but he begged me not to let myself be made hopeful by this talk as the French people were so kind they would say anything to comfort one, and besides lots of Englishmen speak good French and are fair and big in French eyes.

To return to my visit. This schoolmistress was away, the Mayor was away. The villagers would tell us nothing, couldn't answer any questions, everything was despairingly vague. Still we ascertained for certain the fact that a number of unwounded prisoners had been put in the church after the wounded had been put in the hospital. And we ascertained that the English wounded had been in two hospitals. In one of these was an order signed 'Weatherall' in English above the duties of privates in the Officers' kitchens – showing that the English doctor (?) had been allowed to run his own show with his own privates. Outside the hospital was printed in German

'Hospital number –
English department.'

I was very struck with the thoroughness of the organisation this displayed. It was so in every village the Germans stayed in. Everything was thought out.

After one hour at Vivières we went to Puisieux, a village to the right rear of our position. There are some soldiers buried in the Churchyard, one officer among the number. These were Irish Guardsmen, I saw their caps. I could not find out who, but they were buried by the French and their papers and identification discs have all been sent away to Paris – we shall get them in time.

The French at Puisieux also buried another officer in the wood – he fell, wounded in the chest, to the right of our position. He was about 30, the French said, mounted and with spurs – I hope the French Government will secure his things.

Then there are two large graves made by Germans. There is an inscription in German – it makes no reference to English, but it gives numbers. I think there must be some English there as I saw a lot of Khaki caps near. On the first is mentioned '1 Lieut.' but he is not said to be English. Further along there is another big German grave, but no officer is said to be lying there. This grave is to the left of our position. The only grave I could discover to have been made by the English is one at Vivières which has a cross over it and this inscription :

'Here lie the bodies of 13 British soldiers who died doing their duty, May God rest their souls.'

I think this grave must have been made – or at least the inscription – by Irish Guardsmen.

That is absolutely all the really definite information that I brought back from France. But I think I may add that all the dead were buried on Sept. 2nd and that the only exceptions to this were the mounted officer who, lying by himself, was not found and therefore was not buried until 4th September. There has been a particularly cruel story about John Manners which will, I hope, be disposed of by this. I am sorry I have not more to tell you.

I had a telegram from Rotterdam yesterday to say that there was a rumour that George is a wounded prisoner at Aix-la-Chapelle. It is only a rumour. I am not building any hopes on it at all, but I tell it to you as I have heard it. It is the vaguest rumour.

I have asked the French Government to pick up and take care of the little relics left on the ground – the caps, there are never any badges left, the pouches, the litter of a hasty encampment. I have also asked to have an enquiry made more closely in to the prisoners taken to Germany from these villages.

Will you please show this to Colonel Corry, I write it for him as well as for you, knowing his anxiety about his young officers must be very great.

I only wish I could have relieved it.

Yours sincerely,
Violet Cecil.

The second letter, written in November, answers most of the questions. It is from Lord Killanin, the brother of Colonel George Morris, the Commanding Officer of the Irish Guards, who had been killed at Villers-Cotterets.

My dear deVesci,

In response to your request that I should send you an account in writing of what was done in the neighbourhood of Villers Cotterets in France in our search last week for the remains of 'Missing' Officers who, it was thought, had fallen in an engagement there on 1st September, 1914, I send you the following record of my experiences; and perhaps you would kindly send copies to Colonel Streatfeild of the Grenadiers and Colonel Drummond Hay of the Coldstream, as they, too, desired same. Having heard the week before last that some members of the Paris Branch of the British Red Cross Society were about to visit Villers Cotterets for the above purpose, and my brother being one of the 'Missing' officers, I determined to try and go with them, and so left London for Paris on the 14th instant, and after considerable difficulties with the military authorities in Paris, got permission to accompany the Red Cross Party. Accordingly in the morning of the 16th inst., the following left Paris in a Red Cross motor : – Lord Robert Cecil, M.P., Lord Elphinstone, the Revd. H. T. R. Briggs (a Church of England clergyman who lives in Paris), self, and a chauffeur, named Arthur Hughes. We travelled via Senlis and reached Villers Cotterets at about 11.30 a.m. After visiting the local doctor, M. Le Docteur Monfflier, and getting permits from the local authorities to visit the graves in the forest beyond the town and to go as far as the villages of Puiseux and Vivières, we left Villers Cotterets in the early afternoon to commence our search.

About two and a half miles from Villiers Cotterets on the right hand side of the road leading to Vivières and about thirty yards in from the road and in the midst in all directions of a forest, we came to the grave which we had heard of and wished to examine. It had a cross over it and some evergreen wreaths on it, and on the cross there was an inscription in French to the effect that there were 20 English buried there. But this information was evidently taken from purple pencil writing in German on a tree hard by. It was rather illegible, and it was impossible to see whether the figures as to the number buried there were 20 or 200. It turned out that neither number was correct. The grave, or more truly pit, was about 25 feet long and 12 feet wide, and before dusk that evening more than 20 corpses had been disinterred by the six men working for us. And as it was manifest that many more corpses were there, we decided to greatly increase the size of the grave so as to have room to lay the bodies out. In the original grave the bodies were huddled and entangled just as thrown in anyhow, one after the other.

The next day the work of extricating corpses from the pit was continued, and, although over sixty bodies were disinterred and examined, no officer was found among them, but a number of discs were removed from soldiers' bodies. That afternoon Lord Robert Cecil left Villers Cotterets for Paris owing to engagement, and Lord Elphinstone accompanied him. The following morning Mr Briggs and I returned to the grave, and when nearly 80 bodies had been exhumed, the remains of Lt. Geoffrey Lambton of the Coldstream Guards were found. From various signs – the open jacket – collar etc., – it was at once evident that the clothing was that of an officer, and, on lifting the body out of the pit and placing it on the surface of the ground, the disc of G. Lambton, Coldstream Guards, was found on the neck. Soon after the remains of Captain Tisdall of the Irish Guards were discovered and his disc found on him. The next officer whose remains were come upon had no disc on and his long riding boots were gone, but it was clear from the buttons and clothes that it was the body of an Irish Guards officer. As by that time my brother was the only Irish Guards officer unaccounted for after the engagement near Villers Cotterets, and, from the general shape of the figure, I could see that these remains must be his, and any possible uncertainty was removed by finding on one of the wrists and hidden by the sleeve his small gold watch with his name on it. His remains were then placed alongside of those of Lambton and Tisdall. Very soon afterwards, the remains of another officer were found. The buttons showed that it was the body of a Grenadier, but no disc could be found on the body, but we were of opinion, from the description of George Cecil's figure supplied to us and especially from the size of the boots, that it was his body and this was confirmed by finding on the front of the vest the initials 'G.E.C.' which we cut off. As a memento for his mother we took three buttons off his uniform. His remains were placed beside those of the other officers. We then disinterred the few remaining bodies at the bottom of the pit and ascertained that the total number of bodies – all British – buried there was 98 (4 officers and 94 men): and, since we had examined each corpse for discs or other evidence of identity, we had at the end 24 discs of Grenadier soldiers, 17 of Irish Guards, 8 of Coldstreams and 1 belonging to Mark Darking of the East Lancashire Regiment [part of 11 Brigade]. A few books were also taken off soldiers' corpses and the names and numbers, where decipherable, recorded. The others bodies we were unable to identify: and in no case was it possible to identify a body by features – hair, teeth, as owing to the length of time (two and a half months) since burial and to the manner in which these dead had been treated, the faces were quite unrecognisable, often smashed, and were all thickly coated with clay and blood. In the afternoon the bodies of the 94 soldiers were laid out in the enlarged grave, and, since many of them were Roman Catholics, M. Le Doyen Grainblot, the Roman Catholic Dean of Villers Cotterets came out with Mr Briggs and myself at our request and said prayers for the dead by the graveside of the soldiers and over my brother's remains, and Mr Briggs also said prayers for the dead by the soldiers' grave: and the bodies of the 94 soldiers were then covered with earth. The bodies of the four officers, lying beside one another on the surface close by, were covered with leaves for the night, and we returned to Villers Cotterets, after motoring hurriedly round by Puiseux and Vivières in order to see the British graves there and especially Hubert Crichton's. That evening we purchased in perpetuity a grave at the cemetery in Villers Cotterets, arranged for coffins for the officers to be brought out early next morning, and for a wooden cross to be put up on the soldiers' grave recounting briefly the facts which had been discovered about those lying in it and also a wooden cross to be placed on the grave of the officers in the cemetery with the following inscription: –

'Ici reposent'
Quatre officiers de l'armee Anglais,
Le Colonel l'honorable George Morris, R.I.P.
Le Capitaine C. A. Tisdall, de la Garde Irlandaise
Le Lieutenant Geoffrey Lambton,
Le Lieutenant George E. Cecil,
     des Grenadiers de la Garde—
Tombés au champ d'honneur le 1st Septembre 1914 –

herein I made the mistake of describing Lambton as a Grenadier, but this can easily be rectified when a more permanent monument than the wooden cross is placed over the grave.

Early next morning, on Thursday the 19th November, 1914, we returned to the place in the forest where the bodies of the officers lay, and their remains were put into coffins. Inasmuch as plaques, to be nailed to the coffins, which we had ordered the previous evening, had not come, the chauffeur cut numbers on the coffins:— 'I' on my brother's, 'II' on Captain Tisdall's, 'III' on Lambton's, 'IV' on Cecil's. The coffins were then carried by French soldiers to a van on the road, and a pall and flowers, brought by the Monffliers, placed on them. (The doctor and his wife and their son Jacques, gave us invaluable help in every arrangement, and showed us the greatest kindness and sympathy.) Thus the coffins were conveyed to the cemetery at Villers-Cotterets followed by one motor with Mr Briggs and myself and by the Monffliers in their motor. The cemetery was reached a little before 11 a.m., and then the four officers were buried together in the grave which we had bought (the fifth on the left hand side of the path that faces the entrance to the cemetery). The Roman Catholic Dean and Mr Briggs read prayers over the grave. My brother and Captain Tisdall were lowered first, side by side, my brother's coffin being on the left as you look at the grave from the pathway, and Lambton is over him, and Cecil over Tisdall. . . . The Mayor of Villers Cotterets and other civil authorities and a French Colonel and some 20 French officers attended the funeral, although, as we were not many miles from Soissons and the fighting line on the Aisne, they were very busy. During the funeral and all these days the booming of the cannons went on and on. At the conclusion of the funeral Dr Monfflier asked me to follow the French custom, and, as a relative of the deceased, to go and stand at the entrance of the cemetery and, as those who had attended the funeral passed out, to shake hands with them all and thank them for having come to it. This I did, and they made many most kind and touching remarks as to its being the least they could do to endeavour to honour the brave English officers who had fought and died in their country for the common cause etc. That afternoon Mr Briggs and I left Villers Cotterets and returned to Paris. On my return to London, I gave lists of the Guardsmen whose discs or books had been found on their bodies, at the Headquarters of the Grenadiers, Coldstream, and Irish Guards in Wellington Barracks, and the Colonel of the Coldstream kept the 8 discs of the Coldstream soldiers. The other soldiers' discs and Captain Tisdall's I left at the War Office. The three buttons of Cecil's uniform and the initials off his vest and also Lambton's disc I handed to Lord Robert Cecil, and I gave my brother's watch to his widow. A button taken off Tisdall's uniform I gave to you. Irreparable as is the loss suffered by the death of these officers and soldiers and awful

as the work of exhumation was, it is to me an abiding consolation – which I hope it will also be to the other relatives
and to the friends of these officers and men – to know that
their remains were rescued from an utterly unknown grave
and a most indecorous burial, and have been laid to rest under
the circumstances described, when everything possible was
done to show respect and reverence and affection and honour
to their glorious and loved memories.

Believe me,

Yours very sincerely,

Killanin.

4

'Fight in a wood, crossed a river, took a village'

Entry in Battalion War Diary 8 September 1914

THE Battle of the Marne opened on 5 September with the attack by the French 6th Army, under Maunoury, on the exposed flank of Von Kluck's 1st German Army. The Retreat from Mons was ended. During the thirteen days that it lasted it has been calculated that the Army had marched nearly two hundred miles, averaging perhaps some four hours rest in each twenty-four. Now the time had come for the Allies to advance, hopefully pushing the Germans back to their starting point. It was unfortunate that the opportunity thus offered was not followed up more vigorously. It was as a result of the caution displayed in the rather leisurely pursuit that is described in the next few pages, that the fighting bogged down on the slopes of the Aisne.

Sunday, 6 September

Marched off 5.30 a.m. *advancing*. Apparently the Germans have changed direction eastwards, and we and the French are to attack. After three comparatively easy days and *three nights sleep*, the men are fit and hard, and all thankful to get forward. A long delay at the start, but eventually we moved about four miles and halted. Some Cavalry skirmishing in front, but we saw nothing of it. A very long halt near a small château into which we went in turn and had baths, which were *very* welcome. Then we had tea under the trees in the garden. The inhabitants must have bolted in a great hurry, for the whole place was in utter confusion – beds left just as they'd got out of them, and clothes and household goods strewn about anyhow. Later we moved on and bivouacked about 8.30 p.m. just outside Touquin, having covered about eight miles altogether.

Monday, 7 September

Guards Brigade and 41st Brigade R.F.A. [Royal Field Artillery] advanced guard under G. Feilding. A long day's march north-eastwards with very long delays and checks. 2nd Coldstream (vanguard) had a certain amount of fighting with enemy rear-guards, mostly Cavalry, and had a few casualties. We (Grenadiers) had no fighting. The Germans have done a lot of looting and wanton damage before evacuating towns and seem to have done an immense amount of drinking, judging from the empty bottles lying about. Our progress was very slow, as the enemy managed to delay us considerably. From the south bank of the Grand Morin we could see large columns and transport retiring north of the river towards Rebais. We eventually reached Voigny in pouring rain, having marched about thirteen miles. All very wet. We went into billets, getting most of the men into the Church.

Tuesday, 8 September

Brigade with 41st Brigade R.F.A. and 1 Fd. Coy R.E. was advance guard to the Division. Head of main guard was to pass starting point 5.30, and we were all ready and formed up on the road, but owing to the Divisional Cavalry not turning up and then to blocks due to a Cavalry Brigade crossing our line of march, vanguard never got going and a very long delay ensued.

Eventually we got going, but after passing through La Trétoire the 3rd Bn. Coldstream (vanguard Coys) were shelled whilst in column of route, by a battery from the direction of Boitron, and had some casualties. This caused further delay and it transpired that German rearguard was holding the line of the Petit Morin. The 3rd Coldstream were ordered to make good the crossing. The slopes on our side of the river were very thickly wooded and the enemy were holding some houses at Le Gravier, (where the road from La Trétoire to Boitron crosses the river by the bridge), as well as the open high ground on the north side of the river. The Coldstream went forward into these woods and appear to have been held up as soon as they attempted to emerge from them on to the low ground by the river, and the Irish Guards were then ordered forward. They also at about 8.30 plunged into the woods, became much mixed up with the Coldstream, and like them were held up by machine fire when they emerged. About 10 a.m. we (Grenadiers) were moved forward in Artillery formation over the high ground to the west of the Boitron road. We were not shelled, and our 41st Bd. appeared to have silenced the German guns. We closed up under the outskirts of the woods, where we were out of sight and were now ordered by Lieut-Colonel Feilding (acting Brigade Commander) to send a company forward to help the troops in front make good the crossing. Stephen's Company (No. 3) was sent, and they pushed forward to the edge of the woods coming out on the left, and partly overlapping the Irish Guards. They were then also held up, Stephen being badly wounded. We (Grenadiers) were now closed and moved off to our right close under the edge of the woods. Whilst moving to the right we were ordered to send another Company forward, and No. 4 was sent. They disappeared into the woods and we didn't see them again till the afternoon, but they never got into the front line. The rest of our Battalion (H.Q. and 2 Companies) marched down the road (La Trétoire–Boitron), which runs through the woods diagonally north-eastwards. At a point where the roads run out into a wide clearing, running nearly north and south down the river, was an 18 pounder gun, which had been man-handled down to the edge of the clearing and was having snap shots round the corner, so to speak, at the houses by the bridge. Apparently the 18 pounders with their flat trajectory couldn't touch these houses from the high ground, owing to the woods and the slope they were on. We halted about 100 yards short of the turn. G. Feilding was on foot by the gun, rather excited and saying he was being urged by Generals Monro and Haig to get on. At about 11.30 G. Feilding ordered the Battalion to file through the woods with a view to circumventing the clearing (which was swept by machine guns from Le Gravier) and crossing the river further eastwards at Laforge, on which place he had already directed the 2nd Coldstream. The Battalion moved off with Noel Corry at the head and me whipping in at the tail.

When the last files of No. 1 were just disappearing into the woods, G. Feilding who was standing by the gun, thought he saw the Germans withdrawing. He called to me to turn

the Battalion about and to get across the clearing. I shouted
to pass it up and to turn about, but the head of the Battalion
must by that time have been some hundreds of yards ahead
through the trees, and the only ones who came back were a
little more than a platoon of No. 1 with Sloper Mackenzie
and Sgt. Colegate. I formed them up hastily and they followed me in a rush across the clearing. It was at once evident
that the Germans had not gone, and we luckily found a slight
hollow half way across into which we threw ourselves down
for shelter from their fire. We took a breather and when they
had stopped firing we jumped up again and made a dash into
the wood on the far side, getting over without losing a man.
Once over I collected the party and we started to work down
through the woods to the line of the river. There were a few
scattered men of the 3rd Coldstream in the wood, mostly
lost I think, but I saw no officer, and we told the men to
come with us. We got down to the river bank (the wood on
this side runs right down to the river), but could see no
means of getting across. There was still some fire from Le
Gravier and from the opposite slopes, but shortly after we
got to the river (about 12.30) a Howitzer battery began to
shell the houses by the bridge, and after a few shells the
Germans began to withdraw. We could see them dribbling
away on the slopes opposite and also away from the bridge.
My party then worked along the bank of the river and
reached the bridge about the same time as a mixed party,
mostly Irish Guards, but including also some Coldstream and
some of our No. 3, arrived there. I arranged at once with
Stepney (Commanding Irish Guards) to make good the high
ground on the north bank, and as my party was composed
and needed no sorting out, I went straight ahead with it due
north from the bridge. I extended them and went on past
where the road makes a jut inwards. Here there were some
dead Germans and some abandoned bicycles, on which I put
three men and sent them as bicycle scouts along the road,
whilst with the rest I pushed on, and on getting to the top
of the hill, I could see ahead of me what seemed to be a
German battery. It was quite silent and on getting up to it
I found that the guns had been got away, but the waggons
and a lot of ammunition had been abandoned, and a lot of
dead men and horses lay all around. When I got to this
position I halted, as I could see nobody following me and I
had a clear field of fire. Moreover I was rather nervous of
some big woods a few hundred yards away to my left, as

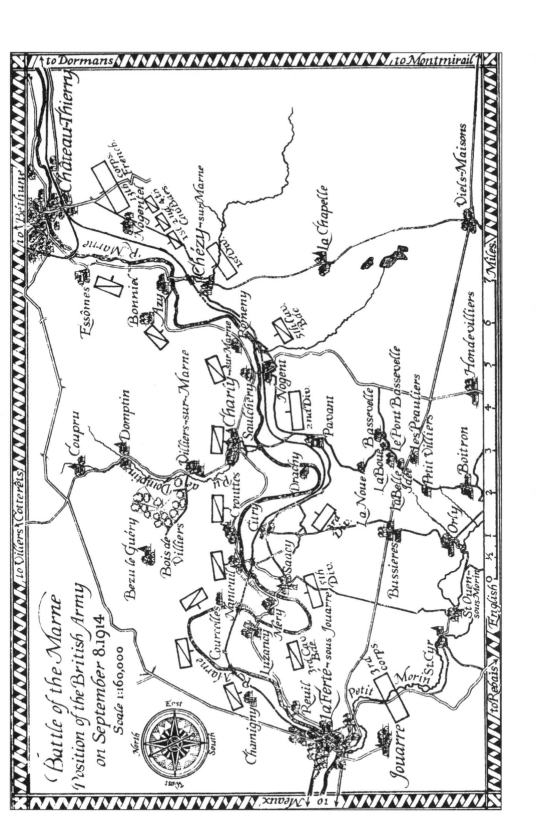

Battle of the Marne
Position of the British Army
on September 8.1914
Scale 1:160,000

they might have been full of Germans. It was now about 1 o'clock and I sent a message back to say where I was. After about half an hour Gerry Ruthven came up to me and told me that the Brigade was being collected in Boitron; that he would send someone to relieve me and that I could then re-join the Battalion. Whilst on the German battery position one of the men was searching dead Germans and found an automatic pistol on one of them. What he did, I don't know – in fact I didn't see he'd got it, but it certainly went off, luckily without hurting anyone. About 2 p.m. we went to Boitron, where we found the Brigade having dinners. At 3 p.m. we went forward, Grenadiers on right, 2nd Coldstream on left, both Battalions in Artillery formation. We (Grena-diers) went straight ahead and could see German troops and transport withdrawing in front of us. Unfortunately our own Artillery shelled our leading Companies, thinking they were Germans, and this caused delay and 2 casualties in No. 2 Coy. The woods on our left (west of Boitron) proved to have Germans in them, and the Irish Guards were ordered to attack them. The 2nd Coldstream advancing over the open ground had already passed them when 'Giant' Hardy, hearing the firing, diverted his Company and took the Germans in the rear, causing them to surrender. They were a complete Guards Machine Gun Company, 7 M.Gs., 100 men, limbers and some good horses. Unfortunately the 2nd Coldstream were also shelled by our own Artillery and 'Giant' was wounded, and several of his Company. Eventually we halted and bivouacked near Les Peauliers in a very damp field of sainfoin. It came on to pour with rain and rained most of the night. We had Stephen badly wounded and 18 other casualties. The rest of the Battalion and the 2nd Coldstream crossed without opposition at La Forge.

Wednesday, 9 September

In the morning orders received for Noel Corry to hand over Command and go home. All the result of the withdrawal at Mons. I still think he was right, and if George Morris had lived, I believe he would have been vindicated, especially as the whole Army was withdrawing a few hours later. I took over command. We were ready to march at 5 a.m., but didn't actually march off till 9 a.m. We were Reserve Brigade and progress was very slow with constant checks, due to

Brigades in front being held up. The rain cleared and it came on very hot in the middle of the day and dried our wet clothes. Eventually we crossed the Marne at Charley, where the other two Brigades had already crossed with little or no opposition. The bridge was undamaged, though prepared for demolition, and the story was that when the time came to blow it up, the Germans were too drunk to do it. As we came down the southern slope towards the river a solitary howitzer shell came over and burst on the opposite bank. Otherwise not a shot of any kind. Down the river, apparently 5 or 6 miles away, we could see a German sausage-shaped balloon. The town had various German bombastic inscriptions chalked in huge letters on the walls of houses. Eventually we bivouacked on a hillside over Domptin. It was raining hard again and we spent a wet and miserable night. Poor little 'Tich' Stephen died of his wounds.

The treatment of their Commanding Officer was a subject on which the Battalion held strong views. Some idea of their feelings may be gained in this extract from a letter written by Jeffreys to the Regimental Adjutant three days after Lieutenant-Colonel Corry's departure:

You will have heard by now that Col. Corry has been ordered home, and I am just writing these few lines to tell you how very sick we all are about it. I have no doubt that he will give you the details himself, but the main facts are that he was ordered by the Divisional General some miles away to hold a position near Mons, which he, G. Morris and I believed to be untenable under the circumstances. That being so, he took the responsibility of disobeying the order on the ground that the issuer did not know the circumstances on the spot. For disobeying this order he was sent home. I want it to be known that the senior officers of the battalion are unanimous in believing that he was right, and that his action probably saved the battalion and the Irish Guards from serious disaster. I do hope he may get some other job.

In the event Colonel Corry returned to France the following year in command of 3rd Battalion Grenadier Guards when they came to join the newly formed Guards Division.

Thursday, 10 September

Ready to march 5 a.m. Marched off 7.30. Orders are to 'Continue the pursuit'. It's a precious slow pursuit and the German rear-guards seem to delay us very successfully, judging from the constant checks. Eventually bivouacked at Brevil 8 p.m. The 6th Brigade (advance guard) had considerable fighting and took a good many prisoners.

Friday, 11 September

Ready to advance 5 a.m. Marched 7.15. Pouring rain and all soaked. The 'pursuit' still slow. We marched by Priez, Sommdans, Larily, La Croix and Breny, and eventually billeted in Oulchy – the first billets for a long time and not enough of them for the Battalion, half of which was put into the Church. We (Battalion Headquarters Officers) were in a fair sized house and I had a clean bed and sheets. The shelter was worth a lot and we got our things dry. Like all these towns Oulchy appeared to have been pretty well ransacked by the Germans and judging by the empty bottles they must have got through an immense amount of drink.

Not everyone had been as lucky as Battalion Headquarters in the matter of billets. Gordon-Lennox gives some idea of the alternative in his diary:

11 September

Off at 7 a.m. and the usual long weary halts with lots of gunning going on all round us. Heavy showers at intervals, but at about 1 p.m. it came on a regular downpour: the wretched men got soaked. No. 2 Company were especially badly off as we had lost all our greatcoats and water-proof sheets at Landrecies. We plugged on in the rain which came down harder and harder. We reached Oulchy-le Château about 5 p.m. where we went into billets. No. 2 had an iron-monger's shop and we soon had fires going, and the men were enabled to dry their sodden clothes. The state of this shop and policies when we arrived was pitiable. The Dutchmen had been in it, and absolutely ransacked the place. Every drawer was overturned and the floors were feet deep with every sort of article, wearing apparel, gramophone records smashed to atoms, food, glasses, etc. and all the tables had glasses and unfinished food: other and less sanitary signs were everywhere apparent – the filthy brutes. We were famished but soon had a good meal of eggs and bacon, and proceeded to divest ourselves of all our clothes, hanging them up to dry.

If the Retreat had been hard for the Allies, it had been no less of a physical effort for the Germans. In maintaining the momentum drink appears to have played a significant part. One of Von Kluck's officers wrote:

> Our men are done up. For four days they have been marching 24 miles a day. . . . The men stagger forward, their faces coated with dust, their uniform in rags, they look like living scarecrows. They march with their eyes closed, singing in chorus so that they shall not fall asleep on the march. The certainty of early victory and the triumphal entry into Paris keeps them going and acts as a spur to their enthusiasm. Without this certainty of victory they would fall exhausted. They would go to sleep where they fell so as to get to sleep somehow or anyhow. It is delirium of victory which sustains our men, and in order that their bodies may be as intoxicated as their souls, they drink to excess, but this drunkenness helps to keep them going. Today after an inspection the general was furious. He wanted to stop this general drunkenness. We managed to dissuade him from giving severe orders. If there were too much severity the army would not march. Abnormal stimulants are necessary to make abnormal fatigue endurable. We will put all that right in Paris.*

The Germans continued to withdraw, fighting hard.

Saturday, 12 September

Ready to move 5 a.m. but did not march till 9 a.m. 5th Infy Bde. (Advance-Guard) had fighting when crossing the Vesle at Courcelles, and this and an awful congestion of transport in Oulchy delayed progress. Again pouring rain and constant checks. Crossed the Vesle at Braine and eventually

---

* Quoted by John Terraine in *Mons*.

got into billets at Vanbeclin just north of Courcelles at 8 p.m. All wet and weary. Bad billets, but much better than none.

Sunday, 13 September

Ready to move 5 a.m. Still raining but cleared soon after we marched off at 8 a.m. About 9.30 a.m. the Brigade halted behind the crest on the high ground south of St Mard, a village just south of the Aisne. Here there was a halt of several hours and dinners were cooked. About noon the 2nd Bn. Coldstream were sent forward to make good the crossing of the Aisne at Chavonne. The other three Battalions remained where they were. At about 12.30 the three C.O.s (Self, Matheson, 3 C.G., Herbert Stepney I.G.) went forward with the Brigade Commander (Feilding) and Brigade Major (Ruthven) to a spur on the high ground south-west of St Mard, in order to reconnoitre the high ground north of the Aisne and the river valley. From this point, which was in a cluster of big rocks on the west side of the road into St Mard we got a good view of Chavonne and all of the high ground north of the Aisne. We watched the 2nd Coldstream attack which seemed to make rather slow progress, though supported by Artillery and by our machine-gun section, which they borrowed. However they got to the river about 3 p.m., and after some delay got across the gap in the bridge, which had been destroyed but had some planks left spanning the gap. Before this we (C.O.s) could see parties of the enemy dribbling back from the slopes above Chavonne and retiring across the high ground towards the Chemin des Dames. The actual crossing of the river did not seem to be opposed, and the crossing was secured about 4 p.m. We could also see shells bursting and fighting apparently going on away to our right and left, but could make out no details. After watching the retirement of the enemy in small parties from the heights above Chavonne, we were surprised to see them, as it seemed, coming back again and moving south across the high ground in long, widely extended lines. G. Feilding sent a message to some Artillery, who were halted a few hundred yards away to the right rear of our party, telling them there was a good target on the heights opposite, and asking them to fire. A reply came back that the guns were not in action, and the horses were being watered, so they could not comply! A further message had the effect of making them get some guns

into action, but before they could fire more than one or two
rounds the enemy had disappeared into the woods and broken
ground above Chavonne. Meanwhile the 2nd Bn. Coldstream
had pushed up through Chavonne and established themselves
in and beyond the northern outskirts of the village, which
had been evacuated by the enemy. Here their forward Companies were shelled, but not otherwise molested. Late in the
afternoon (about 4.30 p.m.) I was ordered to reconnoitre for
crossings in the vicinity of St Mard and to effect a crossing
thereabouts if possible. I moved one Company down through
the woods on the slopes east of St Mard to where the canal
and the river run close side by side. Our patrols were not
fired on and the opposite bank seemed to be unoccupied, so
I brought the rest of the Battalion down under cover of the
woods. We found 3 or 4 small boats under the canal bank
and pushed a small covering party across and eventually got
the greater part of a Company over the canal. Two of the
boats were then dragged across the intervening strip of
ground, and in these we got a few men across the river.
It was a very slow business and I sent Bernard Lennox and
Gilbert Hamilton with a party to a bridge (over the canal
only) opposite St Mard. This however was apparently under
observation, as they were at once shelled, though there was no
interference with us crossing in boats under cover of the
woods on both banks. The woods were shelled intermittently
by Field Howitzers, but it was random shooting and went
near no-one. However by the time about 10 men had been
got across the river, we got orders about 7 p.m. to withdraw
and billet in St Mard. Part of the Company was withdrawn
by the bridge, as being quicker than by boat, and they got
shelled but had no casualties. About the same time 2nd Bn.
Coldstream were also withdrawn across the river and billeted
in Cys La Commune, leaving one Company holding the
bridge. We all wondered why, as they were well established.
Quite fair billets in St Mard: we (Bn. H.Q. Officers) with an
old farmer, who was very friendly, and produced some drink-
able red wine for us. It struck me though as being an odd
place in which to billet – down in a hole and overlooked on
the north bank.

*For one of the Platoon Commanders, Welby, the day made even
less sense. The entry in his diary reads:*

Gunfire still to N.W. Still showery. Looked at old Norman Church. Footling day near canal. Eventually back and billet at St Mard.

On this occasion good fortune in the choice of billets extended beyond Battalion Headquarters. Major Gordon-Lennox noted:

We found an obliging farmer, whose daughter had come home from Paris for a fortnight's holiday, being a dressmaker. I'm afraid her holiday can't have been exactly enjoyable, but she proved to be an awfully good cook, and made us an excellent *bouillon* of vegetables, followed by an equally excellent omelette.

Next day the Battalion went into action again.

Monday, 14 September

Marched off from St Mard 5.30 a.m. with orders to cross the Aisne at Pont Arcy. We were leading battalion of the Brigade and marched along the canal tow-path. There was a thick mist which prevented one seeing more than a few yards, and it was raining steadily. Gerry Ruthven and I rode along together at the head of the Battalion. We talked about the retreat and I asked him if he remembered a conversation we had had at the Depot in the summer about the respective merits of the regiments of the Brigade. He then said that he wished the Grenadiers and Scots Guards were as keen on training as the Coldstream. I said, however that might be, I was certain from my experience of the regiments at the Depot, that our discipline was much stronger than that of the Coldstream, and that I was sure it would tell in war – little thinking that war was so near. Gerry said, 'By God, you were right!' and we both agreed the Coldstream march discipline was much below ours, and below the Irish Guards too. The 2nd Battalion Coldstream have of course been much worse than the 3rd Battalion.

The bridges at Pont Arcy had been destroyed, but the R.E. had made a pontoon bridge and our original orders were to commence crossing at 6.50 a.m., but the 6th Brigade started crossing before us and we sat and waited in the rain. Our Battalion was to be advance guard to the Brigade and my orders were to secure the heights about La Cour de

1. George Darell (Ma) Jeffreys, whom Harold Macmillan, himself a Grenadier who served with Jeffreys, has described as 'the supreme example of a great regimental officer'. This photograph was taken in his office in the Horse Guards in February 1920 while he was GOC London District.

2. Grenadiers at the Guards Depot, 1912. *Standing left to right:* Lt. Hon. R. Keppel, Capt. E. N. Vaughan, Major S. Gallio, RAMC, Lt. E. Gough, Capt. and Qr.Mr. Walker. *Seated left to right:* Lt. Adj. C. Campbell, Maj. G. D. Jeffreys, Capt. W. Ingilby.

3. Reservists answer the call – Wellington Barracks, August 1914.

4. The front line position at Chavonne. *Left to right:* Earl Percy (Staff), Lt. D. Miller, Maj. Lord Bernard Gordon-Lennox, Capt. G. Powell.

5. Inside the Company H.Q. at Chavonne, nicknamed 'The Hotel Billet-Doux', Lt. C. M. G. Dowling, Lt. D. W. Miller, Maj. Lord Bernard Gordon-Lennox.

6. The horse rescued at Landrecies (*page 44*) survived to serve (Ma) Jeffreys as a hunter after the War ended.

7. Wilfrid Smith and (Ma) Jeffreys, early in 1915.

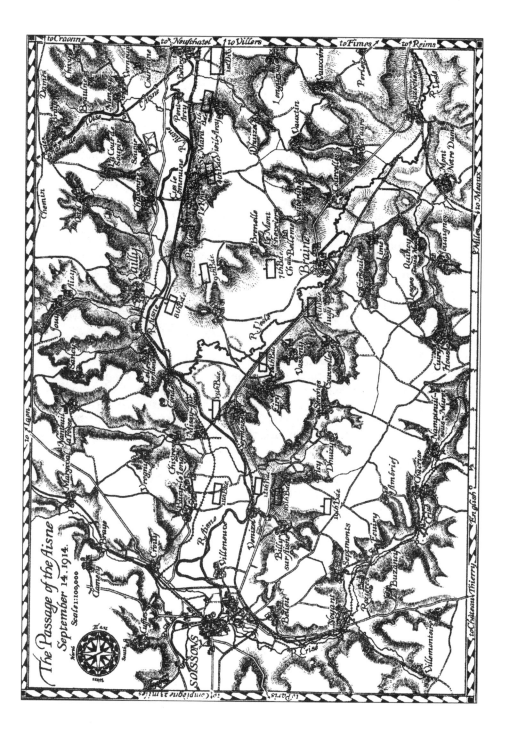

The Passage of the Aisne
September 14. 1914.
Scale 1:100,000

Soupir and to make good the cross-roads east of Ostel (P[oin]t 197). I was given no information, either about our own troops or the enemy, and no-one seemed to anticipate severe fighting. We did not start crossing till 8.30, and when we moved off it was still misty and raining, though less heavily. No. 1 Company (Major G. Hamilton) was van-guard and moved to Soupir village – about two miles west-ward along the river valley: it searched the village and found no signs of the enemy. It then moved forward along the road leading up the hill to La Cour de Soupir. This road runs up a thickly wooded re-entrant, the ground rising very steeply on the west side of the road up to the plateau above Chavonne. On both sides of the road were thick woods and no view could be got from it. There was some delay whilst Soupir village was being made good, and a further delay whilst flanking parties were being pushed out through the dense woods on either side of the road, up which the point of the vanguard (1 platoon under 2/Lieut. Cunliffe) was moving. I moved Battalion Headquarters and the main guard Com-panies to the western outskirts of Soupir village, which we reached about 9.15 and halted there waiting for the van-guard to get on. G. Hamilton now sent a message to say that he was not happy about his left flank. He had sent a platoon up to secure the high ground on the edge of the woods west of the Cour de Soupir road, and this platoon reported seeing considerable numbers of Germans to the westward. I there-fore sent up two platoons of No. 2 and (later), on a further request for reinforcements, the rest of No. 2 to reinforce this flank. One platoon of No. 1 and one of No. 2 (the latter under Prince Alexander of Battenberg) pushed out wide to the left flank in the direction of Chavonne and remained out as a flank guard, eventually joining up with the Cavalry who were sent to fill the gap at Chavonne. The rest of No. 2 and one platoon of No. 1 moved forward on the high ground of the Cour de Soupir road, the point platoon supported by the remaining platoon of No. 1 continuing to move forward along the road. I then moved with Battalion Headquarters and Nos. 3 & 4 Companies along the road into the woods to a point about half a mile south of Cour de Soupir, where a ride runs east at right-angles to the road, getting there about 10 a.m., by which time there was heavy firing in front. On hearing that the Germans had advanced and that they had penetrated into the woods on the east side of La Cour de Soupir, I sent No. 3 Coy, under Gosselin, forward on the

east side of the road with orders to clear the wood and protect our right flank. This Company soon became hotly engaged with the Germans in the wood, but made some
progress. Some Germans had got up into trees and were
shooting from them. Gosselin asked for reinforcements, and
first two platoons and then a third platoon of No. 4 were
sent to him, and on their left they pressed on to the edge of
the wood east of Cour de Soupir. On their right they could
not get on, so that their right platoons were refused [thrown
back] at a sharp angle. Outside the wood they found a considerable number of Germans in front of them, and as there
were still Germans in the wood on and behind their right
flank, their position was far from comfortable. Battalion Headquarters, the M.G. Section, and the one remaining platoon
of No. 4 were on the edge of a small clearing just in front
of the aforesaid ride east of the road, and I and Pike
(Adjutant) went forward to see if we could see anything. We
went up the road, which was now being heavily shelled with
salvos of shrapnel by a field battery taking it in enfilade. The
road was practically the only avenue of communication from
front to rear and we had a very unpleasant walk up it and
back. Owing to thick trees we could see very little in any
direction, except at one point where the road seemed to be
overlooked by a spur (less thickly wooded) on the opposite
side of the valley; from the direction of this spur bullets,
possibly not aimed at us, were coming on to the road. I had
had no message from Nos. 1 or 2 Coys since the firing started,
and by this time practically the whole Battalion was committed and spread out like a fan, Nos. 1 & 2 on the high
ground in front of, and west of La Cour de Soupir; Nos. 3
and three platoons of No. 4 in the northern edge of the woods
just east of the farm, and with their right flank thrown back
through the woods; Battalion Headquarters, M.G. Section and
one platoon of No. 4 on the south edge of the little clearing
in the woods just east of the road. I had hardly any reserve
left and knew very little of what had happened in front.
This was about 10.30. What had happened was that the vanguard on reaching La Cour de Soupir had found the farm
occupied by the Connaught Rangers (5th Infy Bde.). 4th
(Guards) Brigade had never been informed of their presence
there, and much time might have been saved had anything
been known about it. 5th Infy Bde. had crossed at Pont Arcy
the night before, and I believe O.C. Connaught Rangers

occupied Cour de Soupir on his own initiative.* The pity was that no-one else apparently knew anything about it. When Cunliffe and our leading platoon had gone some hundreds of yards past the farm in the direction of Pt. 197, a heavy German attack developed from the northward, and the leading platoon, together with some Connaught posts, was driven back to the vicinity of the farm, Cunliffe being left badly wounded on the ground. Our Nos. 1 & 2 (less their flanking platoons in the direction of Chavonne) had come up on the west of the farm and in front of it, and the Connaughts came out of the farm enclosure and took up positions in front of it and just east of it. The attack was repulsed with heavy loss on our left, but east of the farm the Germans overlapped our right and got into the woods, from which they were only completely dislodged much later and after considerable fighting by our No. 3 and by the 3rd Bn Coldstream and by the Irish Guards. About 10.30 the 3rd Bn. Coldstream began to come up, moving through the woods to avoid the shell-fire on the road. We heard nothing from Brigade Headquarters about them being sent up, but first one of their Companies passed our Battalion Headquarters, moving in extended order through the woods, and then Arthur Smith, their Adjutant, came and told me that Major Matheson, their Commanding Officer, was moving up to Cour de Soupir. I then went and met Matheson on the road by the farm. One company of the 3rd Bn. Coldstream had come into action west and north-west of the farm and with our No. 2 had driven back the Germans, who withdrew some hundreds of yards on this side. As they withdrew an officer was seen to shoot Cunliffe dead as he lay wounded on the ground. This was vouched for by other men of his platoon, who had been taken prisoner when the Germans advanced and were abandoned by them when they retired.† Two other Companies of the 3rd Coldstream pushed up through the woods east of the road, gradually clearing them of Germans, and mixing up with our No. 3, whose centre and right they carried forward with them to the edge of the wood. There

* The Connaught Rangers had occupied Soupir village the night before and had been ordered to hold the village as a secure start line for the operations of 4th (Guards) Brigade next day. The Commanding Officer, however, felt that he would be better placed to assist these operations at La Cour de Soupir farm, and therefore moved up there of his own accord at dawn.

† The German officer concerned was immediately shot by advancing Coldstream.

were still, however, Germans in the woods on and behind
their right flank. Somewhere about 11.0 two Companies of
the Irish Guards, under Captain Perceval (having, I think,
lost direction), went out on to the high ground on our left
and took up a position about the line of the Cour de Soupir
– Chavonne road. The 2nd Company came up through the
woods on the east side of the road, overlapping the right of
the 3rd Bn. Coldstream, and having heavy fighting with
Germans in the woods on that flank. Some of this Company
lost direction and came up into the mixed firing line on the
edge of the wood just east of the farm, but the majority, supported eventually by the remainder of the Battalion fought
their way forward to the edge of the woods, though their
right was unable to get so far, being unable to push the
Germans out of the wood. Up to the time when Matheson
and I met on the road by the Farm, (about 11 a.m.) I had
had no message or order from the Brigade, and we had had
no support from our Artillery, nor had any Artillery Officer
come forward to us. Owing however to the thick trees and
steep slopes it would have been difficult for them to find
positions. The German Artillery fire had now lifted, and was
searching further back down the road and the river valley. At
this time there was a firing line of Grenadiers, Coldstream
and some Connaught Rangers all mixed together lining the
northern edge of the woods east of the farm, the slightly
sunken road just north of the farm, and bending back in a
south-westerly direction on the west side of the farm. A
few Irish Guardsmen were mixed up in the line on the edge
of the woods east of the farm : the majority of the Connaughts were in the farm enclosure, and one company of
Irish Guards and some of No. 2 Coy, Grenadiers were roughly
along the line of the Cour de Soupir–Chavonne road and on
the high ground just north of Chavonne. On the north side
of the farm was a big root field and in it, hidden from view
by the roots, a number of Germans were lying down. We
did not know how many of them there were, but the rifle
fire was now slight and the German Artillery was shelling
far back into the woods and down the Soupir road. Matheson
and I discussed what we should do and decided to attack. He
had one company in reserve, and with this and his company
west of the farm, he would go for Pt. 197, whilst I pushed
forward on the right. At 12 o'clock the order was given to
advance, but as our men got up to go forward a large number of Germans (at least 200), who had been lying flat in

the root-field, suddenly rose to their feet and ran forward with their hands up. It was said that further away to the left a white flag was raised, but I did not see this. Unfortunately men of all units – Grenadiers, Coldstream, Connaught Rangers and Irish Guards – rushed forward to seize prisoners, and though both Matheson and I shouted to them to stand fast, we could not stop them and a confused mass of British and German soldiers was the result. On this mass the Germans in rear at once opened fire, causing a number of casualties. The British, dragging their prisoners, fell back to the edge of the sunken road just north of the farm, and to the edge of the woods east of it; and reorganisation of the troops, now more mixed up than ever, became a difficult matter. I don't believe there was any intentional treachery on the part of the Germans. Their leading line had had enough and meant to surrender. Incidentally they had hardly any ammunition left. Their supports in rear, however, had no intention of surrendering and opened fire when they got a good target. I had no idea what good cover a root field could give to men lying down: they were as invisible in it as partridges.

The German fire now increased in volume, especially from a ridge some 500 yards north-east of the farm, and Matheson and I after again consulting together, decided that he should take the one intact platoon of my No. 4 Coy, and should go round to the eastward through the wood to try and find the Irish Guards, and with them organise an attack to take the ridge just mentioned in flank. I was to remain in command of all the mixed up troops of the Guards Brigade in the neighbourhood of the farm, keeping the ridge under fire, and gaining ground if the turning movement proved successful. The Connaughts were concentrated inside the farm enclosure, a very big one with high walls round it, and the prisoners were moved into a big quarry pit on the edge of the wood just east of the farm. We could do no real reorganisation, but under cover of the wood and the short length of sunken road, we managed to get most of the Grenadiers on the right and most of the Coldstream on the left. Further to the left they remained mixed up. Matheson started off about 1 p.m.; made his way through the woods, and eventually found Major Stepney, Commanding Irish Guards. These had not yet succeeded in clearing the Germans out of the wood, but the C.O. agreed to attack as requested. This attack was made about 3 p.m., and though the Irish Guards never debouched from the woods, yet their movement had considerable effect, a number of Germans leaving the wood and running to their right along the ridge before mentioned, thus giving my troops lining the road north of the farm a very good target, of which they took full advantage to inflict many casualties on the enemy. Prior to this we had been under a constant dropping fire from the ridge and had several casualties: I think our heads must have shown up against the white wall of the farm enclosure just behind. However the fire from the ridge now gradually died away and the Germans appeared to have withdrawn from it, or at any rate to be no longer in force there. I then decided to gain ground to the northwards, and sent two platoons under Lt. Stewart (No. 2 Coy) forward from the road north of the farm about 300 yards to the far edge of the big root field, beyond which were some bare grass fields. These two platoons came under fire from the northward, Stewart being wounded, and they remained on the far edge of the woods. After dark, however, these two platoons, which were right out in front of the general line, were withdrawn.

About 4 p.m. Matheson returned to the farm and we again discussed what should be done. We came to the conclusion that with the Battalions so scattered and mixed up, no further advance should be attempted, especially as we had no Artillery support. The Brigade Major (Major Hon. W. Ruthven) came up about this time, but brought no orders, having merely come to ascertain the situation about La Cour de Soupir. We had had practically no communication with Brigade all day. We had sent them some messages but had had no reply, and visual signalling was hopeless on account of the woods. Ruthven told us that two Companies of 2nd Bn. Coldstream had been sent to Chavonne, where they were in touch with the 1st Cavalry Brigade, which had been sent to Chavonne to fill the gap between us and 3rd Division at Vailly. The two other Companies of 2nd Bn. Coldstream had been sent up on the right to support the Irish Guards, so that this completed a proper mix-up of the Brigade! Matheson and I arranged to reorganise our Battalions as soon as it got dusk – Grenadiers to hold from a track in the wood about 200 yards east of the farm as far as the Chavonne–Pt. 197 road: 3rd Coldstream to hold thence south-westward roughly along the Chavonne road to join up with the 2nd Bn. Coldstream. Grenadiers were in touch with the Irish Guards on their right: beyond the Irish Guards

D

were 6oth Rifles. 2 platoons of Grenadiers were at Chavonne, whence the 1st Cavalry Brigade prolonged the line in the direction of Vailly, which was occupied by the II Corps.

After dark these dispositions were taken up, and the Connaught Rangers withdrew from the farm to the river valley. Stretcher parties were sent out to collect the wounded, of which a considerable number (both British and German) lay out in front as well as a very large number of dead Germans. In front of our left (west of the farm) there lay a whole line of Germans, all dead, and there were a good many bodies in the roots as well as some live Germans, who had been lying doggo and now gave themselves up. We dug our trenches about 100 yards in front of the sunken road north of the farm and curving back to the edge of the wood where we joined the Irish Guards. Our supports were in an old quarry pit on the edge of the wood just east of the farm and dug in behind the south wall of the farm enclosure. The stretcher-bearers reported seeing a good many Germans, both parties and individuals, who did not molest them, but appeared intent on getting away. One stretcher-bearer came up to me and said he had met a German officer with a party of men. He asked in what strength we were, and said that if we were in greater strength than they, he would be prepared to surrender, but that he would only surrender to an officer. The stretcher-bearer had told him that there were 'thousands of us'. I told the man to say, if he saw the officer again, that if he came in an officer would receive his surrender. The stretcher-bearer disappeared and returned in about half-an-hour, saying that he had again seen the officer, but that he would not come with him. He had however met another officer, who had come with him and 'Here he is'. Out of the darkness stepped a tall, smart German Lieutenant, who saluted, said in English, 'I wish to surrender,' and handed me his sword. There was great difficulty in dealing with the wounded. The large farmhouse was full of them, and so were the big cattle byres, barn, cart sheds, etc., and a number were lying on straw in the farmyard, and just outside the gate were a number of German wounded, who groaned and cried out continously through the night. Our wounded on the contrary were very quiet. There were only four or five horse ambulances (no motor ambulances), and the horses, after many journeys up and down the steep hill from the river, were so dead beat that they could hardly move. There were not nearly enough Medical Officers, orderlies etc., at the farm to deal with the wounded, and the farm was not cleared of them until 16 September. . . . We began now to realise our own losses. Of officers, Cunliffe and des Voeux were killed, and Stewart, Gosselin, Welby, Walker, Mackenzie and Harcourt-Vernon were wounded; and we have lost at least 120 N.C.O.s and men. Gosselin and Welby, who were not badly wounded (hand and shoulder respectively) volunteered to remain at duty: the others were all severe wounds. I know too that the other Regiments had severe losses. Percy Wyndham and David Bingham (Coldstream) were both killed: Victor Gordon-Ives was very badly wounded close to me by the farm; I hear Banbury is badly hit too. Arthur Hay and Guernsey (Irish Guards) are both killed, and I saw Guthrie lying badly wounded in the farm. It was late before we got rations up and got everyone some food and hot tea, which was badly wanted. For want of anywhere else I put Battalion Headquarters in a lean-to cart shed just outside the main gate of the farm. It was a rickety place and wouldn't have stopped any missile, but it did keep out the drizzling rain which had now come on again. I tried to sleep, but it was too cold, and a row of German wounded, for whom there was no room in the farm, continuously calling out 'Kamerad', also kept me awake – I had never before realised the meaning of 'My wounds stink and are corrupt'. These undressed wounds did stink and were corrupt! In the middle of the night I was so cold that I got up and went into the farmhouse. Doctors were still at work in the ground floor rooms, but I went upstairs and found a big room with a fire in it. There were two men in it, whom I took for medical orderlies, and I said they must be having a busy time. One of them said, 'Ah! we belong to the Connaughts, but wouldn't you like a cup of tea, Sir?' The Connaughts, who were notorious for straggling in the retreat, were still leaving stragglers behind! However, I couldn't resist the tea and took it gratefully.

One further incident in this day's fighting is worth recalling. It is told here in the words of the Regimental History:

During the wood fighting a young soldier of the Grenadiers, Private Parsons, collected 12 men belonging to a battalion in another brigade, who were lost and had no officer or N.C.O. He got them together and commanded them for the rest of the fight, giving his orders clearly and coolly, and never making a mistake.

For this action Private Parsons was promoted Corporal in the field, and was Mentioned in Despatches on 18 October 1914. He died of wounds on 28 October.

Tuesday, 15 September

Soon after daylight we sent out stretcher-parties again, but they were fired on by the Germans, and we had to withdraw them. After an interval of two hours we tried again, but they were again fired on, and we could not collect the remaining wounded until after dusk. Men who had fallen dead or wounded in the dense woods were very difficult to find, and probably some wounded men died through not being found. I was anxious about Alexander of Battenberg, of whom we had no word last night, but found he was at Chavonne, where he and his platoon had been sent as flank-guard by Gilbert Hamilton. We were shelled intermittently all the morning but did a lot of work deepening and improving the trenches, which about noon were shelled pretty heavily. My cart-shed felt very insecure, but wasn't touched. Feilding (acting Brigade Commander) came up in the afternoon and talked to the German wounded prisoners, who were in a large cattle-shed on the north side of the farmyard. Our Corporal in charge of them pointed out one man and said, 'This man is troublesome, Sir. He keeps getting up and I keep putting him down, and he says he is an officer.' G.F. spoke to him in German, and it transpired that he *was* an officer, and all he wanted was to get up and go to the rear! We got a good many of the wounded away from the farm during the day, but not nearly all. After dark we buried all the dead we had been able to collect, by the cross-roads just east of the farm – all Germans in one big grave and all the British in another. We couldn't get a Chaplain, so I read part of the Burial Service with Pike holding an electric torch on the book. We sent the dead officers down the hill to bury them in Soupir churchyard.

Wednesday, 16 September

We again sent out stretcher-parties at dawn and managed to get in a few more wounded – all in a pitiable state – but the stretcher-parties were again shelled. Ridley with two men had a sniping post on top of a big corn rick just east of the farm. Eventually he must have been spotted, as about 11 a.m. a shell hit the rick, wounding both the men and setting fire to the rick, from which Ridley made a hasty descent, dazed by the explosion but otherwise none the worse. The shelling now increased and about midday the Germans began to shell the farm itself, which they had previously left alone. All the British wounded had been moved, but there were still some German wounded in the big shed on the north side of the yard. We moved Battalion Headquarters down into the quarry, and as the sheds now caught fire, we ordered all men out of the farm into the quarry. I didn't want a stampede, so stood in the road opposite the gate and made the men walk (not run) across, and this they did very steadily. I don't think we lost a man. One young Coldstream rushed across and I caught him by the collar and said, 'Didn't you hear me say "Walk"?' He said 'Yes Sir' and walked quite slowly on. We formed everybody up close under the steep slope at the bottom. A party of the 3rd Coldstream very gallantly got the German wounded out of the big shed into comparative safety behind the south wall of the farm. Two companies of the Oxford & Bucks Lt. Infy., who had been sent up to support us were also in the quarry. Early in the afternoon the shelling became very intense both on the trenches and on the woods in rear. All kinds of guns were firing, from field-guns to very heavy howitzers. We got all the troops closed up close under the steep north bank of the quarry: the bank was not too steep to climb and had little ledges on it, on which a certain number of men sat. As the shelling seemed to portend an attack, I moved No. 2 Coy up to just below the top edge, so as to be handy for counter-attack. I sat with Pike (Adjutant), Bernard Gordon-Lennox, and George Powell near the top of the bank, so that we could look over occasionally. We sat there for over an hour quite unscathed, while the shells roared and screamed overhead and crashed into the wood further down the slope. The trenches were mostly shelled with light stuff, the heavy shells going further over. The noise was so continuous that one couldn't hear any single shell, and we were smoking our pipes and getting quite used to it when the unluckiest thing possible happened – a heavy howitzer shell just cleared the edge of the quarry and burst amongst the troops at the bottom of the slope, killing and wounding a great number, both of those at the bottom

and of those sitting up the slope. Neither I nor the three
officers with me (Bernard Lennox, Pike, G. Powell) were
touched, though we were right in the blast of the shell. It
was an awful sight – dead and wounded men lying all round
– and I shouted for the doctor – Huggan, R.A.M.C., attached
3rd Coldstream – whom I had seen just previously. There
was no answer, and I shouted again, 'Where's that Doctor?'
Someone said, 'Here Sir', and I saw that he was dead. There
was no other doctor and the stretcher-bearers tied up wounds
as best they could with 1st Field dressings, and we moved
some of the wounded into some small caves in the quarry
bank. No other shell came into the quarry, but the shelling
(by far the heaviest we had experienced) went on for some
time, and then in the late afternoon an attack was made. It
was very half-hearted and withered away directly it was met
by our rifle-fire. The shelling ceased altogether shortly after,
but we had had a bad day. That one shell in the quarry
killed and wounded some 40 of our men and also about 50
of the Oxford L.I., besides Huggan, R.A.M.C., and a few
Coldstreamers – over 100 in all. The trenches got off sur-
prisingly lightly with about 30 casualties, but we lost two
valuable officers killed – poor 'Stag' Cecil shot in the throat
and Welby, who had been wounded in the shoulder on Monday, but stuck to duty as his Company was so short of
officers. Gosselin, too, who though in great pain had stuck to
his Company, had now to go to hospital.

Thursday, 17 September

We were relieved during the night by the Oxford &
Bucks L.I., the relief being completed just before dawn, and
we went back into billets in Soupir village. We were all dead
tired and slept most of the morning. In the afternoon we
cleaned up and I went to the hospital and saw poor 'Cakes'
Banbury lying on straw in a stall in a stable. He died soon
after. Victor Gordon-Ives is dead too. Alexander of Battenberg is in hospital with a chill. He stuck the retreat much
better than I expected, but he's not a heaven-born soldier
and is rather a responsibility to have on one's hands, so I
asked our Doctor, Howell, R.A.M.C., if he could get him
sent home. He said they had more cases than they could
deal with and very little accommodation, and that they
would be glad to get him away! In the evening we buried

our dead officers – Cecil, Welby, des Voeux and Cunliffe – in the cemetery. Then a quite good dinner and a good night's sleep.

A nice description of the hospital is given in the following extract from Gordon-Lennox's diary for the same day.

17 September

I went to see Drino* in hospital. He is bad with jaundice and chill, and will have to go to the base. The hospital is the Château, a magnificent place belonging to the Mme. Barsomme, or some such name: she is Calmette's mistress and the *Figaro* appears to be a paying concern. I don't think the good lady will like the look of her place when she returns from Pau. The Germans ransacked the place on their retreat and we have had Cavalry and Artillery galloping all over the gardens and Dutch shells bursting in & about the grounds.

It was clear by now that further advances were impossible, and the necessary steps were taken to consolidate the line, and establish a routine of reliefs.

Friday, 18 September

Battalion took over the sector on the left of our old position from the 3rd Bn. Coldstream. Nos. 1 & 2 in trenches just east of the Cour de Soupir–Chavonne road, Nos. 3 & 4 in reserve behind the steep slope down to the Cour de Soupir–Soupir road. Battalion Headquarters in a big limestone cave close under the brow of the hill. Very safe and good visual signal communication with Brigade Headquarters in Soupir. Germans did not interfere with relief, which was complete by 8 a.m. We could see them digging some 600–700 yards away. Later shelling began. In a lull about midday I went to go round the trenches, taking Howell, R.A.M.C., with me. We got some way round, walking on top of the ground, as the trenches were not continuous, when they began to shell us steadily. We dodged from one short length of trench to

* 'Drino' – nickname for Alexander of Battenberg, one of Gordon-Lennox's Company officers.

another, finally taking refuge in Bernard Lennox's trench, where we stopped till it got quieter, and then made a bolt back. Our doctor, who is short and fat, didn't enjoy his walk. The shelling went on most of the afternoon, but didn't do much harm; a good deal of it went over the slope, but our reserve Companies had mostly got into caves like our Head-quarters one, and those who couldn't get in were all dug in, so we had few casualties. Just after dark the Germans made an attack, but it was half-hearted and easily beaten off, being caught in flank by the fire of the Cavalry above Chavonne, as well as by us in front.

For the whole of this period the German shelling was intense, and came to dominate the lives of everyone. Some idea of what this meant to those in the trenches may be gained from the following extracts from Gordon-Lennox's diary entries for 18 and 20 September.

18 September

We were subject to a hell of a bombardment all day with shrapnel and Black Maria. So far this has been an unequal contest, as our guns have practically not come into action yet, being unable to find a position or target, and whenever they do open fire from the valley below, it only draws a hail of shrapnel and high explosive on it at once: and the Dutchmen seem to know exactly where they are. The place must be full of spies. We could from the trenches see a good deal of the German position and could see them digging like blazes too, but their guns are awful hard to find. Throughout the day shrapnel was bursting right over and on us, but I had only one man wounded in the arm. Some of our guns were directly behind my hole, so I had the whole bombardment from both sides going on just above me. They turned on Black Maria in the afternoon, & she planted some shells within a few yards of us without doing any damage. She makes a hole in the ground big enough to bury 3 or 4 horses in. The only incon-venience suffered was a bad head, as the high explosive seems to daze one when it bursts close. Ma and Howell (Doctor, an excellent fellow) came to see me in the trenches in the morn-ing when all was quiet 'just for a stroll': they had hardly got in when they started shelling like blazes, and their visit was greatly and inconveniently lengthened, the more so as my hole was not meant to house three persons. Howell says he is giving up 'going for strolls'. . . .

20 September

Donald Miller and I started to dig and improve our trench as soon as it was light. I had just taken my overcoat off and laid it on the back of the trench about 1 yard away, when there was a tremendous explosion just above me. The man in the pit next door was badly hit by a shell, and has since had his arm off. My coat had the right arm nearly taken off at the shoulder and the left sleeve cut to bits, and it was only a yard off me, but I am thankful to say I was not inside the coat at the time. After that they left us pretty well alone till the afternoon. The battery which is plastering us like this is so close that one has no warning of the shell coming along: the only thing one hears is the burst and then woe betide you, if you aren't down in the bottom. Our gunners have been looking for this battery for five days now, but so far have failed to knock it out. Donald and I had a few shots ourselves at some Dutchmen who came up to within 500 yards of us on our left, in a gap in the wood, and we made them double back pretty fast. In the afternoon we underwent our usual bombardment and had another narrow escape, a bit of shrapnel landing at the back of the trench and making a good hole.

A new Commanding Officer arrived to take the place of Colonel Corry. Jeffreys's diary continues.

Saturday, 19 September

Still in the same position. Wilfrid Smith arrived from England to take over command of the Battalion, so my brief command ended. Sorry to lose command, but glad to serve under such an old friend as Wilfrid. He brought out (amongst other very good young officers) W. Bailey and Beaumont-Nesbitt and Congleton. Cavan arrived to take over the Brigade. Everyone full of confidence in him. In the afternoon and shortly after Wilfrid had arrived we were very heavily shelled – as heavily as on the 16th. The trenches didn't suffer much (7 casualties), and Battalion Headquarters and supports were in caves. The bulk of the shelling went over into the woods and valley.

Having taken over, Lieutenant-Colonel Wilfrid Robert Abel Smith commanded the Battalion until being killed in action on 18 May 1915 during the Battle of Festubert. He proved to be an outstanding Commanding Officer, who very quickly gained the deep respect and affection of all who served under him. The combination of Colonel Smith as Commanding Officer and Major Jeffreys as Senior Major gave the Grenadiers a partnership in command that was often considered to represent the ideal. In this extract from a letter to his wife, written two days after his arrival at the front, Colonel Smith gives an account of what he found:

> I write in a sort of cave, safe I hope from those horrible shells. Yesterday we had an extra dose of them. I suppose just to show what they could do. They had been going all the morning as usual, but from 2 till 6 they fairly let fly. One of the Brigade staff told me last night that they had been amusing themselves by counting them, and they averaged 50 a minute. It was like hell let loose, and the gunners calculated the afternoon's amusement must have cost them £35,000 in ammunition. In the evening they made a feeble attack, and we wiped them out. I was thankful the men have learnt at last to dig and burrow in like rabbits. I don't know what others lost, but we lost only 2 killed, and 4 wounded, entirely owing to good digging. It is a gruesome business burying the poor fellows at night, but somehow it seems better that it should be ended for them than that they should be badly wounded. The men are splendid and I think their bravery in disregarding danger is largely due to British stupidity. I don't think they realise their danger, which is a great blessing for them, and makes them stand like rocks, when the highly strung foreigners can't stick it. But the men are tired, I can see that. They have not had one day's rest since they started, to refit and wash etc., and the difficulty of keeping them awake at night is extreme, in fact the officers (and I have only 10 Company Officers) have to keep at them all night to keep them awake.

By now the Battalion was well established in the routine of trench life, and had time to catch up on the general situation.

Old friends, some of them Grenadiers seconded to other regi-
ments, began to make their appearance in the line.

Sunday, 20 September

In the same position. Again heavily shelled, but only four
casualties. German counter-attack at night easily beaten off.

Monday, 21 September

Relieved just before daybreak by Irish Guards, and went
back to Soupir and billeted. Gradually beginning to hear
something of the rest of the Army. We are across the Aisne
on the whole front from Bourg to Soissons, but except on the
right have rather a precarious hold on the north bank. The
1st Brigade too have had heavy losses – Poor old 'P.G.' is
missing too and believed to be killed. He took a message from
the Brigadier to 1st Bn. Coldstream; started back, and was
never seen again. Stephen and Willie Wickham (Scots
Guards) are killed: John Ponsonby (Commanding 1st Bn.
Coldstream) wounded. Ardee has been sent out to command
Irish Guards – very hard on the 1st Battalion just as they
are starting on active service. Francis Scott has been sent as a
Company Commander to Irish Guards: this too is very hard
on the Regiment at such a time as this. The Irish Guards,
however, have practically no reserve of Officers to fall back
on to replace casualties. Had a quiet day in billets and a clean
up. Went to Brigade Headquarters, which is in the Château,
a big, pretentious building with appalling furniture and
decorations. They got shelled there, but otherwise are comfortable.

Tuesday, 22 September

Marched to Chavonne at 4 a.m. and took over new positions from the 1st Cavalry Brigade, who were put in there
on 14th to fill the gaps between us and 3rd Division at Vailly
and protect our left flank. They are clamouring for bayonets
as they don't like the idea of being without them when dismounted and at close quarters. We had two Companies in
trenches north-west of Chavonne, and Battalion Headquarters
and two Companies in reserve in Chavonne, which is in

terraces up the steep hillside. Battalion Headquarters Officers in the school: we use the large schoolroom as a mess. We watched the Cavalry ride away: the enemy shelled the canal bridge with a few shrapnel as they crossed but, so far as we could see, did no damage. We took over from 11th Hussars under Pitman. Our line runs approximately along the Cour de Soupir road from a point just north of Chavonne to its junction with the main Vailly road a mile west of Chavonne. Then there is a gap of some hundreds of yards between our left and the 3rd Division on the other side of the valley. We are in touch on our right with the Irish Guards, who are in our old position, where they relieved us.

Wednesday, 23 September

Chavonne. Some sporadic shelling during the day on the trenches and river valley, but nothing serious. The village hardly gets touched, as being close under the slope, it is not under observation, and shells just miss it and burst in the valley below. They have got, however, some nasty high explosive shells with time fuses, which burst in the air and cut straight down (not forward). They have masses of white smoke with a greenish tinge in it, and the men call them 'Woolly Bears'. The heavy shells make a black smoke, and the men call them 'Black Marias' and 'Coal Boxes'. The splinters of the 'Woollies' can touch us, but nothing else does to speak of. Deepened and improved all trenches.

A new position meant new problems requiring solution. One example is to be found in the Gordon-Lennox diary on the same day.

23 September

So far every night the Dutchmen creep up after dark and snipe us: the jumpy ones reply and the whole line takes it up – result everyone stands to arms etc. The more we fire, the more we get in return as they fire at our flashes. I returned to have a quiet night and gave orders to Donald Miller on the left trench which is their favourite line of approach, not to fire at all unless absolutely necessary. This he carried out – result a quiet night.

Considerable ingenuity was exercised in elaborating the front line.

Thursday, 24 September

Chavonne. Still improving trenches, which are getting much better. In No. 1's Sector, which runs through woods, Gilbert Hamilton is thinning (not clearing) the trees very artistically so that enough are left to screen the trenches, but they are thin enough not to interfere with our view and fire. A Battery of 6″ Howitzers came into action today near the bridge. They have just come out and we can now do something to answer the German heavy Howitzers, which are 5.9″ and some even 8″. The 6″ Howitzers are just below us and fire straight over the house. They make an awful row and shake the house, but thank goodness they have come. Practically all our Field Batteries are back on the south side of the river.

Noise was not the only hazard associated with our own Artillery, as this extract from the Battalion War Diary, again for 24 September, indicates:

Section R.F.A. attached to No. 4 Coy. Their Major telephoned up to ask why they were doing nothing, so they opened fire with the inevitable result of drawing German shellfire on No. 4.

The new arrivals quickly drew a similar response from the enemy:

Friday, 25 September

Some shelling all round. The 6″ Howitzers are beginning to get it, but they go well over us. Still improving trenches and erecting obstacles. The Germans do a certain amount of sniping by day, but it is more annoying than harmful.

Saturday, 26 September

Usual scattered shelling. Ridley was wounded, but very slightly and stayed at duty. Some anti-aircraft pom-poms

have come out. They may frighten the German aeroplanes,
of which there are a lot, but they never look like hitting
them. Their nasty little shells, however, come down and
burst, and might easily do us harm.

*Ridley's own account of his wounding clearly illustrates the
chances taken by those bored with the routine of trench life:*

During a lull I went out to look at an English aeroplane
being shelled, heard a shell coming and bolted for cover.
Shell too fast and burst above me and to left. Lyddite. Got a
cut in back of head and hit between shoulders. Head bled a
bit. This was 10.30 a.m. At about 12 noon, during a lull,
walked down and got it dressed. Ordered to remain down till
relieved.

*Much of life in the four years to follow is foreshadowed in
Jeffreys's next entry:*

Sunday, 27 September

Much as usual. We lead quite a regular life. A daily walk
round the trenches and meals at regular hours. We've got
quite a good mess going – Wilfrid, self, Pike (Adjutant),
Cunninghame, Howell (R.A.M.C.) – and are reasonably comfortable. We get mails and papers regularly. Colston has
been invalided home. He was sitting on top of the bank of a
sunken road in the left Sector and was blown by a shell into
the road. Taken to hospital much bruised and developed
appendicitis!

*Colston was succeeded in command of No. 4 Coy by Ridley,
who noted:*

Poor Ted Colston down with appendicitis and ordered home
for operation. Took over Company from him. A very good
Captain who thought a lot about the men and believed in
digging. Hence our recent freedom from casualties under
heavy shell fire.

*New and often surprising German enterprises helped to vary
the monotony of their existence:*

Monday, 28 September

German snipers getting very active in front of our left Sector, and also some *very* small shells, (apparently fired from close range) are fired at us here. There is a little spinney about 200 yards in front from which the firing seems to come. No. 2 Coy send out patrols to try to stalk the snipers, but without success so far. On various occasions from the left Sector, a German band could be heard playing not very far away up the Ostel valley. Our men were very indignant when they played, 'God save the King' – 'our tune', as they called it.

By now the war on the Aisne had reached stalemate, and life in the trenches had settled down into a routine that was not to alter much for the next four years. At this time, however, it was still something of an unusual experience. Devastation of the area was not yet total, and there was still room for the unexpected. The activities of those days may be seen in the following extracts:

I am sitting now at the back of the local school house in a garden facing due south. It is a glorious day and you can imagine me with no hat and in my shirtsleeves. The Doctor is sitting beside me reading the paper of the 12th. inst. which has just come, and as he says, if it was not for the continual roar of the guns one would imagine oneself miles away from this war. There is a valley in front of me and a river and then hills on the other side. Our guns are on the other side of the river firing bang over my head at the Germans who are behind on the hills to the north. The shelling goes on all day and at night there is always a good deal of rifle fire from our trenches and from the Germans. We have been lucky lately and lost, I am glad to say, very few men, being in trenches saves them, and also the German rifle fire seems to be high and wild at night. It is awfully cold at night now but it is hard to couple a lovely day like this with all this terrible war, bang, bang as I write and the whistling of the guns as they go over my head. The Germans are not applying much at this part of the line. Yesterday Lord Cavan, who commands the Guards Brigade, the Commanding Officer and I were going round the trenches in the morning when suddenly they opened with shrapnel; you should have seen us running for cover. They put one of our machine guns out of action, that was all. The German line in one place is only about 700 yards from us and I was watching them yesterday moving about. You can see them quite plainly, they are digging like anything and I expect laying mines. I had my first warm bath for 5 weeks, the day before yesterday, and it was nice to be fairly clean again. I also had my hair cut by a private soldier and not at all badly.

Letter from Captain Pike, dated 23 September 1914

The sort of food luxuries we want are such things as potted meat, small plum puddings, soup squares, possibly cakes if they will travel, but they must be sent in small quantities, a huge parcel is no good as we can't carry them. We get very good rations, heaps of jam, biscuit and often bread, and when we can buy them butter, eggs etc. but they are difficult to get. You might order Fortnum & Mason to send me 2 lbs. of coffee every week, if possible, to be ready for making. We never get it, and it is a capital thing in the early morning. One gets tired of perpetual tea. . . . I never get my clothes off, and very seldom my boots. If ever I take my boots off at night there is sure to be an alarm, so I have given it up altogether. . . .

A parson has just turned up, so I hope I shall have to conduct no more funerals. I dislike it extremely, it is such a distressing job.

Yesterday we got a goose, being Michaelmas Day, but we couldn't manage the stuffing or the sauce. We get plenty of papers but about 10 days old as a rule.

Letter from Colonel Smith dated 30 September 1914

N.C.O. and 2 men crawled out to woodstack which was hollowed and loopholed by German snipers. Fired at by Germans they returned the fire, killed 2, burnt the woodstack and returned, though the N.C.O. was badly hit. The Brigadier (Lord Cavan) had a piece of his breeches taken away by a shell splinter.

Battalion War Diary dated 10 October 1914

A parson arrived yesterday, Fleming by name – the first time a parson has seen the Battalion since the beginning of the war. We had a service this morning in the Church here, lent by the French curé – just a Communion service. It was an odd experience with shells backwards and forwards all the time. I was astonished at the number of men who turned up, particularly as they had been in the trenches all night, and I am glad to say several officers came. . . .

We often see the aeroplanes returning from the German Lines. It is most exciting to watch them. The Germans turn on their guns, and I have seen 20 shells burst near them at times, generally nowhere near them, but now and again most unpleasantly close. I do not think they have ever been hit.

Letter from Colonel Smith dated 2 October 1914

. . . We have our meals as follows: breakfast 7 a.m., lunch 12.30 p.m., tea 4 p.m. and dinner 7 p.m., generally in bed by 9.30, and up about 5 if there is no alarm during the night. Lately things have been much quieter at night . . . and so for the last 3 nights I have taken off my boots and socks. Everything always ready to jump up and be off any moment.

Letter from Captain Pike dated 6 October 1914

. . . If the Germans get Antwerp they may try and send airships to drop bombs on London in which case don't stay there, but go into the country for a bit. . . . We got a tremendous shelling yesterday and one shell killed 3 of our horses, no man badly hurt. I went out to try and shoot a partridge in a turnip field the other side of the river, and missed the shelling which was all over this village. I lay flat in the turnips and watched it. A wonderful sight, to see it going on you would never imagine that anyone could remain alive under it. I was only about 500 yards away and at times could hardly see the village at all because of the smoke.

Letter from Captain Pike dated 7 October 1914

Jeffreys sums up this period from 29 September to 11 October as follows:

Tuesday, 29 September–Sunday, 11 October

One day very much like another. Nearly always some shelling, but seldom very severe. We watch them shelling our Batteries on the far side of the river, which they sometimes do very accurately. One day they shelled our left Sector very heavily, but did little damage, most of the shells being 'overs'. Bernard Lennox reported, 'The ground in rear of my trenches resembles a Gruyère cheese' – a very good description of the effect of the shell-holes. Prince Arthur of Connaught [then Colonel of the Regiment] came one day and paid us a visit.

He sat for some time and had tea. The 6" Battery was firing, and every time a gun went off he jumped nearly out of his skin, so fear he didn't enjoy his visit! A new sort of projectile has appeared. It is fired from quite close range and you can see it coming and turning over and over in the air. It bursts with a tremendous noise and seems as big as a 5.9" shell. So far, however, it has done no damage. We have had few casualties this last fortnight – about 9 or 10 in all, and the trenches are now strong and good, and well wired. We are to be relieved by the French tomorrow night, 12 October.

Monday, 12 October

French Infantry [Territorials] arrived to relieve us in the line about 8 p.m., and all our Companies were back from the trenches by about 1 a.m.

Gordon-Lennox described the handover thus:

12 October

They [the French] turned up at 11.40 p.m. and it took a long time to carry out the relief. They only brought 150 men and one Officer – all there were of the company of Terriers. The Officer was very funny and whenever I showed him my posts etc. he said, '*Oh la la: je n'ai pas les hommes*' – no more he had. One thing they would find hard and that is to fire out of our loopholes, as they were not of Guardsmen stature. I have no doubt the Dutchmen will be surprised when they see them in our trenches in the morning.

5

'You may yet save the Army'

(Message from Brigadier-General Lord Cavan to 2 Grenadier Guards 31 October 1914)

WITH the fighting bogged down on the Aisne, both the Germans and the Allies started a series of movements to the north in an attempt to outflank the opposition. As the line to the left was lengthened, the position of the B.E.F. in the centre began to present difficulties. Their lines of communication now crossed those of the French Armies of the left with all the attendant risks of confusion. It was agreed therefore that the B.E.F. should be relieved in its present position by French Territorials, and should move up to Belgium. The operation began on 3 October, and was completed on 19 October when I Corps, of which the Grenadiers were part, finished detraining at St Omer. By this time the opening moves in the First Battle of Ypres had already been made.

Tuesday, 13 October

Marched 1 a.m. back through St Mard to Perles (2 miles north-west of Fismes), and billeted there 6 a.m. Understand all British being relieved and moving to left flank of French in the north.

Wednesday, 14 October

Entrained at Fismes between 4 and 6 a.m. As we were entering the town in the dark a French sentry challenged, '*Qui va la?*' I answered '*Troupes Anglaises*', hoping it was the right thing to say, and it apparently was, as he let us go on. All day in the train. Round Paris there has been a lot of cutting of trees – presumably to clear a field of fire. Amiens 8 p.m., and then all night in the train.

The break from the trenches met with keen appreciation. Echoing the feelings of many British soldiers, both then and later, Wilfrid Smith wrote:

> . . . It is resting to see civilisation without guns. It seems so odd to be fighting in this sort of country, we have always associated war with the tropics in the past. . . . How odd all the outskirts of Paris look – all the trees cut down to prepare for its defence, and yet everything going on apparently as usual. We have just left, having stopped there for twenty minutes – all the people waving frantically at the men – and well they may, for we saved Paris.

There seems to have been little sense of urgency about the move.

Thursday, 15 October

Arrived Hazebrouck 8 a.m., detrained and billeted. We (Battalion Headquarters) are in a villa on the outskirts of the town, owned by an old bourgeois – not a bad old sort, but very fussy and apprehensive of what we shall do to him and his house. He reels off strings of petty complaints and invariably ends up, 'Enfin – c'est la guerre!' Our transport are in a field close by, and one of our horses broke a leg and had to be shot. No sooner was he dead than crowds of inhabitants came rushing with knives and plates and dishes from every direction and in an incredibly short time he was cut up and every bit of meat taken away! Apparently they are great horse eaters hereabouts. Everything seems quite peaceful and there are good shops in the town, and the only sign of war (apart from troops) is the sound of heavy gunfire coming from the south-east. In the evening just as it was getting dusk, a French Cavalry Division rode through the town. They *look* much better than their infantry, but in the twilight one couldn't see to what extent they and their horses were clean or otherwise. All were in pre-war uniforms – cuirassiers complete with cuirasses, brass helmets, long plumes and red breeches. Quite like a Meissonier picture and rather imposing to look at. Comfortable night in a bed.

Friday, 16 October

Hazebrouck. Douglas Loch came to see us from G.H.Q. and told us a little about the situation. Apparently the Germans are prolonging their line northwards as fast or faster than we are, and everywhere we advance we find Germans in front of us. The present fighting is mostly in a flat country cut up by dykes, and Douglas Loch says every crossing over the dykes has a German machine gun firing down it, so that our progress is not so fast as could be wished. The 2nd and 3rd Corps are doing the fighting so far, but we are sure to be in it before long, probably in the direction of Ypres. Orders to move early tomorrow came in the evening, also a fine present of tobacco, cigarettes, socks etc. for the men from the Officers, past and present, of the Regiment.

Saturday, 17 October

Marched 7 a.m. about ten miles to Boeschepe. A dull, cool day and mostly *pavé* roads, which are bad to march on. The men marched well considering how little practice they've had of late. After we got into billets we could hear firing in the distance north-eastwards. Wilfrid and I rode on to have a look about, as we have been told absolutely nothing of the situation. We rode north towards Poperinghe, and as we came in sight of it, we could see troops busily entrenching on the slopes south of the town, i.e. facing us. After a good look we saw they were French and apparently preparing a position facing the wrong way! The country is now flat and enclosed, except for some big hills south of Boeschepe, one of which is called Mont des Cats. We are billeted on an old woman – most unprepossessing and with a raucous voice. She is eternally scolding a youth, whom we took to be her son, but who turned out to be her husband! The Belgian frontier is just ahead.

Sunday, 18 October

Still in billets at Boeschepe.

Monday, 19 October

Boeschepe. A draft arrived to join the Brigade. Wilfrid and I rode out to meet them. Frank Maitland, Ralph Cavendish, Jack Hughes, Ivor Rose and Crawly de Crespigny for Grenadiers, but Crawly is to be Staff Captain of the Brigade. As we saw the draft approaching, we saw a curious figure in front of it – very fat and with a rolling gait. It turned out to be old Harry Pole Gell – his figure more than ever like the Queen Mother, and very footsore!

Maitland went to command No. 4 Company. Cavendish was sent as second Captain to No. 3 Company, and Rose and Hughes were sent as Platoon Commanders to Nos. 2 and 1 Companies respectively.

The care which the officers of the Regiment took of their men is well illustrated by this extract from a letter written by Wilfrid Smith to the Regimental Headquarters at this time:

Will you kindly cash the enclosed cheque for £1.10.0, and have it conveyed to the wife of No. 13493 Pte. F. Toon. He was wounded about 10 days ago, and we don't know where he has gone – but he has been our mess waiter for some weeks, and the enclosed amount is due to him for wages. I understand that his wife is going to be confined shortly, so she will probably be glad of the money. . . .

I Corps was now ready to be committed to battle.

Tuesday, 20 October

Marched off 6 a.m. to Ypres, through which we marched. Crowds of people in the streets to see us march through, and there seemed to be a tremendous lot of priests and nuns. Rather a nice old town with narrow, cobble-stoned streets, and some fine buildings. We marched through to St Jean (about a couple of miles north-east of Ypres), where we took up a position and entrenched, facing north-east. Some French troops about and some of their guns came and took up a position close to us. The Battery Commander had an elaborate expanding ladder, which he erected close behind his guns and observed from. Saw a few patrols of Household

Cavalry coming and gathered they had had some skirmishing towards Houthoulst forest. A lot of firing to our left front in the afternoon and all night, but we saw no enemy. A pouring wet night.

Wednesday, 21 October

Marched 6 a.m. to a position of assembly near the Haane-beek brook near St Julien, where the Brigade concentrated. A long wait here – many rumours and no information. Finally orders for 2nd Bn. Coldstream on right of 3rd Bn. Coldstream on left, to advance in conjunction with 5th Infy. Bde. on our left and 7th Div. on our right. We (Grenadiers) and Irish Guards in support and reserve. Coldstream Battalion's first objective the line of Zonnebeke–Langemarck road. Then to advance in direction of Passchendaele. They met with considerable opposition, but got to the line of the road. A gap having developed between them, one company of our Battalion was ordered up to fill it. The rest of the Battalion was in reserve between the crossroads ½ mile south-east of St Julien and the Zonnebeke–Langemarck road – spread about in small packets. St Julien was getting heavily shelled, and what looked like a factory was constantly hit, sending up clouds of red brick-dust, but though a few shells were broadcast about the country, they didn't hurt us. By about 2 p.m. two Companies 3rd Coldstream on left, one Company 2nd Grenadiers in centre and one Company of 2nd Coldstream on right, were east of the Haanebeek; one Company of 2nd Coldstream was thrown back on right trying to keep touch with 7th Division, who were hard pressed in Zonnebeke, and one Company of Irish Guards was sent to close the gaps between 2nd Coldstream and 7th Division. We remained in these positions for the rest of the day, and dug in at nightfall. After dark the whole sky to the east was lit up by the glare of fires, presumably started by the Germans, who made a counter-attack on our positions about 10 p.m. As they approached, someone called out, 'Don't fire, we are Coldstream', but as their spiked helmets could be clearly seen against the light of the fire, our men were not taken in, and they were repulsed with heavy loss. But they are clever in getting to know who is in front of them. If we did know we should probably get the name of the regiment wrong, if we tried such a trick. That night I was sent back to Divisional Headquarters to report the situation. Road crowded with trans-

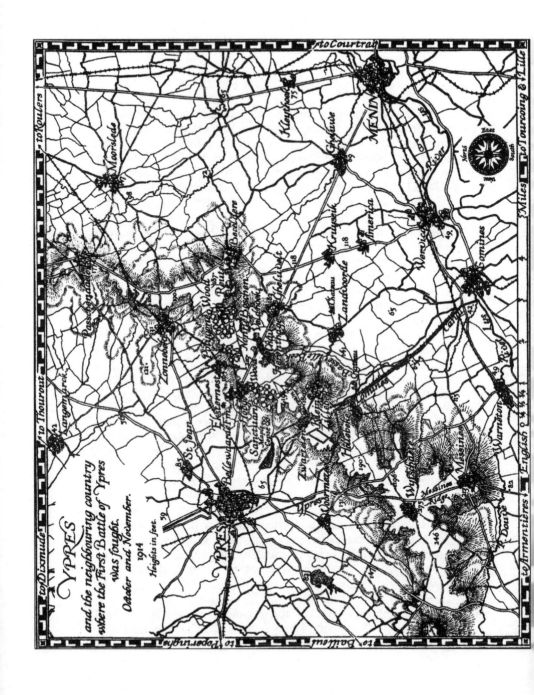

YPRES

and the neighbouring country
where the First Battle of Ypres
was fought.
October and November.
1914
Heights in feet.

port moving up and odds and ends moving back, and I was tired and wet. Got to Headquarters eventually and was received by Monro, who was as nice as ever. He was full of confidence: said the German troops in front of us were a raw lot – 'mostly cooks and waiters'. I wonder!

Monro also said that large Russian reinforcements are on their way and have already landed in the north of England. However, both we, the 7th Division on our right, and the 1st Division and French on our left have been checked today.

A more pessimistic, and perhaps realistic, view of the situation than the Divisional Commander's was taken by Wilfrid Smith, who wrote home the following day:

Our Flyers are wonderful, and if they had faster machines could drive the Germans off altogether as a German now will not let them come near them if they can help it.

We had a battle yesterday, but did not get on very far – our line is so long that one part cannot get too far ahead of another – and some are very sticky; we got on further than anyone else. But it is all rot saying we have nothing in front of us. There are heaps of Germans, and, as an army, they are very good, and their gunners are perfect. The Belgians have never done any good, I am told. They will not stand the shelling – no more will any but highly trained and disciplined troops. The French and Belgians who are not far from us are most unreliable. I expect our advance will be very slow unless something unexpected happens. No doubt we will kill heaps of Germans but there are always heaps more. We got a lot last night after dark. The Germans attacked one of my platoons shouting, 'We are Coldstream', but we let them have it, and picked up 100 this morning. They are up to every dirty trick. It was all over in two minutes. I have the greatest faith in the men at night if they are well dug in (and they do dig now, like rabbits!). They shoot so well that all I have to see to is that they have plenty of ammunition, and no German will ever reach the trenches.

The crowds of refugees are the saddest sights imaginable, miles and miles of them, and the Germans like to get among them and come with them, but we are up to most of their tricks now. The Germans have burnt all the houses for miles. Last night the sky was all lighted up, and it looked like an inferno. They do it, I suppose, to prevent us attacking, but it is very foolish of them, as they attack us, and we give them toko. If we advance we shall find no houses to sleep in. There is not a soul left in the country. All the farms are deserted, and the cows and pigs wander about aimlessly. The men milk them in the intervals of shelling! The crops are splendid, but wasted, it is as if a plague has passed over the land.

Despite optimism at the highest level it was becoming increasingly clear that the Allied advance had been checked.

Thursday, 22 October

Entrenched and consolidated last night's position. Front and support lines shelled a good deal and a lot of rifle fire, causing a good few casualties. Our Battalion Headquarters in a small farm halfway between St Julien and the Zonnebeke–Langemarck road. The 3rd Bn. Coldstream lost most yesterday – G. Feilding, the C.O., wounded and poor Charlie Monck killed. We hear that Sam Ashton, 2nd Life Guards, is missing and believed killed, and Robin Duff killed. No news of our 1st Battalion, but 7th Division have been having a bad time, and their 22nd Brigade on our right was driven back last night, the enemy occupying Zonnebeke.

Friday, 23 October

After quiet night very heavy shell-fire in morning along whole line and we expected attack but none developed though the shelling continued. A message came to say that French troops were to attack through us in the afternoon with the object of taking Passchendaele and that 'an officer who could speak French' was to be sent as Liaison Officer to General Moussy, the Commander. Wilfrid sent me and I went off and met General Moussy on the Wieltze Road just as his Infantry were beginning to come out on to the more open ground south-east of St Julien. He received me very kindly and told me to come along with him. He had two Staff Officers with him – both very smart, especially one (a Cavalry-man) in a light blue tunic with silver lace and red breeches. He seemed to have no Headquarters, as we understand them, to which reports could go, but he walked about amongst his troops with the two staff Officers, and seemed more like an umpire at a Field Day than a Commander of

8. The Hon. W. Bailey and A. K. S. Cunninghame.

9. *Left to right*: Capt. Lord Desmond Fitzgerald, Irish Guards, Brigadier-General Lord Cavan, not identified, Lt.-Col. Hon. J. F. Trefusis, Irish Guards, not identified.

10. The grave at Villers-Cotterets (*page 66*) **where Lt.** George Cecil and three other officers were buried in November 1914.

11. The Prince of Wales.

2 G. G.

Well done — Hope you have got
my memo re calling on 1st
Coldstream at once if necessary —
now in the wood along side of you —
+ you must use them to help
both yself + Irish Guards —
when used up. Let me know —
am turning all Artillery on
to wood in yt. front.

Cavan B/G.

1.15 pm   17 Nov.14

I have no means of communication
left except orderlies —

12. Facsimile of field service message written by Lord
Cavan during the fighting on Tuesday, 17 November,
before Ypres.

13. Officers of the 2nd Battalion Grenadier Guards at Meteren, December 1914. *Standing left to right:* Mervyn Williams, J. Hughes, Hon. W. Bailey, A. K. S. Cunninghame, J. Buchanan, F. Beaumont-Nesbitt, F. G. Marshall. *Seated:* Capt. R. Cavendish, Capt. P. A. Clive, Major G. D. Jeffreys, Lt. Col. W. R. A. Smith, Capt. Sir M. R. A. Cholmeley, Qr.Mr. Skidmore.

14. At the end of 1914 the moving war gave way to the static world of trench warfare, a situation which was not to change until 1918.

attacking troops. As his troops came into the open they split up into little columns on either side of the road and went forward in Artillery formation. They did this very well. As they approached the Zonnebeke–Langemarck road they began to come under shell-fire, which did little or no damage, but caused them to check. General Moussy walked about among the groups, and whenever he saw one halted he went up to it and spoke to the men – '*Allons, Allons, mes enfants. En Avant! En Avant!*' to which they always replied, '*Bien, mon Général!*' and got up and advanced, but as soon as he had turned to go to another group they dropped down again. In between he kept explaining to me that he had lost many officers and had nothing but *sous-officiers* and promoted *sous-officiers*, and that these were no good. However, he gradually got them forward, sometimes joking with them saying, '*Il faut absolument arriver a Passchendaele ce soir, ou pas de souper, pas de souper!*'

Eventually the leading troops crossed the Zonnebeke road and passed through our front line, those on the right retaking Zonnebeke. However, they only got a very short way beyond our front line and in some places they stopped in it, drawing everywhere very heavy fire. General Moussy went forward and stood at the cross-roads on the Zonnebeke–Langemarck road, a most unhealthy spot, as it was being shelled and a machine-gun from the direction of Passchendaele was firing straight down the Wieltze Road. However, he showed not the slightest sign of fear, and nor did his two Staff Officers, who laughed and joked at the bursting shells. I think these two, at any rate, were determined to show me that they didn't care, and I (though inwardly hating it) was equally determined to show them that I didn't care either. There was a good ditch with a bank towards the enemy along the Zonnebeke road, and in it was Gillie Follett and his Company of Coldstream. He said to me, 'Why don't you get in here with us?' I asked the General if he wouldn't get into the ditch, and after at first demurring, he did get into it, followed by the other three of us. I was very glad to get there. The attack was definitely held up by about 5.30 p.m., and after dark General Moussy and Staff Officers came back with me to our Battalion Headquarters in the little farmhouse, where we gave them some supper, which they seemed to appreciate and Moussy said he thought we lived very well. I liked him and admired his gallantry, but could not make out how he thought he was commanding! He did the work of a regimental officer; had no communication; received few, if any, reports, and on the rare occasions when he issued any sort of orders, he sent a Staff Officer with a verbal message. That night the French relieved our Division. Actually they had practically done so by their attack coming to a standstill in and about our front line, and we withdrew about 11 p.m. During the day Mark Maitland was wounded, a bullet going through the top of his head, but missing the brain, and Donald Miller was killed by a shell. We went a few miles south and bivouacked in some farms about Eksternest. I was very tired and slept in a hay-barn in good clean hay – very comfortable. All our officers in the same barn.

The events leading up to the wounding of Captain Maitland were described by Ridley in his diary:

Turned out early after a cold but quiet night. . . . Enemy suddenly appeared 1400 yds. to front and started to entrench. Fired a few shots at them to get range. Sniper about 500 yds. off began to take us on. He was a good shot. Mark came along and eventually sat on back of trench. I had got him to take his cap off to not draw fire when he was suddenly hit by the sniper on the right side of head above ear. He bled a bit, groaned, but suddenly was quite all right. I tied up his head and advised him to remain in trench but he would not, and got up and ran back to Coy. H.Q. and eventually to Bn. H.Q. and hospital. The sniper then gave it us hot, fired every time we showed an ear. I could not get out. I think he was a sportsman and did not fire at Mark when he saw he was wounded. Eventually I had to go to stop the expenditure of ammunition. Got out by crawling and went to Sgt Fremlin's trench where the sniping was not so bad. From there to Stock's from which I could get at the whole line.

The next day was quiet.

Saturday, October 24

Remained in reserve about Eksternest. Could hear heavy firing all day and again at night to the eastward. There seems to be no longer much question of our outflanking the Germans, or in fact of our attacking, and we seem to be heavily attacked all along the line. The country about here is very wooded and enclosed, and there is a great number of small farms and cottages.

Ridley's version of the day's activities was more down to earth:

Halted at a farm and remained all day doing nothing. Was very tired, too tired to sleep in the fowl house we had as Coy. H.Q. Hungry too, and did not feel well enough to eat the bully I was offered.

The Battalion was soon in action again.

Sunday, 25 October

Orders early to be prepared to advance through 5th Brigade on Reutel. I was sent on to reconnoitre towards Reutel and Becelaere. I rode on round a big wood of young fir trees – Polygone wood – and skirted a thick belt of wood running south from it. H.L.I. in this belt. At the south end of it across a stream was a château, Polderhoek Château. Here I found Alexander, Irish Guards, also sent ahead, and we went across a small bridge and into the château grounds. Quite a nice garden with a terrace facing south and big stables on the western edge. Not a soul about. We went into the house. It was deserted and we climbed up to an attic, which was full of apples; there was a shell-hole in the attic wall facing east, and through it we got a wonderful view of Becelaere and the German trenches in front of it, but we could make out nothing in the woods between us and Becelaere (which is on a hill overlooking them) except that a clearing about 100 yards wide runs through the Reutel woods. A good few Germans moving about Becelaere, but we could see no British. We went down into the grounds again, but they were unoccupied, though a trench in the garden showed that troops had been there. We went on to the terrace and again got a wonderful view of the country to the southward, which is far less wooded than about here, and we could see troops moving (apparently British) away on the lower ground towards Menin and Kruyseik. The troops we saw were about 1½ miles away and seemed to be first advancing and then falling back. We could see no troops near us. We were starting to go back when the enemy began shelling the château grounds and we took refuge in the

trench in the garden until the shelling ceased. Then we started
back, having found out very little except the lie of the ground
and that Polderhoek château would be a wonderful Artillery
O.P. Riding back over the open ground south of Polygone
wood a shell landed in a ploughed field about twenty yards
from me. My horse jumped several feet sideways, but we were
not touched. All this ground is under observation from
Becelaere church, which is on top of a hill overlooking the
woods. When we got back to the western edge of Polygone
wood we found the Battalions preparing to go forward.

We were ordered to attack at 3 p.m., but there was never
a hope of our being ready by that time, as it was 2.45 when
we got the order to start from the west side of Polygone wood.
The Battalion advanced in artillery formation over the open
ground south of Polygone wood and closed up behind the strip
of wood between Polygone wood and Polderhoek château.
We sent two platoons into the château grounds to hold them
and protect our right, and pushed No. 2 Company forward
into the Reutel wood, No. 1 Platoon working along the stream
running along the north side of the château. About 150 yards
into the wood was a clearing about 60 yards wide along
which another stream ran. This clearing was swept with fire,
as was the line of the Polderhoek stream, down which a
machine gun was firing. After struggling through the first
belt of wood No. 2 were held up by this fire, and as darkness
was coming on, entrenched practically on the line held by
H.L.I. (5th Brigade). We never really located the German
line. Irish Guards on our left had much the same experience.
We took over from the 5th Brigade, who withdrew. Some
Germans approached our position twice in the night and were
received with heavy fire, but doubtful if they were anything
more than patrols. Our Battalion Headquarters in a peasant's
cottage on west edge of the wood. Very stuffy and smelling
of onions, but warm and out of sight of the enemy. Peasant
and wife still in it, also 2 large and surly dogs. Very wet
night.

A vivid account of the fight was given by Gordon-Lennox:

At 3 p.m. we advanced and got up as far as the trenches.
I sent out scouts followed by a section. The Bedfords kept up
communication on my right. We managed to get about 150
yards along the stream when we came under a heavy cross-

fire which luckily did remarkably little harm. The Bedfords retired back to the trenches. We stopped where we were and Dowling came in to report the situation to me. The situation was that my Company were attacking a strongly fortified position on a one man front which didn't seem quite sound, so giving the Bedfords time to collect themselves, I went back and reported to Headquarters the situation. The Irish Guards had got no further than I had, and everything stood by. It was now dark and seemed quite futile to attempt to take a strong position in a thick wood on a dark night when no one had the remotest idea where their trenches were, or how strongly held, but I had a very good idea as to the latter item. I therefore took over the trenches of a company of the Oxford L.I. having the H.L.I. on my left and R.S. Fusiliers on my right. It started to rain and blow and we had really a most unpleasant night. Gilbert brought up a platoon of his company and occupied the R.S.F. trenches on my right which I was glad of. During the night we were attacked three times, about 9 p.m., 12 midnight and 3 a.m. (sounds like a prescription on a medicine bottle). Very heavy firing each time, but I don't think they really meant to come on. The last attack, however, was so strong that I felt justified in sending back to Headquarters suggesting a company being sent up closer in support if necessary as they would probably come on again at dawn if at all. They didn't however.

Further progress was now clearly impossible.

Monday, 26 October

Same position all day. A lot of sniping on both sides, and the château heavily shelled and knocked about. We improved our trenches, but this difficult as the ground low-lying and wet. A quieter night. Hear 7th Division have had a bad time and been forced back on our right, and that 1st Division has relieved them on part of their front.

The lesson, taught on the Aisne, that in order to survive troops must dig, and dig deep, was strongly reinforced at Ypres. It had become the Battalion's creed, as illustrated by this extract from Gordon-Lennox's diary, dated 26 October:

Found us in trenches and digging like mad to improve them. Can't make out why every Battalion doesn't dig itself in properly. If they did they might never be turned out of their trenches like some of them have been lately.

Jeffreys's next entry shows that from the earliest days of military aviation the problem of aircraft recognition has beset the ground forces:

Tuesday, 27 October

Same position. A lot of shelling and rifle fire. Our two reserve Companies relieved 3rd Coldstream away to the left. Whole Brigade now to be relieved by the 1st Brigade. 1st Division fighting between us and the Menin road. During the day a British aeroplane flying low over the lines and dropping lights was mistaken for a German and heavily fired on by Black Watch, who brought it down in flames, all the men cheering as it came down. A dreadful sight, as we (Wilfrid and I) were watching and realised it was British. Relieved at midnight by Black Watch (1st Bde.), but relief not complete until 5.45 a.m.

Wednesday, 28 October

Relief completed 5.45 a.m.: very long business owing to difficulty of getting to trenches and getting touch through thick woods. Went back before daybreak to Nonne Boschen wood about 1½ miles. Orders to march 9.30 a.m. to support attack on 6th Bde on Becelaere. Attack made no progress. Bivouacked in western edge of Polygone wood, near 6 cross-roads at its S.W. corner. Brigade Headquarters in a little cabaret at these cross-roads, and we too had our food there. We dug trenches for shelter inside the wood, and also some along its southern edges for defence if necessary. Information from Div. Headquarters that XXVII Res. Corps would attack early tomorrow.

As the war progressed the shortage of machine guns was becoming a severe problem. A principal target for the enemy, they suffered heavy casualties. Communications were another prob-

lem exercising Wilfrid Smith's mind when he wrote to the Regimental Adjutant at this time:

We want machine gunners badly, having had rather bad luck with them. Signallers do not matter – I think after the war they will be obsolete. We use them as messengers, and little else except for telephone work. I wish we had telephones in every Battalion, they would be invaluable and save many lives as we could communicate with the trenches without sending orderlies who often get sniped. Wherever we go we dig, and communication is very difficult without telephones.

It was now the turn of the Germans to attack.

Thursday, 29 October

At 5.30 a.m. tremendous shelling of Gheluvelt started and 1st Division heavily attacked. From our position we could see Gheluvelt and it did not seem as though anything could live in it in such fire. No. 4 Coy ordered to the woods west of Polderhoek to support Cameron Highlanders (1st Div.), and sent two platoons into front trenches. They were not again attacked but had a few casualties from the shellfire. We heard that 1st Division had been driven back and also the left of the 7th Division (on right of 1st Div.). Our front line still in front of Gheluvelt. Wet but quiet night.

Wilfrid Smith wrote home that night:

The noise of the guns and shells has become positively boring. Of course, one is semi-conscious of the danger – but the feeling of boredom is uppermost. One would like to get away for a few days from the never ceasing din. I can't see how these battles are to end. It becomes a question of stalemate. With a line of this length you can't get ahead anywhere (or else you get in a dangerous position) unless the whole line can get on, and you can't get on because there are no flanks, and you cannot therefore get round them. As soon as you outflank, an aeroplane gives away the show, and the enemy meet it, and vice versa with us, so it is a neverending business. You get to within a few hundred yards of each other and dig, and there you stop, sniping all day and shooting all night at imaginary or real night attacks.

E

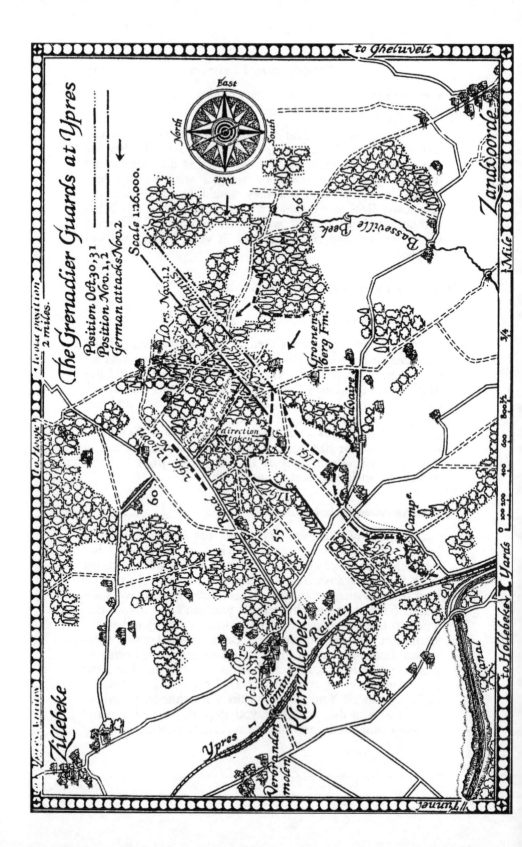

The Grenadier Guards at Ypres
Position Oct. 30, 31
Position Nov. 1, 2
German attacks Nov. 2

Scale 1:26,000.

Next day the German pressure increased.

Friday, 30 October

6th Brigade on our left and 7th Division away to the right again heavily shelled and attacked. At 3 p.m. we and the Irish Guards were ordered off to the right and moved at first across country southwards from the Menin road and then along a road to [Klein] Zillebeke. The road was parallel to the line and hidden from the front by thick woods. As we were halted by the roadside a number of Gordon Highlanders came dribbling back from the line, some wounded but not all. I stopped a Corporal, who with a man was escorting a slightly wounded man well able to walk, and asked him if that was the custom in the Gordons. He said 'No Sir' and turned round and walked back. At Kleinzillebeke we were told we were to relieve the Cavalry who had been hard pressed all day, towards Zandvoorde, and we sent Company Commanders forward to reconnoitre the line. The Cavalry trenches were very poor and we agreed that they should remain in them as covering position while we dug an entirely new line 300 yards further back. Our men dug in up to their necks, mostly in ploughed fields – really good deep trenches – and finished about midnight, when the Cavalry withdrew. Wilfrid and I stood and talked for a long time with Gordon Wilson (Commanding Blues) and Foster, his Adjutant, while they were waiting for their regiment to be relieved. Irish Guards in line on our left. Our right on the canal in touch with Cavalry posts on opposite bank. Cavalry on west bank hold in front of Hollebeke and along Messines ridge. Just before midnight we went into a cottage in Kleinzillebeke, in which we had established Battalion Headquarters, and got a bit of sleep. Heard that our 1st Battalion, the 1st Bn. Coldstream and 2nd Bn. Scots Guards had had heavy losses, but no particulars. [In the fighting around Gheluvelt on 29 October 1st Battalion Grenadier Guards was reduced, by nightfall, to a strength of four officers and a hundred men.]

Saturday, 31 October

Soon after daybreak I went to have a look at the line. The night had been wet, but the trenches had kept fairly dry and everyone seemed all right. On the right No. 2 Coy were in

touch with the Cavalry (4th Hussars) on the opposite bank
of the canal, and I spoke to the Sergeant in charge, who said
they were all right. It was rather misty and all quiet as I
was going around, but very heavy shelling began just after
I got back to Battalion Headquarters. We had not dug any
shelter for Battalion Headquarters, so we established them
in the ditch on the western edge of a strip of wood running
at right-angles to the canal. Nos. 2 and 1 Coys' Headquarters
were on and just in front of the front edge of this wood. We
had not been in our little ditch for more than a few minutes
when four heavy howitzers' shells burst just in front of us,
distributed along the edge of the wood, and looking as if the
Germans had it taped. Luckily none of us was touched, and
Wilfrid withdrew our Headquarters party about 100 yards
to where we found a big hole dug (probably for a mangel or
beet clamp). We got into this and stayed there for some
hours, whilst a really terrific bombardment went on, not
only on the front trenches, but also on the wood and far
back to the rear. Though a bit cramped we were all right in
our hole and kept in touch with the Companies by runners,
who were extraordinarily gallant and clever at getting backwards and forwards through the shell-fire.

All Companies reported that they were holding all right
and that the shell-fire, though terrifically heavy, had so far
done little damage to our trenches, which were short, deep,
with no parapets but the earth thrown out in front so that
they were difficult to spot in the ploughed fields. During
the morning some French troops came up, apparently to
counter-attack through us. They seemed to have no definite
objective and just stumbled forward through the shell-fire in
little groups, which never reached our front line and dumped
down in shell-holes and depressions in the ground wherever
they could find any shelter. Some of them came to us and
asked Wilfrid to let them have some tools, as they had none,
but Wilfrid was adamant and absolutely refused to let them
have any, saying that we should never see them again if we
did. About mid-day the bombardment lifted off our front
trenches and the German infantry moved forward, but they
were met with such heavy fire from our line that they were
stopped at once. Early in the afternoon we received messages
from the Brigadier telling us that the situation was critical,
and that the line had been broken further to the north, and
urging us to hang on at all costs. He even said that Sir D.
Haig relied on us to save the First Corps and possibly the

Army! Actually in spite of the tremendous shelling our men were holding on without excessive difficulty, and the enemy attempt to assault had been completely crushed. Only George Powell (No. 3) asked for reinforcements and was told that none was available and he must hold on. Wilfrid, however, decided to move the Battalion Headquarters forward, and accordingly we went up to No. 1 Coy's Headquarters, where Wilfrid and I and Pike fitted ourselves into Gilbert Hamilton's very inadequate trench on the reverse slope of some rising ground on the east side of the strip of wood. There was no room for our orderlies, who had to shelter behind the bank of a wood a few yards in rear of us. We were lucky to get up through the wood without having anyone hit, as it was being heavily shelled and the slope by Gilbert's Headquarters was being searched by time shrapnel. The bombardment got, if possible, heavier in the early afternoon, every sort of shell, big and small, screaming and droning over. There seemed to be no reply from our own guns, but it was difficult to hear them in the general noise. Some of our forward posts of No. 2 Coy had their trenches blown in and fell back on the support line, and at about 3 o'clock the Germans advanced in force (against No. 2 and No. 1) especially, but were again completely stopped by our rifle fire, and our line held everywhere. There was no further infantry attack, though it looked as though another was contemplated when the Germans brought up some field guns and fired on the trenches at close range. They did no damage however and were soon withdrawn. About 4 I went to visit Bernard Lennox (No. 2), who had his headquarters on the eastern edge of the wood close to the railway and canal.

I went along the edge of the wood to get to him and found him all right, though his trench had been knocked about a bit. One of his forward trenches had been hit direct by two big H.E. shells and several men had been killed or buried. One of the latter was Ivor Rose, who was dug out alive, but cut and scratched and badly concussed. He was got back successfully. I stayed a bit with Bernard, who had more room than Gilbert Hamilton, and as it got dark the shelling died down and we were able to stretch our stiff limbs and look about us. It had been an awful day – far the heaviest shelling since the Aisne, or in fact during the War so far, and it was more than anything their good digging which enabled our men to hang on. Our short lengths of deep trench were very difficult to

F

spot and only a very few got direct hits. The men were as steady as rocks and when the German infantry came on they withered away under our rifle fire. The ground was very cut up by the shell-fire and some houses just behind our centre had been set on fire by shells and were blazing furiously. Our losses had been very light considering the heavy fire – only about 40 – though we were all weary and stiff after the long hours in narrow trenches. Sgt. Hutchins (No. 4) did very well in charge of our left post, which was heavily attacked, and in maintaining touch with the Irish Guards on our left. The shelling had gone far back to the rear and had disorganised transport etc. One of our S.A.A. [small arms ammunition] carts was blown up by a direct hit and we didn't get our supplies up till midnight, by which time everyone even more sleepy than hungry.

Gordon-Lennox's account of the day was as follows:

31 October

As soon as daylight came we were subjected to a terrific shelling: the enemy's captive balloon was observing and I regret to say they got the range of No. 2 Company's trenches, which were in the open. Ivor Rose had a wonderful escape, a high explosive landed absolutely in his trench and buried the whole lot. He was dug out just in time and dreadfully shaken, with cracked ear-drum. 2 or 3 men killed and others buried. Shortly after another one arrived and demolished another of my trenches. The Frenchmen had meantime arrived and started off, while their supports started digging in immediately in rear and in front of my line of trenches and drew a lot of fire. I therefore determined to withdraw temporarily behind them to my support trenches. The French attack did nothing: they came back and occupied our trenches, and for the rest of the day we were subjected to a terrific shelling. To our left our centre had to give way a bit and I received a message saying, 'Our centre has been driven in: the safety of the Army depends on the Irish Guards and the Grenadier Guards holding on at all costs.' That was all right. The Germans advanced and came into a wood in our front, but No. 1 Company took tea with them and they didn't advance any further. I had established my own Headquarters in a trench immediately next to the railway, a spot they hammered at incessantly all day, and towards evening brought up a couple or so of some field guns and fired point blank at me. Towards morning we were relieved by more Frenchmen and retired about a mile into bivouac. Everyone dog beat.

The relief was short-lived, as the Battalion went to patch the line elsewhere.

Sunday, 1 November

At 3 a.m. we were relieved in the line by French troops and we went back and bivouacked in a larch plantation by the railway and got 2 or 3 hours sleep. Soon after daybreak the shelling began again, but nothing came very near us. Various reports reached us of heavy attacks further to the north, and of the German break-through, and after standing by for some time the Battalion was ordered to go and report to General Bulfin, who was said to be in a wood ¾ mile south-west of Herenthage. East of Zillebeke and north of Klein-zillebeke is a mass of woods and we were doubtful as to where to find Bulfin. We marched along a road running north-east, in column of platoons with 50 yards distance between platoons as the road was being intermittently shelled. One shell landed almost on the feet of a man a few yards in front of me and the blast made me stagger backwards. I ran to pick up the man expecting to find him at least badly wounded, but he wasn't touched – only dazed – , and said, 'Thank you Sir' to me and went on! Wilfrid sent me ahead to try to find General Bulfin and find out what the Battalion was to do. I rode on about a mile and found some Staff Officers and asked for General Bulfin and was told he had been wounded and that Cavan was taking over command of all troops in the neighbourhood. I was told that the Germans had broken our line and got into the big wood to the eastward – Kleinzille-beke wood – and that no one quite knew where our line was or how far the Germans had got; also that except for our Battalion there was no reserve anywhere near. A few strag-glers of British Regiments were the only troops to be seen, and there were some shells dropping about. Standing near by with only an A.D.C. was Major-General Sir T. Capper, commanding 7th Division, but he gave me no orders. I said, 'I'm afraid your Division has had a bad time, Sir.' He re-

plied, 'Yes, so bad that there's no Division left, so that I'm a
curiosity – a Divisional Commander without a Division.' He
seemed to treat it almost as a joke.

[By the following day the 7th Division had been reduced
to one fifth of its original strength, with an average of
fourteen officers and 770 men in each of its three Brigades.
It continued in action however until relieved on 5 November.]

I went and met the Battalion coming up and gave Wilfrid
such scraps of information as I had received, and almost
directly came orders from Cavan for the Battalion to clear
the wood south-east of the road at the point of the bayonet.
Wilfrid formed the Battalion up parallel to the road facing
south-east. He ordered the men to take their packs off and
leave them, and then launched the Battalion, three Companies (1, 2 and 3) in front and one Company (4) in support,
with orders to clear the wood and make good the eastern
edge. The first bit of wood was not very thick underwood:
then it became thicker and in front of our left Company
(No. 2) there was a very thick plantation of young fir trees,
which they didn't attempt to push through but went round.
Beyond this was a straight ride running at right-angles to our
line of advance and with an avenue of fine old beeches. Here
we corrected our line and pressed forward, driving out parties
of Germans who seemed to have lost cohesion in the wood
and offered little resistance. Jack Hughes's platoon of No. 1
pushed out into the open beyond the eastern edge of the
wood and was held up with some casualties. It was withdrawn after dark to the edge of the wood, and we established
a line just inside the edge of the wood with the left thrown
back in touch with troops of various Battalions, who seemed
a good deal mixed up. After dark Wilfrid sent me to report
to Cavan, who had taken over Bulfin's Headquarters in the
wood to the northwards of us. I don't know how I found him,
but I did somehow. On the way I crossed a ride running
roughly east and west and with a tremendous lot of dead
Germans lying in it. One had fallen into a kneeling position
and looked as though he was prepared to fire, – very lifelike,
but quite dead. It was moonlight and a very eerie sight!
Spent the night in a ditch on the edge of the fir plantation.
It kept the wind off but was damp. All very weary, but at
10 p.m. were woken up with orders to take over more front
on our left from Gordon Highlanders. Put in No. 4, so all
our Companies now up. New line runs back at an angle to the
rest of our line. No. 4 had to dig new trenches as what there

were had fallen in. New trenches not completed till 3 a.m., but after yesterday's experience men will dig till any hour, sooner than not get well down!

Monday, 2 November

Started early to make splinter-proof dug-outs for Battalion Headquarters – one for Officers: one for Other Ranks. D/Sgt. Littler very efficient in charge of digging party. Made quite good dug-outs roofed with branches covered with earth. At 8.45 and 11 the Germans attacked, each time after a short and heavy bombardment. I don't think they had quite located our trenches, but the second attack got fairly close. However, each was stopped by our rifle fire. Luckily we didn't site our trenches on the actual edge of the wood. At 2 another bombardment and attempt at an attack, which never really developed. After dark Wilfrid and I were going round the line and were just approaching No. 4's line, when about 5.45, firing broke out and we saw shadowy figures of Germans coming forward through the trees. Almost directly a message was passed down the line from the left, 'Stop firing: the Northamptons are going to charge.' The men did stop firing for a moment, but we shouted to them to go on, which they did. God knows what started the message, which might have been disastrous; probably it was just some fools going on passing a message which started far away and went far beyond where it meant to. The Germans were close up and Wilfrid said he would go back and collect what re-inforcements he could, and ammunition, and told me to stay with No. 4. I got into the nearest trench and found the men very steady. We could see the Germans very close now (there was a slight moon): they were coming on very slowly and seemed to stagger back before our rifle fire, but always came on again a few paces. With them was a Drummer, who was beating his drum all the time and not, like the others, taking cover behind the trees. I never saw him fall and I believe our men didn't shoot at him. The attack gradually died away before our fire, but they got too close to be pleasant. On our right were the two machine guns of the Oxfordshire L.I. I don't know how they came to be in the middle of our line, but they did good work. Our firing went on after the attack had been repulsed and we could no longer see Germans, so I got up and went along the line and told them to hold their fire until they could *see* Germans and then give them hell.

Nothing more happened except some scattered firing, which as good as told us that the attack had failed. But the Germans must have found out now just where our line is. Luckily their Artillery can't observe their fire. On the other hand, owing to the trees, our own guns can't give us any support close in front of our line. A quiet night after quite a good meal of hot coffee and hot porridge brought up by Sgt. Martin. 17 casualties. Enemy heard digging all night.

Tuesday, 3 November

Position unchanged. At 1 a.m. No. 4 Coy relieved by a Company of Oxfordshire L.I., who reported finding 300 dead Germans in front of our lines! Not much shelling today but a good deal of sniping, so that walking up to (especially) No. 2 Coy's line is none too pleasant. We have now heard more details about the 1st Battalion's losses, which are dreadful. Dear old Stucs, 'Wisher' Forester, Dick Wellesley, 'Beef' Colby, Philip Van Neck (amongst others) all killed, and very many wounded, including Ruggles-Brise (the Brigadier).

The losses of the 1st Battalion were a sad blow. Gordon-Lennox noted in his diary the next day:

4 November

In support in dug-outs. A German aeroplane came over about 8 a.m. and discovered us, shortly after the worst shelling we have had was administered to us: it went on all day unceasingly and we had many casualties. Poor old Mary – Noel's horse – got one on the head and was killed: also 4 or 5 other horses. I had 2 men killed and 7 wounded, some of them being of the draft of 10 who had only joined me the night before. Steere also joined the Company. The shelling subsided at nightfall and we were all thankful to get some relief from the eternal din. It came on to rain just about nightfall and poured in torrents: altogether a most disagreeable ending to a most disagreeable day. Our trenches are all in wet clay and marshy ground, which makes things even more disagreeable than they might be, but there is a certain amount of satisfaction in knowing things are equally if not more disagreeable for the Dutchmen. We heard today of poor Teddy Mulholland's death – a dreadful loss and think of poor

Joan. I suppose one gets inured to seeing all one's best friends taken away from one and can only think one is lucky enough to be here oneself – for the present.

This was to be the last entry. Major Lord Bernard Gordon-Lennox was killed by a shell on 10 November.

Wednesday, 4 November

Same position. A day of very heavy shelling, but no Infantry attack. Enemy now entrenching line along whole front 300 yards away. Very wet night and miserable for all in trenches.

Writing home, Wilfrid Smith said:

It has been a most critical week, and our losses are very heavy. . . . They say the Emperor has been here in person urging on his men, and my word, they are brave. We have killed hundreds the last few days, and these woods are full of them, poor things. It has been a most trying time for nerves. I had one man went mad the other day for a bit, but he pulled himself together after a time.

The tempo slackened for a while, as the Germans regrouped.

Thursday, 5 November

Same position. Another uneventful day, though with intermittent shelling and sniping. We have Irish Guards on our right, Oxfordshire L.I. on our left. Moussy's French Division is on right of Irish Guards. Cavan's Headquarters are now in a house on a hill about 800 yards back from the western edge of Kleinzillebeke wood. A road runs roughly north-east and south-west along and through the rear edge of the wood. This is known as the 'Brown Road', as being metalled it is coloured brown on the map. We have strengthened our positions a good deal, and dug a series of redoubts as supporting points behind the front line. We have thinned, not cleared, the underwood in front of our positions, so that we can get a clearer view, though enough is left to screen our trenches from enemy view. It is worth any trouble to

make good deep trenches, however tired the men may be.
Many of the very heavy losses of British and French Regiments have been due to bad trench digging, and the losses
have been terribly heavy, and our whole Army has been
very hard pressed and has become very mixed up. Cavan
commands a mixed force of various units hereabouts, with
only ourselves and Irish Guards of his own Brigade. The two
Coldstream Battalions were left near Reutel. The Kaiser is
reported to have arrived on this front and we hear that his
reputed Headquarters have been shelled. There is constant
talk of our being reinforced, or possibly relieved by French
troops, but nothing materialises. Our dug-out is not too bad,
but having been dug among pine roots, they leak gum, which
is messy. It is boring too, sitting for hours with nothing to
do but talk and write letters. Eben Pike is convinced that the
War will be over by Christmas. Wilfrid and I don't agree.

Friday, 6 November

Early morning misty, but when it cleared very heavy
shelling began, followed after two hours by Infantry attacks
all along the line. The first attack was everywhere repulsed,
but the next attack drove the French from our old positions
of 31 October, thus uncovering the right flank of the Irish
Guards next on our right. We heard of this just after 1 p.m.,
and almost directly followed the news that the Irish Guards
too had given way and retired in disorder. This left our right
flank (No. 1 Coy) in the air, and most of our positions there
enfiladed. No. 1 Coy lost heavily, but managed to swing
back so as to form a flank to the right with their right on
the Brown Road. Here they held on under 'Bill' Bailey and
Sergt. Thomas, and did great execution by picking off Germans as they came to the road. But the Germans pressed
through the gap left by the French and Irish Guards and
from our Headquarters we could see them behind our right
rear. As soon as he heard that the Irish Guards had given
way, Wilfrid sent Congleton and his platoon of No. 3 and
Tufnell with his machine gun section with orders to act
against the flank of the Germans pushing through the gap.
These were our only Battalion reserves, and they did splendid work. Cavan sent for the Household Cavalry, who were
in reserve in 'Sanctuary Wood', and they came up to
Brigade Headquarters at a gallop, dismounted, and did a first
rate Infantry attack and drove the Germans back and closed

the gap. They saved us, but poor Gordon Wilson (Blues) was killed and Hugh Dawnay (2nd L.Gds.) too, and they had heavy losses of all ranks. Congleton and his platoon went forward with the Cavalry, but poor Tufnell was shot through the throat and died soon afterwards. He was a first rate Officer and is a great loss. All the rest of our line held, but No. 3 had to swing back their right to conform with No. 1. When the Household Cavalry went up, No. 1 swung forward its right again, but not up to its original line. Eventually Cavan sent up some fresh troops to establish a new line in front of, and parallel to the Brown Road, and when this was established the Household Cavalry were withdrawn. Our Nos. 4 & 2 remained in their original line, but No. 3 & No. 1 had to dig new lines to connect with the new line covering the Brown Road. The night was pitch dark and the men dog-tired, but they began to dig soon after midnight and were well dug-in by 4 a.m. What a day! We had about 80 casualties, mostly in Nos. 1 & 3. Dowling was wounded, the only other Officer besides Tufnell. The Irish Guards went into reserve. They have had a bad time – a lot of casualties, including nearly all their Officers – and they were very shaky even before today. Irishmen don't stand hard pounding like Englishmen! Our men are as steady as ever. The Oxfordshire L.I. and R. Sussex helped us with such few men as they could spare. They are good Battalions.

Saturday, 7 November

A misty morning, for which we were thankful as it kept the German guns and aeroplanes quiet, and we could get about the line. The men very tired, but wonderfully cheerful and confident. We could *all* do with a wash and clean clothes and our boots off for a bit. I have managed to shave and wash hands and face every day, as there is a tiny stream just behind our Headquarters from which Hill gets water, but I don't dare think how dirty I must be otherwise. The 3rd and 22nd Brigades were brought up today to counterattack and regain some of the lost ground. Both owing to losses are terribly weak, and the counter-attack only partially successful. We were shelled most of the day, and once the enemy's Infantry advanced, but were met with heavy fire and stopped. We had 63 casualties, but some of them were yesterday's.

Some idea of casualties, and of the impact of individual deaths may be gained from this extract from a letter written by Captain Pike, dated the next day:

Do you know, this Battalion has lost about 800 men so far in the war, and about 20 officers, out of 1000, and 28 respectively. The Irish Guards have only 3 officers and about 150 men left. The 1st Battalion Coldstream have I believe no officers at all left, and about 100 men, and our 1st Battalion only 5 officers and 200 men, and the other Battalions very much the same. The 22nd Brigade which should consist of about 4,100 men, now consists of 3 officers and a few hundred men. . . . Poor young Tufnell was killed the day before yesterday. He is the second mechanic gun [sic] officer we have had killed, and was engaged to a girl in England. Poor chap, he was always so excited about the post coming and getting his letters.

It was the continuous German shell fire that affected the British most. Wilfrid Smith noted:

We have taken considerable toll of the Germans here, but their beastly guns are what cause the casualties. They go on all day, and though they waste heaps of ammunition, some must take toll. The only small consolation is that every shell costs them heaps of money, which will, I hope, help to bleed them to death. The Infantry is beneath contempt compared to ours. They are brave enough, jolly brave, but at night it is too much like shooting a flock of sheep, poor things. They have discipline, and do what they are told, but their attacks at night in this wood developed into the poor devils wandering rather aimlessly about under our terrific rifle fire. The Germans are fighting this war with guns and machine guns, and jolly good they are. They require skill and experience to avoid them even to such a small extent as one can avoid them, but I'm afraid new troops will pay a heavy price to them.

One of the problems of inter-allied co-operation is well illustrated in Jeffreys's next entry.

Sunday, 8 November

Same position. Another misty morning and a comparatively quiet day with only intermittent shelling and a good deal of sniping. At night the London Scottish relieved the Oxfordshire L.I. who held positions on our left and right. Germans shelled the French apparently about a mile to our right and the French guns replied with rapid fire, which is more than ours ever do, though we are said to be short of gun ammunition. A good many French troops about behind our line. Yesterday a Grenadier private appeared at our dug-out leading a Zouave and said, 'Beg pardon Sir, but we've found about 60 like him digging in our wood. What shall we do with them?' He was quite surprised to hear that they were our Allies and had a right to be there. There are a few pheasants in these woods and one of our men in one morning shot 4 pheasants and 7 Germans, all running across a ride he was watching from his trench. Quite good shooting – from 70 to 200 yards. He picked the pheasants up after dark and we (Battalion Headquarters) had one for dinner.

Monday, 9 November

Same position. Quiet day except for some sniping & a little shelling. About 6 p.m. a sudden outburst of rifle and machine-gun fire from enemy line. It was answered at once by a roll of rapid fire, which told us all was well. I don't think the enemy Infantry ever left their trenches and I don't know what the object of their heavy firing was. Casualties in Battalion: – 1 killed, 6 wounded. In the afternoon I went and took over Bernard Lennox's Company in the line to let him get back and have a bit of rest and food. He is very tired and wants rest badly.

There were a few redeeming features: Pike wrote at this time:

We managed to feed very well; there is a farmhouse close by where we used to cook our meals but just after we had had breakfast and gone back to our trenches the other day the Germans put a shell into it and killed 2 men and 3 horses, so now we have our meals cooked in the farm and brought down after dark, and before daylight; for breakfast porridge, Quaker Oats, cold tongue and bread and marmalade and coffee; lunch, cold potted meat, and bully beef, and bread and cheese, generally no tea and hot stew for dinner with bread and cheese. Then I have got some old brandy and they give us ration rum, and last but not least, the greatest luxury of all, I have been able to manage to have a cigar almost every evening. The fighting still goes on and we hold on here like grim Death, there is a tremendous fight going on on our left. It has been going on continuously all night and it is now 10 a.m. The weather is now raw and cold, typical November weather. The London Scottish are here beside us, and are doing splendidly.

The next day was a bad one for the Grenadiers.

Tuesday, 10 November

Same position. After a quiet night terrific shelling started soon after daybreak and lasted practically without inter-mission throughout the day. Our trenches on the right where the line was thrown back were taken in enfilade and badly knocked about, and as they have now located us pretty well there were a few direct hits and consequent casualties. The trees too were knocked down and what with fallen trees and shell-holes, movement was very difficult. Ridley, who was slightly wounded, sent a message, 'The trees about my line look like a lot of spillikins', which exactly expressed it, as they were heaped up and mixed up in every direction. The Battalion hung on grimly through it all, but with heavy loss. Poor Bernard Lennox was killed, also Congleton (a first rate boy), and Stocks. Tudway badly wounded in the head, and George Powell completely buried by a huge shell which hit the parapet of his trench. He was dug out just in time, black in the face, cut and concussed, but still alive, and he should pull through. Besides these we had 21 killed, 37 wounded and 16 missing, who must be buried and dead. At dusk the shelling died down, but it had been a terrible day. After dark we went round the line – Wilfrid took the right and I the left, and it was a terrible job in the dark, falling into shell-holes and stumbling over fallen trees, but the line was intact and the shelling had caused such an abattis of fallen trees in front of it that I don't think an enemy assault would have been possible. I was with Ridley's Company (No. 4) when Foulkes, an R.E. Major, arrived, saying he had orders to help repair the trenches and if necessary dig new ones with his Field Company. I showed him the line, but he had the utmost difficulty in getting his men up through the debris of fallen trees. About midnight the Munsters and Welsh came up to relieve us in the line, the former a wild-looking lot in the old-fashioned black greatcoats. We were relieved by soon after 2 a.m. and went back into Corps Reserve at Bellevaade farm, north of Hooge. We got there about 5.30 a.m., and were told that we were to have some rest. We had some food and lay down and got a little sleep.

Ridley's own account of the day's action runs:

At about 10 a.m. a most violent shelling began. Time H.E. and Black Jane. The right trenches were destroyed and Coy. H.Q. made a hell. An enormous number of trees were cut and fell all over the ground and trenches making communication very difficult. We lost a lot of men. Poor Stocks was killed and Tuddles wounded. I had a job to get the latter in and got covered with blood. The same shell that hit him wounded me in the back and I bled quite a lot. They sniped us all the time and no one could do anything but be in the bottom of the trenches. I could not get away the wounded owing to the fire. About 2 p.m. shell fire slackened, and I got some men back into trenches. Sniping very heavy and a few Black Janes. Went and saw Bernard whose line is now very weak. In evening got up all supports ready for attack which never came. At 10 p.m. relieved by Welch R. and Munsters who had great difficulty owing to the obstacles.

There was little time for rest.

Wednesday, 11 November

At 8.30 a.m. orders received to be ready to move at short notice. Wilfrid rode to Div. Headquarters to see General Monro and returned just in time to find the Battalion falling in with orders to move to a 'position of readiness' in a small wood just north-east of Hooge Château. The German Guard Corps was reported to have attacked our positions on either side of the Menin road and to have broken the line opposite Polygone wood. We were to be ready to support the 1st Division. I was sent as liaison officer to the Headquarters of

one of their Brigades in a small house looking out on Hooge
street and close to the Château. Lieut.-Colonel Lovett
(Gloucester Regt) was in temporary command with 'President' Grant (Coldstream) as Brigade Major. Lovett seemed
dog-tired and rather bewildered, I thought. Through the
window saw some prisoners of the Guard Corps being taken
down the road – very fine looking men. I went to see the
Battalion and found one Company in the wood and the others
in the adjoining Château gardens, all in hastily dug trenches.
A battery of Field-Howitzers was in action on the forward
edge of the wood, which was being intermittently shelled.
It was cold and dull and drizzling. Having no news to give
them I went back and sat for a long time with the Brigadier
and C. Grant, who could get no very definite news as to
how far the enemy had got. Then at 3.15 orders from
Division for us to go forward to support a counter-attack by
the Sussex, Gloucester, and Oxfordshire L.I. We moved along
a narrow lane running east from Hooge Château until we
got to an open ploughed field on the west side of Nonne
Boschen wood. Here we turned south across the plough and
halted close under the west edge of the wood, leaving our
horses and pack animals in the lane. The ground rose to the
southwards and we could see nothing of what was going on
in front. We had no orders except that we were to be at the
disposal of Brig. General FitzClarence, commanding 1st
(Guards) Brigade, whose Headquarters were in a farm on a
track running eastwards along the south edge of Nonne
Boschen wood. Wilfrid sent me forward to find FitzClarence
and report. I went forward, following the edge of the wood
and seeing nobody but a straggler or two. I got to the farm,
in which were one or two men, who told me they thought I
should find the Brigade Major in a trench in the wood. I never
saw anybody so pleased to see me as he seemed to be! He said
the Brigadier had gone out and left him and he had since seen
no one and heard no news. He had no news of the counter-
attack, but said he knew the Brigadier would be delighted to
know the Battalion was handy. I started back and met Wilfrid
coming up himself. He went on to see Charles [Corkran,
the Brigade Major], and if possible FitzClarence, and I went
back to the Battalion, which was spread out in Artillery
formation over the plough. There was a good deal of shelling
and soon after I got back a shrapnel shell burst just in front of
where I was standing with Eben Pike and he was wounded
in the stomach. How it missed me I don't know. He fell into

my arms and I and an orderly got him into a hole, where stretcher-bearers tied him up and took him away. I caught myself almost envying him, as he was taken away, for getting out of this. It was getting dark and to make matters worse an icy rain began to fall in torrents and we were all wet through directly, and plastered with mud off the ploughed field. I sent an orderly for my mackintosh which was on my saddle and I then heard that my poor old black horse had been killed.

It was soon pitch dark and we heard that the counter-attack had been stopped by darkness. However we got no orders and lay there in the mud and rain till after 8 p.m., when we got permission to withdraw the Battalion to Hooge and give them a meal, prior to moving up to make a night attack at 2 a.m. We had had between 30 and 40 casualties from the shell-fire. We went back to the Château grounds and the cookers came up and the men had a good meal and got some shelter in stables, outhouses, etc.. We (officers) went into the Château. It had been the Headquarters of the 1st and 2nd Divisions but had been shelled and evacuated after General Lomax (1st Div.) and others had been wounded. It was now empty, and we got a fire going in the kitchen and got a hot meal and tried to dry our clothes. My jacket got fairly dry, but one sleeve got burnt in the process. We were all dead tired and after food lay down and got what sleep we could. I went into the drawing-room, which was well-furnished, and hesitated before laying down in my dirty things on the sofa. But I thought it would probably be smashed up before long and that I might as well make use of it while I could, so I had an hour's good sleep. At 1 a.m. we started off again and plunged through the mud and rain back to Fitz-Clarence's Headquarters. Wilfrid and I went in and found there the acting C.O. of the Irish Guards, one Webber, whom we had met in the Soudan in 1898. He had only just come out and seemed quite at sea about everything. Fitz-Clarence explained what he wanted us to do, which was apparently for us (Grenadiers), after being led to a position on the flank of the trench captured that day by the Germans, to pass along it in file shooting any enemy met with either in or out of it. As FitzClarence himself was apparently the only man who knew where this trench was, he proposed to lead the Column and put us in position to start. The Irish Guards were to follow us, but for some reason they were to precede us, led by FitzClarence in column of route to the assembly point, which was the south-west corner of Polygone wood. It seemed a mad plan, we thought!

At 3 a.m. we started off in column of route down the muddy lane running east and skirting the south edge of Nonne Boschen wood. FitzClarence marched at the head of the Irish Guards, who were very shaky, and we followed, Wilfrid and I marching at the head of our Battalion. There was a thick, high thorn hedge on the right of the lane and beyond it open fields. When we had gone two or three hundred yards a man in the rear section of fours of the Irish Guards suddenly turned round, let off his rifle in the air, and started to run back. I caught him by the collar and kicked his backside harder than I've ever kicked anyone before, and pushed him back towards his place. But the moment I let go he made a dash for the hedge on the right and dived head-first through it. I caught him by one leg and one of our men got him by the other, but we had to let go as he bolted into the darkness the other side! Unfortunately his shot attracted attention and there were some shots fired in front. FitzClarence halted the Column and went forward himself. After a pause we went on again and reached the west edge of Polygone wood, which was held by British troops, Connaught Rangers. There had been some more firing from in front and FitzClarence had been killed. No one knew what to do nor exactly where the German trench was, except that it ran south from the south edge of Polygone wood. Colonel Davies, commanding Oxford L.I., now appeared and after consulting with Wilfrid decided as senior Officer to abandon the attack as impracticable. I think he was right and that, at anyrate after Fitz-Clarence's death, we hadn't a chance of success. Making a detour to the north we went back to the Brigade Headquarters, after detailing a Sergeant and two men to bring FitzClarence's body in, which they had great difficulty in doing, as he was a heavy man and the mud was sticky and ankle-deep. Webber was also wounded, so his time with the Irish Guards was brief. MacEwen (Camerons) came to take command of 1st Brigade and decided to dig a new line between Nonne Boschen wood and Herenthage wood on the Menin road. Ridley's Company (No. 4) was told off to help the Gloucesters dig and occupy this. They knew the importance of being in by daybreak and dug for dear life and got well down in time. We and the Irish Guards went back to Hooge Château grounds, getting there at 6 a.m., after our first day's 'rest'.

Thursday, 12 November

We were preparing to lie down and sleep when a Staff Officer arrived with orders for us to move to Herenthage wood on the south of the Menin road. We were still to be in Corps Reserve and were not to take over line, but we were close behind the front line, which was held by several weak Battalions hereabouts. We dug ourselves into shelter trenches in the wood. We (Battalion Headquarters), i.e. Wilfrid, I and Bill Bailey, who had taken over the Adjutancy after Eben was wounded, shared a shelter with the Battalion Headquarters of the Scots Fusiliers (commanded by a very good Captain Barrett), the Northumberland Fusiliers and the Sussex Regiment. It was barely splinter-proof, but kept out the rain and we were a weary and not very merry party in it! We got no rations, as we had to move without having a chance of drawing any, but we found some tins of bully-beef dumped by the road-side, enough to give some to every man and keep body and soul together. A good deal of shelling during the day, but no heavy attack on the line in front of us, though there was a heavy attack away to our left. Wilfrid was two or three times appealed to by other Battalions to take over line, but he obeyed his strict orders to keep the Battalion intact. It was a miserable day and we were all cold, wet, tired and hungry. At night Wilfrid sent me with an orderly to report to Colonel Cunliffe Owen, who commands this group of Battalions. We had great difficulty in finding the cottage where his Headquarters were, stumbling through the mud across country to get there, and being dead beat by the time we got back. Our rations came up after dark, which made us all feel better. A quiet night and we got some sleep.

Friday, 13 November

An uneventful day with intermittent shelling and sniping, but no attempt at an attack. Another wet and cold day. At 9 p.m. one Lyttelton (a Staff Captain in 1st Division) appeared with orders for us to move to a fresh position in Corps Reserve. He led us for some way down the Menin road towards Hooge and then turned south through the woods to a white Château, which seemed undamaged. We halted some time in the wood behind the Château, while Lyttelton went for further orders, and finally he took us to yet another wood south of Hooge, known as Sanctuary wood, as it had so far not been shelled. We got there about 2 a.m. and dumped down and got 4 hours sleep of sorts, but it was bitter cold and damp.

After all the activity of the previous three days the Commanding Officer at last had time to write home:

I luckily got off my letters to the bereaved parents just in time the other day, when I had half an hour to spare. It is a sad heartbreaking work writing them, but it is all one can do for them. I feel these poor boys' deaths dreadfully, but we live with constant death round us, and must accept it. When I think of poor Bernard's utter weariness some days ago (I left him in his trench in the early morning, and wished I could take his place, he was so done) and alas! never saw him again. I think of him now at peace, away from all this noise and misery, and though it is terrible for her, poor thing, it can't be bad for him, and must comfort her to feel that he can rest at last. I can't bear seeing my friends go day after day, and when Eben (Pike) was hit, my heart sank, but I must face the difficulties, and hope for the best. If I didn't put my trust in God, I couldn't have lasted as long as I have, but I feel I shall be helped as difficulties arise. . . .

It was with relief that the Battalion came out of Corps Reserve, and returned to their Brigade:

Saturday, 14 November

We found some shelter trenches in the wood, dug by some other unit, and we improved these and dug some fresh ones. A battery of Field Howitzers had just come into the wood before us. The battery Commander said he had been shelled out of every position he'd taken up, and hoped he wouldn't be spotted here. But he was, and the wood was duly shelled. Gilbert Hamilton had his dug-out knocked in and was buried. He was dug out unconscious and will have to go home. Dowling too was wounded. A beastly day; cold, wet and raw; with nothing to do except to squat in a cramped and damp dug-out. We've none of us had our clothes off for nearly a month, and our feet from being constantly wet are swollen and chilled. We had no news, but so far as we know there was no big attack today, and I hope there will be no more for a bit. We've hung on by the skin of our teeth and caused the Germans great losses. But we too have lost very heavily and many Battalions are down to 100 men and everyone is tired and wants rest badly. We must have reinforcements, or there'll be nothing left of us. At night came welcome news to move back to Cavan's force and take over line in Klein-zillebeke wood, and we relieved Munsters on left and 60th Rifles on right by 1 a.m. The line not the same as we held before. Munsters held roughly our line of 10 November, but drawn back a bit. The Cavalry were holding a line thrown back across the Brown Road. Then on their right the 60th continued nearly to Hill 60. Nos. 1 & 2 took over from the 60th; then Cavalry remained in between; No. 4 and 2 platoons No. 3 took over from Munsters. 2 Platoons No. 3 in reserve with Battalion Headquarters, which we took over from 60th. Phillips, C.O. 60th, seemed in depth of depression and we were quite glad when he departed. Nos. 1 and 2 had to dig hard as the trenches of the little Riflemen only covered them up to their waists!

Sunday, 15 November

Remained in position. Bitter cold rain and snow. A good deal of shelling and sniping, and we had about 6 casualties. 'George' Edwards with 1st Coldstream (about 150 men, chiefly drafts) allotted to us as Battalion Reserve. G.E. nearly as gloomy as Phillips and convinced that all was going wrong! Good news that I Corps is to be relieved by the French within next few days. Just about time too.

Monday, 16 November

Same position. Cold and wet. Some shelling and about 6 casualties. We dug new Headquarters in a clump of pine trees. Drill Sergeant Littler full of energy and organised digging parties. He is first rate. G. Edwards and 1st Coldstream withdrawn to Brigade Headquarters.

Tuesday, 17 November

Terrific shelling started about 8 a.m. and went on all the morning. About 1 p.m. the enemy attacked in force, but was everywhere driven back with very heavy loss. The brunt of the attack fell on Nos. 1 and 2 Companies, and Symes Thompson commanding No. 2 was killed. Lee Steere took over command and sent back to say he was running short of ammunition. Wilfrid told me to take up our two reserve platoons of No. 3 under Ralph Cavendish and a supply of ammunition. I took them through the wood to a point about 200 yards from the trenches and halted them under cover. There was still some firing from our line and I could see the Germans lying down about 100 yards in front, but no reply seemed to be coming from them, though little explosions with puffs of smoke came now and again among them. I had a good look and came to the conclusion they were all dead, wounded or shamming, and I told Ralph to extend his two platoons and take them up. They got up without casualties, but when he got up Ralph found Lee Steere had also been killed – a very good boy, who had only lately come out. But the men were in good heart, absolutely steady and full of confidence. The German line now in the edge of a bit of wood about 500 yards to his front (our trenches (No.2's) ran over an open field here). I went back to Battalion Headquarters having made sure Nos. 2 & 3 were all right. Shortly after, another heavy bombardment opened and the German Infantry again advanced, but were completely stopped by our rifle fire. All about our Headquarters heavily bombarded and 6 of our ammunition pack animals killed. The neighbourhood of Brigade Headquarters also heavily shelled and the farm, in which they were, destroyed. The Brigade Signal Officer was killed and 13 out of 15 orderlies were killed or wounded. All the Brigade Headquarters horses were killed. Jack Hughes (No. 1) sent a message to say they too were running short of ammunition, and Wilfrid sent me with a party of orderlies to carry some boxes up, all our pack animals having been killed. We started off to the right through the wood and though there was a good deal of shelling the mud and snow were the chief obstacles and we were pretty blown when we got to the foot of an open slope about 100 yards long in rear of No. 1's position, which was on the front edge of a belt of trees about 30 yards wide. The open slope was a kind of clearing in the wood which surrounded it on three sides with the belt on the fourth. Norman Orr Ewing (Scots Guards) with the Headquarters Irish Guards, which he was commanding, was in the wood at the foot of the slope and told me they were in touch with No. 1 and all right. The slope was slippery with mud but the men managed to get the ammunition boxes up to the trenches, though we had one man wounded by a shell whilst doing so. I went up and spoke to Jack Hughes, who was all right. No. 1 had had a great shoot and had fired 24,000 rounds of ammunition and like No. 2 had killed no end of Germans. The shelling went on till dark, but there was no further attack. The Germans were extraordinarily brave in the way they advanced, and their losses were very heavy. After dark we went over their dead, which lay thick in front of us, for marks of identification and found out the cause of the little explosions I saw. Each man carried on him a hand grenade and these when hit by bullets exploded. A vile day – shelling, snow, mud and cold: we were all stiff and tired, but felt we'd really hit the enemy very hard. Alf Cunninghame and Sergt. Martin brought up rations about 8 p.m. and we were glad to get them.

In a subsequent account of the day's fighting Cavendish wrote:

I mention the following . . . as showing the spirits of the men, dead beat as they were. In the afternoon . . . when all was quiet, I was awakened from a doze by firing, and looking out saw the right half of the mixed 2 and 3 Coys. standing up behind the trench shooting at some Germans who had lain down in a slight fold in the ground when their attack failed, and were now trying to crawl away amid rapid fire and roars of laughter.

This was the Battalion's last major engagement at Ypres.

Wednesday, 18 November

Same position. Shelled, but not so heavily as yesterday. About 24 casualties. Relieved in line about midnight by 3rd Bn. Coldstream who (with 2nd Bn. C. G.) had been at Reutel for more than three weeks until relieved yesterday and had not had much heavy fighting since 21 October. We marched back into reserve at St Jean. Battalion billeted in a farm, with luckily good straw ricks. Snowing hard when we got in.

Thursday, 19 November

Very cold, snowing and sleeting. We all had our clothes off for the first time for a month and had a good wash. A calf feeding tub made a good bath. We (Officers) are in the farmhouse: the men in sheds and out-houses and some burrowed into the straw ricks. The whole country a sea of mud but covered with snow. A good rest today and no shell nearer than 500 yards. The whole Corps except our Brigade has been relieved by the French, and we were to have been relieved tonight, but now the news is that they are jibbing at taking over any more British lines, and so we may have to stay indefinitely. The whole country seems to be swarming with French troops, who don't appear to be doing anything, and they really ought to relieve us. Since this Ypres fighting started we've had 7 Officers killed, 1 (Tudway) died of wounds, and 6 wounded; and something like 400 Other Ranks killed and wounded. Barring Cunninghame (Transport Officer) I am now the only Combatant Officer left who started the War with the Battalion.

The contribution that the Battalion made in these critical days is perhaps best summarised in the following account by Wilfrid Smith, written shortly after their relief:

On the afternoon of 30 October the Grenadiers and Irish Guards and the Oxfordshire Light Infantry were sent under Lord Cavan, from the Polygone de Zonnebeke wood, to help the line which the Germans were forcing back somewhere between Zandvoorde and Klein Zillebeke. The 2nd Battalion were told to go and reinforce the Cavalry, who were holding a line very lightly somewhere north of Ch. de Hollebeke. It was just dusk when we arrived at Z of Klein Zillebeke. I went forward to see what the Cavalry were holding and found they were holding a long line very lightly on a forward slope which appeared to me to be an untenable position. After a considerable delay, owing to the darkness, I arranged with the Cavalry to hold their present line, while I dug in in rear of them. My right was on the railway, my left on the Klein Zillebeke road in the following order, from right to left: No. 2, No. 1, No. 3 and one platoon No. 4; the rest of the Battalion and H.Q. being north-west of the wood between the railway and Z. of Klein Zillebeke.

We got up teas and supplies, ammunition, etc., and were well dug in by about 1 a.m., when the Cavalry withdrew and went to the rear. The Irish Guards were continuing the line north of the Klein Zillebeke road.

On the 31st the French were ordered to attack through my Battalion, the Irish Guards were told to join in, and I was ordered not to leave my trenches. The French advanced at dawn and immediately very heavy shelling commenced. The French never got beyond the line of my trenches. Some of them got into my trenches, some dug new trenches in front of and behind my line. Many wandered back through the wood where the shelling was so terrific that I had to move my H.Q. back and dig in again behind a hedge about 300 yds. from the wood. About midday the Germans appeared to be going to attack us, but they all eventually moved northwards. The shelling continued throughout the whole day till just after sunset, and was simply terrific. Early in the afternoon I got a message from the Brigadier to say that the Germans had broken through the line on the left of the Irish Guards. Another message came shortly afterwards, as far as I can remember in these words: 'The situation is extremely critical, you are to hold your ground at all costs. Sir D. Haig relies on the Grenadiers to save the 1st Corps, and possibly the army.'

I had been suffering casualties from shell fire, and No. 3 particularly had been having a bad time, and I had already had to support them with one platoon. On the receipt of the Brigadier's message I took up the remainder of my supports, and every available rifle, to the line of the trenches, the supports remaining about 400 yds in rear of No. 3. It was then about 3.30. I informed the Brigadier what I was doing and I got the following message back: 'Splendid, you may yet save the Army.'

Meanwhile the Germans had broken through as far as the Brown Road. Later on I got a message from the Brigadier to the effect that the situation was easier, and that the Oxfordshire Light Infantry were coming up on the left of the Irish Guards. Shortly after dark the shelling ceased and I went round the line. It was an extraordinary sight; a farm in the middle of my line was blazing, the hedges were all torn to bits, and the whole place was ploughed up with shells. I found everybody quite happy, though very tired, and I found my casualties were extraordinarily small. This I venture to put down entirely to the good digging of the men, and to the fact that our position was rather concealed, owing to the nature of the ground. Rose had been buried by a shell, but was dug up again. Otherwise my casualties were only about 40 N.C.O.s and men.

During this day I had been very anxious about my right. My right rested on a high railway embankment beyond which was a small wood, and it was very difficult to keep up communication. There were a few British Cavalry there, and I was told that the French were coming up to help them, as the Germans were said to be attacking towards the Canal Bridge. (The Canal was dry). I do not think the French ever arrived, and I was very anxious all the latter part of the afternoon. However, the German attack never developed, and all was well by dark.

During the night 31 October to 1 November, we were relieved by the French and withdrew about 4 a.m., with reserve in rear of the village near Z. of Zwartelen. We had not been in reserve many hours before we heard that the Germans had broken the line again, and I was ordered to go and report to General Bulfin, who I found in a wood near contour 60, three-quarters of a mile south-west of H. of Herenthage. By the time I got the Battalion there, General Bulfin had been wounded and it was difficult to find out what the situation was, and what I was required to do. Eventually Lord Cavan took over the command, and ordered me to clear the wood, south-east of the Brown Road, with the bayonet. I was ordered to leave my kits at the farm in rear of the wood. (Eventually, when I got back the kits that night, many of them had been looted).

I launched the Battalion into the wood, which was very thick, and I was very much afraid I should get the Battalion hopelessly lost. We found the Germans were not in the wood, but they evidently had been as there were many dead lying about. Near the far edge of the wood I managed to find three companies out of the four, and eventually found No. 2, who had reached the front edge of the wood. One platoon of No. 1 had gone beyond the wood, and suffered severely from Maxims. I found No. 1 had touch with the Oxfordshire Light Infantry on the right, and No. 2 had touch with the same regiment on the left. No. 3 was filling up the gap between No. 1 and No. 2. I cannot say enough about the good

leading of the Captains on this day. We were launched into
the wood in a great hurry, the wood was very thick with very
few rides, but somehow the Captains had their companies all
together at the far edge of the wood. No. 4 was with me in
support of the Battalion.

As soon as it was dark, the Germans did their best to set
the wood on fire. Thank goodness, they did not succeed, although there were one or two fires blazing not far from us. I
went round the line and arranged where we were to dig in.
The position was a very nasty one and very difficult to hold
and the Germans were very close to us. We dug in and got
food, etc. About 10 at night I was ordered to take over with
my reserve company the line held by the Gordons on the
left of the Oxfordshire Light Infantry. I had a look at this
line and found no trenches worth speaking of, and the line
very lightly held. I took No. 4 over there and we dug in just
in rear of where the Gordons had been.

On the night of 2 November this Company was very
heavily attacked. It was shortly after dark. Jeffreys and I were
going round the Companies to see how they had fared during
the day. We had hardly reached No. 4 when very heavy
firing broke out on the line held by No. 4 and the Oxfordshire Light Infantry on their right. The Germans attacked
with the beating of drums and the blowing of small horns.
A curious thing happened during this attack. At one time
firing almost died down and it passed down the line, 'Don't
fire, the Northamptons are going to charge.' (The Northamptons were on our left.) We shouted to the men to go on
firing: fire was at once taken up, and went on until the
attack died away. I tried next day to find out where this order
started from, but could never ascertain anything. I have not a
doubt in my mind that it was started by the Germans, some
of whom got within a few yards of the line. This part of the
line was taken over by the Oxfordshire Light Infantry during this night. The next morning they reported to me that
they counted 300 dead in front of this Company.

During the next day or two the Germans moved across our
front several times towards the Irish Guards. On each occasion we took heavy toll with rifle fire and once with
machine guns.

On 6 November it was reported that the Germans were
moving in large numbers towards the right, i.e., the Irish
Guards and French who were on their right. Sometime early
in the afternoon I got a message from the Irish Guards that

the French on their right had been driven in. Almost at the same moment I had a message from Hamilton that the Irish Guards had also been driven in, and that his right was in the air. He also informed me that he had sent a platoon to block the Brown Road on the right where it entered our wood. Shortly afterwards I heard the Germans had reached the Brown Road on my right, and some were advancing round my right rear. At the first alarm I had posted Tufnell with one machine gun on the Brown Road to guard a ride through the wood, across which the Germans would have had to come to get behind my line of trenches. I also sent Congleton with one platoon to stop the Germans getting through 'the gap' on my right rear. For some reason, that I have never been able to get an explanation of, Tufnell took his machine gun with Congleton's platoon. I believe the machine gun had one good target, but Tufnell was unfortunately hit at this time and I never found out exactly what did occur.

After a very anxious afternoon, about dusk the Household Cavalry arrived, made a most gallant charge with the bayonet, and drove the Germans back about the Brown Road, above the Zwartelen wood. For some hours during the afternoon, the right of No. 2 had been absolutely in the air. The men of No. 1, who were on their right, had been practically all killed or wounded by shell fire shortly after the Irish Guards withdrew. Sergeant Thomas, who commanded the right platoon of No. 1 remained at his post after the Irish Guards had gone, till he had only three men left. During this time this N.C.O. was twice buried by shells and had three rifles broken in his hand: he then withdrew with his three men to the Brown Road. It was during this time that Sergeant Digby was very severely, and I believe mortally, wounded. He was never seen again. As soon as it was dark I sent Captain Powell with a part of No. 3 to get in touch with No. 2. This was eventually done, to my great relief, and the line was once more safe. During this very anxious afternoon Colonel Davies, who commanded the Oxfordshire Light Infantry, helped enormously on my right, with the few men he happened to have in reserve. I went to see the Brigadier, as soon as I knew the line was safe, to find out what line he wished us to hold under the circumstances. He ordered me to throw back my right towards the Brown Road. (I omitted to say that a Company of the Sussex was sent to help me during the afternoon and they largely helped to save the situation on my right.)

I went back and let the men have their teas before digging the new line. About this time Congleton appeared and told me he had successfully stopped a lot of Germans getting through the gap. He reported he was holding the gap between the Sussex and, I think, the Cavalry. He had lost several men, but said he had collected several Irish Guardsmen with his platoon, who, however, had no rifles or ammunition. He collected rifles from casualties, and carried them himself, with an orderly who carried ammunition, back to arm these Irish Guardsmen. He held this gap during the night and withdrew in the morning. The intelligent way in which this officer handled his platoon during this afternoon was admirable, and I sent in his name specially to the Brigadier. We arranged the new line about midnight, and I left the men to dig about 1 a.m. When I returned at 4 a.m. I found the men splendidly dug in in spite of the trees and the pitch darkness of the night. I considered this a fine performance as the men were very tired, had suffered heavy losses, and the Companies (1 and 3) were much disorganised.

On 10 November we had a terrible shelling and, owing to my right being thrown back, we were badly enfiladed by the German guns. The shelling continued throughout the whole day all over the wood, many trenches were blown to pieces, many men were buried, and the trees fell in dozens.

During this day Lennox and Stocks were killed by shells, Congleton was shot through the heart, Tudway was hit by a shell on the head and died a few days afterwards. Powell was buried by a shell, was dug up and brought to my dugout by two gallant men under very heavy shell fire. He was in a very bad way. That night the wood was in an awful state. Fallen trees made it almost impossible to get about, and I had great difficulty in getting away my wounded, none of whom could be got away during the day.

On the night of 10 November we were relieved by the Welch Regt. and the Munsters, who took over our line at Klein Zillebeke wood. It took most of the night to relieve and get away and it was about 5 a.m. when we reached Bellewaarde farm, N. of Hooge, where the Bn. went into 'dugouts' in the wood and H.Q. into the farmhouse.

About 7.30 a.m. I rode over to the H.Q. 2nd Division to report to General Monro. He was very kind, congratulated the Bn. on the good work it had done, sympathised with our losses, gave me breakfast and said we were to rest that day, and that the next day he would come over and say a few words to the Bn. I rode back to H.Q. and looked forward to a wash and a good sleep.

When I got back, I found that the Bn. had been ordered to be ready to move at a moment's notice, and very shortly afterwards I was ordered to move to a wood N.E. of Hooge Château. I was told that the line had been broken and that we were to be ready to help. I was told to put the Bn. in the wood, but I found some guns hard at work there, which of course meant that we should be shelled. I put one Company in the wood and the remainder of the Bn. were scattered about the grounds of the Château in comparative safety from shrapnel. We were shelled pretty well all day, chiefly by shrapnel and 'Woolly Bears' and we had a few casualties. About 3.45 p.m. I was told an attack was to take place to retake the trenches the Prussian Guard had captured in the morning, and that the Bn. was to support the attack. The Sussex, Oxford L.I., Irish Guards and Gloucesters were taking part in the attack. The trenches the Prussian Guard had captured were S.W. of Polygone wood, close to our old Brigade H.Q. We crossed the open ground towards the wood E. of Hooge Château in 'artillery formation'. The G.O.C. 5th Brigade insisted on my going forward at once to see General Fitz-Clarence (1st Guards Brigade) whose H.Q. I was told were at the S. corner of the wood. I went on to the corner of the wood where I expected to find General FitzClarence but he was not there and I sent Jeffreys on to see if he could find him. Meanwhile it was getting dark, no attack seemed to be going on and I halted the leading Company. I got another message to go and see General FitzClarence and at the same time I got information from the subaltern in the 15th Hussars exactly where he was. About this time they began shelling us with shrapnel. I got safely to a dug-out in the wood where I found Jeffreys and Corkran (Brigade Major, 1st Guards Brigade). The latter told me that he had never heard anything about the proposed attack, that he had no idea we were anywhere near and that General FitzClarence had gone off somewhere and that he could not find him. He asked me to wait till the General returned. It was then getting dark and began to rain hard. I sent Jeffreys back to collect the Bn. Shortly after he had gone the shelling was rather heavy and I was wondering whether he had got back safely when some officer came into the dug-out and said, 'Your Battalion has rather caught it from shrapnel.' I said, 'Did Jeffreys get back all right?' 'Yes,' he said, 'but the officer with him was hit'. My heart sank, as I knew that must be Pike, and so it turned out. I found afterwards we had lost about 30 men crossing that field.

Trefusis turned up about this time with the Irish Guards and he and I waited in the dug-out while Corkran went to find his General. Time passed and nothing happened, so I went to see what had happened to the Bn. I found Jeffreys had managed somehow to get them together in the dark. It was a pitch dark night and pouring with rain. I went back to the dug-out and getting tired of waiting I went to a house close by where I was told H.Q. 1st Brigade was. There I found General FitzClarence who told me that the Oxford L.I. were to take the German trenches, and if they did not succeed, my Bn. and the Irish Guards were to take them. I asked if I might feed my Bn. first, and was eventually allowed to and ordered to be back at 2 a.m. He told me his general intentions. (I must say I did not like it a bit. We none of us knew exactly where the trenches were, nor had we seen the country by daylight. The men were dead-tired, it was pouring with rain and the mud was awful. However there was nothing for it.) I went back to the Bn. and after great delay, owing to the dark, we got back to the Château grounds, and I sent on for the cookers to come up. The Château grounds I found full of Gunners, Sappers and all sorts of oddments. We were all wet through and you could not see your hand in front of your face. With the greatest difficulty we got the Bn. more or less together, and after a long delay the cookers arrived. We gave the men food and Bailey (whom I had just appointed Adjutant) arranged for the Officers in the Château. Meanwhile a thunderstorm came on and it rained harder than ever, after which it cleared up. We had some hot food in the Château and we got about an hour's sleep. We paraded at 12.30 a.m. and marched back to the H.Q. of the 1st Bde. The slush and mud were awful. I had gone forward with the Adjutant and General Fitz-clarence explained his plan. He had not heard whether the Oxford L.I. had succeeded or not, but we were to move at 3 a.m. The Irish Guards leading in fours, followed by the 2nd Bn. Grenadier Guards. On arriving at Polygone Wood, the Irish Guards were to halt on the W. side of the wood in fours facing S.E., and the Grenadiers were to be in the same formation just beyond (i.e. W. of the I.G.). At 4 a.m. the Grenadiers were to advance, and go straight for the German trench, taking it in flank. The I.G. were to follow the

Grenadiers. About 3 a.m. we started, the General and his Staff leading at the head of the I.G. We walked down the muddiest lane I have ever been down and kept the Bn. pretty well together. After going about ¼ mile some shots were fired. We halted and waited to see what was going to happen. All the time a certain amount of bullets were flying about but the Bn. was perfectly steady. After a short time we advanced again and got to the W. edge of the wood, Corkran having come back and told me where to go. We got into a ditch on the edge of a wood, and Corkran went to try and find General FitzClarence. He had hardly left me, when Bailey told me that the General had been hit badly close to us. The next thing I heard was the General was dead. After a few minutes I saw some men approaching us, who turned out to be the Oxford L.I. I recognised the C.O., Colonel Davies, and called to him. I asked him if he had attacked the Germans and what had happened. He said 'No, I haven't and I'm not going to.' He then told me he had carefully reconnoitred the position, that the Germans were well wired in front, that another trench in rear was full of Germans and most probably machine guns, and that in his opinion the job was a hopeless one. I said that this was exactly what I had expected to be the case, that the General had been killed and we had better consult as to what was to be done. He asked my opinion and I said that I thought the best thing would be to get the Bn. back behind the wood (i.e. W. of Boschen Wood) before it got daylight and that we had not much time to spare. This we eventually decided to do and we gave the necessary orders to our Bns. and went to see the G.O.C. 5th Brigade, who was at a farm not far off. The G.O.C. 5th Bde. (Col. Westmacott) agreed that the attack must be off and arranged to hold a new line a few hundred yards further off (i.e. W.) from the trench the Germans had taken. I went back to the old 1st Brigade H.Q. where I found Corkran, who had sent for Col. MacEwen, O.C. Camerons, to take over Command of the Brigade. The Gloucesters had been told to dig during the night the line it was now settled to hold, but they were not strong enough to hold it and I had to find a Company to help them. This Company (No. 4), under Captain Ridley, found the trenches had not been dug in their section, and had to dig them. Tired as they were, they dug for their lives and got well dug in by about 6.30 a.m. or 7 a.m.

I was told to take the rest of the Bn. back to the Château grounds, where we had been the previous day. This I did, sending Jeffreys to see No. 4 had all they wanted. We got back to the Château, much to my relief, and so ended one of the worst nights, if not the worst, I have ever spent. I now found that I had lost one Platoon of No. 1 and the whole of my H.Q. They had got lost in the dark and goodness only knows where they had got to. I was then nearly driven off my head. Within an hour I was put under 4 Generals and received orders from all of them: G.O.C. 1st Bde., G.O.C. Cavalry, G.O.C. 5th Bde. and finally G.O.C. 1st Div. The latter (General Landon) came to me personally and told me to take the Bn. and the Irish Gds. to the wood on the Menin Road ¼ mile E. of B5, where we were to remain in dug-outs and counter attack the Germans, if they got through the line again. Off we went again and eventually we were put under another Commander, Col. Cunliffe-Owen, who was given Command of that section of the line. Of course we had to dig in again more or less, and then I think the men slept soundly most of the day, in spite of considerable shelling. We had our H.Q. with 5 other regiments, who were holding this portion of the line with Bns. of very much reduced strength, and we stayed there the whole of the 12th and 13th. The wood we were in was shelled continually the whole of this day, but except for the noise, which prevented any sleep, we came to no harm.

On the evening of the 13th, I was ordered to move the Bn. to some dug-outs about ½ mile back (West); my Company in the trenches was relieved and we moved off after we had had food about 10 p.m. When we arrived at our destination, and had just settled where to put the Companies, a Staff Officer appeared and said we were to go to another wood where we could rest in peace. They called this wood 'Sanctuary Wood' because it had never been shelled. After some delay we reached this wood ¾ mile off, and at last got to sleep about 3 a.m. About 6 a.m. I had a look round, and saw some guns just in rear of us, so I wandered down to see what they were. They turned out to be some Howitzers and the officer told me they had been shelled out of every place they had been to by guns with a range of 14 miles. Sanctuary Wood or not, I knew we were in for another shelling, and it began fairly early and went on all day. Gilbert Hamilton left us on this morning, his dug-out having fallen in on him. About 2 p.m., the 14th, I got orders to be ready to move at once, as the line had been broken. Thank goodness nothing came of it and we were left in peace and at night the shelling ceased. I got orders about 5 p.m. to move back to the 4th Bde. that night. Although this meant another march all night, it was hailed with joy by all ranks, nobody wanting any more Corps Reserve. We started about 8 p.m. and got back to our old Bde. H.Q. about 1 a.m., took over a part of our old line and got settled about 3 a.m. on the 15th. During our 'Rest', we had marched about 3 nights out of 4, and been properly shelled every day.

During the 20 days, 31 October to 19 November, the Battalion lost 12 officers and 466 men. At the end of this period I had 6 Company Officers and about 350 rifles. I had also lost a great many horses.

Lord Cavan, their Brigade Commander, described their work in the following terms:

No words can ever describe what the devotion of men and officers has been under the trials of dirt, squalor, cold, sleeplessness and perpetual strain of the last three weeks. . . . We came into this theatre 3,700 strong, and we shall go back about 2,000, but nothing finer to my mind has ever been done by human men. I really should cry if the Germans got into Ypres before we go. . . .

And in more formal terms:

[The Battalion] leaves the line intact, and in spite of great loss and untold sufferings and hardships, it fought the battle of 17 November with as good a nerve as the battle of the Aisne. . . .

I can never express what I think of the great courage and endurance shown by officers and men during the defence before Ypres, and I should like to put on the regimental records not only my sense of pride at being their Brigadier, but my debt to the Battalion for their great devotion to their duty. The men have all kept up a respectable appearance, which has been an example, considering that it has been absolutely impossible to change an article of clothing for four weeks. . . .

6

'A question of stalemate – the year's end'

(Wilfrid Smith – letter, 29 October)

BY the time that the Battalion was relieved, and marched off to rest and refit, it had become clear to everyone that the war on the Western Front was deadlocked. As Wilfrid Smith remarked, 'You can't get on because there are no flanks, and you cannot therefore get round them.' Both sides settled down on a front that stretched from the Channel to the Swiss border and was to alter only in detail over the next four years. The memory of more open warfare lingered on, especially tempting to the Cavalry officers who made up so many of the senior officers in the Army. Tactics however were dictated by the realities of the situation. Trench warfare, of the type that had first appeared on the Aisne and the lessons of which had been hammered home in the dark days of Ypres, had come to stay.

First, for those Battalions decimated at Ypres, there was a chance to recover in the comparative peace of Northern France.

Friday, 20 November

Still at St Jean. Hard frost and snow. Relief really to take place today. Hear poor Dick Dawson, Coldstream, has been killed by shell. We were to have marched at 4 p.m., but the French were late, and we did not get off till 10.45 p.m. Then the Herts Territorials, who are attached to our Brigade, were missing, so further delay and we did not get on the move till nearly midnight. We, Irish Guards and Herts marched as a Column under Wilfrid Smith. Freezing hard and roads very slippery.

Saturday, 21 November

Progress very slow and roads blocked with guns and transport, so that for some way we had to march in file or even single file. About 2.30 a.m. we halted at Onderdoman, whither our transport had preceded us, and where huge fires had been lighted, and there we had hot tea. About 3.30 a.m. we moved on. Progress still very slow owing to congested and slippery roads, and a good many stragglers of some regiments. Our men were still marching like soldiers: a good many others were not. Many Battalions are reduced to 100, or less, tired, muddy men. How the Corps will ever be reconstituted, goodness knows. About 8.30 a.m., we reached Meteren – 2 miles west of Bailleul – and went into billets. Officers in small, working-class houses in the village street, the men mostly in barns etc. A Staff Officer met us on the road an hour before we got in and anounced that there was to be 4 days leave home for the Officers of each unit who had been out longest. Almost too good to be true! Spent the day washing, sleeping and reading the papers, which seem to think we had an easy job beating the Germans at Ypres! ! ! Still bitterly cold and snow on the ground. Heard that I am definitely to go on leave tomorrow.

Sunday, 22 November

Started 8 a.m. with Ridley and 'Tubby' Howell, R.A.M.C. in General 'Joey' Davies's car, which he kindly lent us, for Hazebrouck, where we got a slow and crowded train for Calais. The train very late and we missed the connection to Boulogne. Very afraid of missing the boat and asked Station-master how we could get on. He said no train, but if we liked to walk down the line to the junction there might be a goods train or an engine! Walked down the line and sat in the snow by the signal box. Signalman very civil and promised to stop anything that came along. Eventually an engine appeared and was stopped and the driver said he would take us to Boulogne. We sat on the coal and he stopped on the embankment at Boulogne to let us get off and we walked to the 'Maritime' Station and caught the boat at 4 p.m. Very rough crossing and arrived late at Folkestone. London about 9 p.m. and to Hans Place, where D. awaiting me.

Ridley's account is rather more colourful, and gives a clue to the effects of the strain under which commanders at all levels had been working in the past weeks.

Up at 2.30 p.m. and was ordered to go on leave at 7 a.m. tomorrow for a fortnight. I can hardly believe I am awake. . . . Had dinner and early bed. Very cold. Slept like a log. Dreamt less than usual. This time it was being unable to find my Company, wanted for immediate attack. I also got lost, I think. Up 6 a.m. in dark and collected a little kit and souvenirs. Breakfast 7.15 and at 8 got into car lent by Gen. Davies to Hazebrouck and there entrained in the 9.6 for Boulogne. Half hour late. . . . Train rather full. With Ma and Howell into a 2nd Class with an Ensign A.S.C. and a Sergeant of French interpreters from an R.F.A. Bde. Very slow journey. Arrived at Calais to find the connecting train gone ½ an hour. Eventually we got onto a light engine. Slow and cold journey. Saw Belgian Infantry in occupation. Ice apparently bearing. To Boulogne and reported to Base Commandant and was ordered to embark. Good lunch. Return fare £1.9.2d. Boat off about 4.30. Bad crossing.

The leave was all too brief.

Monday, 23 November/Tuesday, 24 November

In London – warm, comfortable, happy! in plain clothes.

Wednesday, 25 November

To Burkham for the day. Back 8 p.m.

Thursday, 26 November

In London, which seems just the same, except for many men in uniform.

Friday, 27 November

Started 8.30 for Victoria. Crossed Folkestone–Boulogne. Travelled with Philip Runloke, who is a King's Messenger. He introduced me to Baker-Carr, who is on the Staff at

G.H.Q., and took me in his car to St Omer. He then sent me on in the car to Meteren, where I arrived about 5 p.m. Weather warmer: all snow gone but plenty of mud and slush. The Prince of Wales, who is at G.H.Q., came in after tea to see us.

Saturday, 28 November

Wilfrid Smith started on 4 days leave home. No draft for the Battalion yet, but the men are getting new clothes, which are badly wanted. Our casualties since the beginning of the War have been:

        17 Officers killed
        15 Officers wounded
       739 Other Ranks killed and wounded
       188 Other Ranks missing.

Total 959

Practically the strength of a whole Battalion. The missing must nearly all be dead, for, except at Villers Cotterets and on 6 November there could have been no prisoners, and the Germans abandoned their wounded prisoners, taken at Villers Cotterets, when they retired. On 6 November we know of no prisoners, but some wounded may have been left when we threw our right flank back. Some of the missing were probably hit direct by big shells, or buried. Others may have dropped in the woods and not been found. Walked to Bailleul and lunched with Alick Russell, who is G.S.O. 2 at II Corps Headquarters there. Warm and muggy, and I got quite hot walking.

Sunday, 29 November

Church Parade in the morning. Lunched with Boy Brooke (Brigade Major) at Headquarters 1st Guards Brigade, now commanded by 'Meat' Lowther. 'Bulgy' Thorne, Staff Captain, Alick Russell and Gathorne-Hardy, both on Staff of II Corps, came to dinner with us.

Monday, 30 November

A draft of 465 men under Monty Cholmeley and Percy Clive, with two new Special Reserve Officers, Buchanan and

Williams, arrived to join the Battalion. Still damp, muggy weather.

Tuesday, 1 December

The draft is settling in. They are mostly older class reservists with a certain number of serving soldiers from 3rd Battalion, including a few joined in August. A fine lot of men and the Battalion again about 900 strong. Douglas Loch came to lunch and took me in a car to the II Corps observation post on Kemmel hill, whence one could see most of our now shortened line in the flat country below. Nothing much going on except near our old position by Zillebeke, where the Germans were shelling briskly. Otherwise they have been strangely quiescent of late.

Wednesday, 2 December

Walked into Bailleul. Have started doing a little drill, musketry and route marching daily. Just enough to keep the men fit and soldierly, and to harden their feet. Dined with 2nd Bn. Coldstream.

Thursday, 3 December

The King inspected the Brigade, which was drawn up in the road. He afterwards assembled the C.O.s (myself, Torquil Matheson, MacGregor and Jack Trefusis), and was very complimentary on the work of the brigade out here, and said he was very proud of his Guards! The Prince of Wales, in Grenadier uniform, was with him and came and talked to me afterwards, and asked after everyone. He is a very nice boy and a very keen Grenadier. I think the King coming out has done a lot of good throughout the Army. Monty Cholmeley and I walked into Bailleul, which is a big town and full of troops. There is a fine Cathedral and Town Hall, and the biggest fruit gardening establishment I've ever seen, with acres of glass. The owner told me he supplied huge quantities of fruit to Covent Garden in normal times, and we bought some lovely white muscat grapes from him. Most of his glass-houses have troops billeted in them, and they are very comfortable with the heating on.

During his visit the King presented medals to those N.C.O.s and men of the Brigade who had been awarded decorations as a result of operations since September. Among those Grenadiers who received the D.C.M. were Lance Sergeant L. Thomas, for the burning of the woodstack used by enemy snipers at Chavonne, Private Cooney, for 'gallantry carrying out his duties as a stretcher bearer after he had been twice wounded', two men for their work as orderlies, carrying messages at Ypres, and Sergeant G. H. Thomas, for the action described on page 148. (Sergeant Thomas was killed three weeks later in the trenches near Festubert. Wilfrid Smith, writing to Regimental Headquarters on 29 December, said, 'He came out as a private, and has worked his way up to acting Sergeant by sheer merit. He was a gallant man, and a great loss to No. 1 Company.')

Friday, 4 December

At Meteren – Rain, mud and slush.

Saturday, 5 December

At Meteren – Rain, mud and snow. Frost at night.

Sunday, 6 December

Church Parade 11.30. The Prince of Wales came to tea with us. Monty C. and I go for long walks together. It is very nice having him out here and we have great talks of old times from the Eton days onward. Wilfrid Smith and others returned from leave at 10 p.m. They have had a week, where we (first lot) only got four days!

Monday, 7 December

Pouring rain all day.

Tuesday, 8 December

Walked with P. A. Clive to Bailleul. Old P.A. still very much the M.P. but also a very keen soldier! Had tea with Alick Russell at II Corps Headquarters.

New skills were learned. Lord Cavan wrote to the Regimental Lieutenant-Colonel:

Our chief work of late has been to learn three things. 1st. How to make our own charcoal and how to carry it and use it in the trenches when made. 2nd. How to throw hand-grenades – curious work for Grenadiers. 3rd. How to shoot at aeroplanes, but the trouble here is – birds are scarce, and our guns have very long waits between the beats! We are now trying to dig in a machine gun and work it on a pivot – but so far we have not had a try at a real enemy flier.

Ridley had just returned from leave:

Went and saw grenade practice. It was quite like old times to see a good explosion quite close. . . . It has been an awful wrench coming back: much, much more than going out the first time. I gather it is the same with the others.

It was a good time to be out of the trenches.

Wednesday, 9 December

Very wet.

Thursday, 10 December

Rained hard. Sidney Clive came to see us. He is at the French G.H.Q.

Wilfrid Smith went into more detail in a letter home next day:

I saw Sidney Clive yesterday for the first time during the war. He was very well, but is very hard worked. Most of what he told us was not for publication. They all seem quite happy about Russia, and say that the German losses have been enormous. Kitchener says the war is going on for two years, but they think he does not realise what it would mean to every country but England, who as yet has not been touched by the War. In other countries all trade is practically at a standstill, and it is impossible to believe that the world can stand such a thing for two years.

Traditional rivalries found their outlet in sport.

Friday, 11 December

Played football – Officers 2nd Bn. Grenadiers versus Officers 2nd Bn. Coldstream. Ground like a quagmire. Result – 2G.G. 5 goals – 2C.G. 2 goals. Teams – *Grenadiers:* Jeffreys, de Crespigny, Cholmeley, Cavendish, Ridley, Bailey, Gerard, Nesbitt, Hughes, Buchanan, Cunninghame. *Coldstream,* Mac-Gregor, Towers, Clark, de Trafford, Taylor, Verelst, Feilding, Ramsay, Burn and 3 N.C.O.s.

Saturday, 12 December

Walked to Bailleul. We now live well with plenty of food in the Mess. The men too have been sent by the Regiment and others any amount of tobacco, food and comforts – probably more than they will be able to carry when we move. The Prince of Wales came to see us, and has given some footballs to the Battalion.

Sunday, 13 December

Church Parade in the morning. Warned to be ready to move 9 a.m. tomorrow.

The Commanding Officer held firm views about Church parades:

I went to Church this morning, a fine large Church, but very gaudy inside, and it was chock full of men, entirely voluntary. It bears out my theory that a good parson will get as many men to Church as they get now compulsorily. I think it speaks well for the French R.C.s that they almost always allow us to use their Churches, and I believe it is a thing that the R.C.s are very particular about. We had a good organ this morning, which was a great pleasure. . . . . . . The Prince came again last night. Poor boy, he is very miserable at Headquarters with nobody of his own age, and no special job to do.
We have no orders to move yet, but it cannot be far off

now. We shall never get the war over if we sit here doing nothing all the time.

This last sentiment is echoed in Jeffreys's next entry:

Monday, 14 December

Standing by all day. The French made an attack towards Hollebeke and our II Corps one on Witschaete. These reported successful. I was President of four Courts Martial. The country a sea of mud, and we are getting bored.

The Battalion had another visit from the Prince of Wales, recounted by Wilfrid Smith:

. . . The Prince arrived here late last night in high glee. He had seen a fight (at a fairly safe distance) and had got a prisoner in his car! I never saw a boy so happy. The prisoner was in his car, guarded by his 'bear leader' while he talked to us in our house. Eventually he left, his prisoner (a lieutenant) looking very comfortable, and having the time of his life, being driven by H.R.H. himself. He always drives himself in an ordinary car, with a hood and tremendous headlights.
. . . We shall never beat the Germans unless we get on with it. We are, however, doing something, though I mustn't say what. The weather is so bad, no weather for fighting.

The waiting seemed interminable.

Tuesday, 15 December

Still standing by. It is said that we have lost most of the small amount of ground gained yesterday and that the French failed at Hollebeke.

Wednesday, 16 December

A draft of Officers, 'Mis' Churchill, and 5 Special Reserve Officers – Hopley, Rumbold, Nevill, E. Williams and Craigie joined the Battalion from home. All the S.R. Officers seem very good fellows. 'Mis' just the same as ever and full of zeal!

Thursday, 17 December

Still at Meteren and nothing doing. The weather and sodden state of the country make any considerable or quick movements impossible.

Friday, 18 December

Meteren. Very wet. V. Vivian has taken over as Brigade Major from G. Ruthven.

Christmas was close, and brought its own attendant problems for Commanding Officers:

Everything seems hung up just now for all the Christmas parcels, which are becoming a positive nuisance. I am told that the rations of the Army are to be held up for twenty-four hours to enable the Princess Mary's presents to come up, and I have had reams of orders as to their distribution. I don't know what I am not responsible for in connection with this present. It was the longest order I have had since I have been out, and it seems rather ridiculous to make such a tremendous business of it when, after all, our first business is to beat the Germans. Our enemy thinks of war, and nothing else, whilst we must mix it up with plum puddings!

The period of rest was nearly at an end.

Saturday, 19 December

Meteren. Football. Grenadiers versus Coldstream: 5 Officers and 6 Other Ranks on each side. Grenadiers 2 goals – Coldstream 1 goal.

Sunday, 20 December

Meteren. Rode to Mont des Cats in the afternoon. Mervyn Williams (one of our S.R. Officers) came. He says the language these Flemish speak is like the South African Taal. It is certainly very ugly.

Monday, 21 December

Ordered to be ready to move at one hour's notice. News that the Indian Corps very hard pressed and have lost some trenches not far from Bethune. In the evening orders to move at 7 a.m. tomorrow.

Tuesday, 22 December

Marched at 7 a.m. by Merville to Bethune. Bitterly cold. I was riding in rear of the Battalion as we went over the level crossing at Merville, when who should appear but ——— in Grenadier uniform. I said, 'Hullo ———! When are you coming back to the Regiment?' He said, 'Good God! you don't think I'd be such a fool as to do that! I've got a good job.' He's an arch-shirker and brazen-faced about it in the bargain. He's a draft-conducting Officer on the railway, or something of the sort. The Prince of Wales marched with the Battalion all the way after Merville, and apparently enjoyed it, but I doubt if the Staff Officer with him did – trudging along in the mud! It was dark for the last two hours of the march and we could make out the position of the line by the lights and star shells sent up by the Germans. Battalion billeted in Bethune Boys' School, having marched about 17 miles. Considering it was their first long march, they got along well, though all tired when we got in.

No. 3 Company had good fortune that night. Cavendish noted:

Slept in Bethune in a draper's shop. Draper most attentive, slippers, cigars, coffee, a spirit heater, cognac and finally a hot water bottle!!

Next day the Battalion went back into trenches.

Wednesday, 23 December

Marched off in the dark at 7 a.m. and bivouacked at Le Touret in readiness to support 2nd Brigade (1st Division) holding the line in front, as a German attack was anticipated. However, nothing happened and we hung about waiting in the cold (rain and sleet). A good many Indian soldiers about.

They looked utterly miserable and curled up with the cold!
The Prince of Wales came with us, but just as we were going
to move on at 3.30, General Monro appeared and, in spite of
his protests, carried him off in his car. He is tremendously
keen and seems to like turning out in the dark on a winter's
morning and marching (on his feet) with the Battalion. He is
not to be allowed in the line for the present, much to his dis-
gust! After dark we took over the line in front of Rue des
Cailloux from the R. Sussex Regiment. A dreadful line in
low-lying waterlogged country. Many of the trenches simply
wet dykes into which the Indians had been driven when they
lost their trenches. Such trenches as existed were full of
water and mud and no better than the dykes. Several men
had to be dug out of the mud into which they had sunk.
Enemy continually sniping and the flat country swept by
bullets in all directions. Battalion Headquarters in a small
and smelly farm with a bottomless pit in front of it. Very
cold night: alternately snowing and raining. 2nd Bn. Coldstream on our left: 1st Division on our right. Our line runs
roughly north-east to south-west and about 250 yards south-
east of Rue des Cailloux. Our right on the Bethune–Quinque
road. Many villages hereabouts are called by the name of
the road they are on.

Thursday, 24 December

I went round the trenches early. The water up to my
waist in some places. Daylight showed our trenches to be
very badly sited as well as full of water and mud, which
made communication slow and difficult. The country quite
flat and featureless, and intersected with dykes. A ridge about
6,000 yards to the eastward, whence the Germans can over-
look us, and about 1½ miles to our right front we can see
Givenchy hill, held by our 1st Division. It took me over two
hours getting along the line, wading a good bit of the way.
We found that the enemy has sapped up to within 10 yards
of our front trench in two places and his snipers were very
active. Also he is using trench mortars (*minenwerfer*), which
throw heavy bombs. One can see them coming, turning over
and over in the air, and so can often avoid them, but it is
impossible to move quickly in this mud and water. I went
around again later and had only just left Monty Cholmeley
(who had an awful cold), and got back to the support line,

when about 11 a.m. the enemy blew in No. 2's trench with a land mine (or perhaps a *minenwerfer* bomb) from one of their saps and rushed in behind the explosion. There was a general scramble in the mud and water and Nos. 2 and 3 retired from their front trenches into the second line, which the enemy then attacked but was driven back with heavy loss. But we lost heavily. Dear old Monty Cholmeley killed (shot through the head): also Nevill, a very good S.R. Officer recently come out. Another young S.R. Officer, Goschen, was badly wounded and left in the trench when the Germans got into it, as they could not get him away through the mud and water. We are afraid he may be dead too. Other ranks, 15 killed, 29 wounded and 9 missing, of whom 5 known to be wounded. We ought never to have held such a line, but taking over in the dark we could not see the lie of the land. There was continuous firing for the rest of the day and a good deal of bombing from the *minenwerfers*, but no artillery fire. No. 1 Coy. on the right had remained in the forward position when No. 2 came back, and we could get no communication with them. At night Wilfrid decided we must dig a new line and finish it by daylight. I superintended the work, and it was a ticklish job, as every few minutes the Germans sent up flares which lit up everything, and each time they did so we threw ourselves flat, and got up and went on digging as soon as the light died away. It was a hard frost and the ground was getting hard and the men tired and stiff from being so wet, but by daylight we had it done, and withdrew our right into it, the men there having many of them been up to their waists in icy water for 36 hours. One platoon of No. 1 was still left out on the right in wet dykes and no communication with them possible.

Friday, 25 December

Hard frost and ground as hard as bricks. Dykes frozen over. At daybreak a few Germans put their heads up and shouted, 'Merry Xmas'. Our men, after yesterday, were not feeling that way, and shot at them. They at once replied and a sniping match went on all day. 'Mis' Churchill was particularly busy sniping and I think exposed himself too much, as he got shot in the head, the bullet making a deep groove in his head, from forehead to back. I saw him carried back and never thought I should see him again, but he is getting

better and they think he will live. In the middle of the day
the sniping died down. From our front line I could make out
the isolated platoon of No. 1 about 150 yards to our right,
and I decided to try and get to them. I got along an old dug
dyke for a bit, but then came to flat open ground. There was
no firing and I got out and walked across, not a shot being
fired at me. Possibly the Germans were having dinner and
not looking out. Anyhow I got to them and they seemed glad
to see me. They were in a dyke, lying on a rather sloping
bank just above the ice. They did not know where Battalion
Headquarters were and had no means of communicating.
They had got their rations direct from the rear at night. I
told them to expect relief at night, and then had to face
getting up and walking back, but again no one shot at me.
However, I was very glad to get back to our trench, and I
think I was a fool to do it. In the afternoon there was again
a good deal of sniping, and we had several casualties in the
day. About 6 p.m. we were relieved by 3rd Bn. Coldstream
and went back into reserve at Le Tournet. The only billet for
us (Battalion Headquarters) was a very cold kind of store-
house but we were too tired to look for anything else and
sat down to our Xmas dinner muffled up in greatcoats. My
feet were so swollen and painful from wet and cold that I
had great difficulty in getting my boots off, and still more
difficulty in getting them on again, and we had 57 cases of
frost-bite (or something like it) and many more of badly
swollen feet in the Battalion.

Saturday, 26 December

Sent out Alf Cunninghame (Transport Officer) and Skidmore (Qr.Mr.) early and they found us quite a fairly good
farmhouse to get into (which they ought to have done
before), and we made ourselves reasonably comfortable and
had a proper Xmas dinner with a turkey sent by Lord Derby,
port sent by Dorothy, and a bottle of old brandy sent by
Colonel Streatfeild. Every Officer and man got a Xmas card
from the King and Queen, and also a metal box from Princess Mary, with tobacco, a pipe and cigarettes in it. The
people of the farm are very boorish Flemish peasants, quite
decent people in their way, though not attractive. A good
fire in the open fire-place in the kitchen. The men mostly in
barns with plenty of straw.

Back in reserve, Wilfrid Smith summed up the reconstituted Battalion's baptism of fire:

. . . I am quite overwhelmed with letters, my own and many for the Battalion. Such a quantity of Christmas things for the Battalion, which have to be thanked for, but I shall get through it in time. Having to dish out all these things has been a great burden, and came at a somewhat harassing time.

. . . We went into the trenches on Wednesday night, and had a real bad time – most cruel luck for these poor boys to have the first time they have been shot at, the result was of course trouble and anxiety. The country about here is dead flat, the most horrible looking country you can imagine. We took over the most horrible trenches, they were so wet and muddy, and you cannot approach them without being shot at, so all communication has to be by trenches, which are sodden and mostly under water. On our way there, four men sank in up to their hips. It took nearly four hours to dig them out, and they all fainted several times from cold. Eventually we got the line taken over, but it took eight hours – the going was so awful. Poor Monty's Company were in a trench with water above their knees, and to get to it they had to wade up to their middles. In the morning we were in trouble, the Germans were in many places up to ten to twenty yards of us, which we had never been told when we took over in the dark. They threw bombs at us, and shot a horrible explosive bomb, which was nearly as bad as a shell. The shelling was very slight, and our guns are splendid and improving every month, as they get more ammunition and bigger guns. To make a long story short, the beggars got into our trenches. The whole place, trenches and inside, was like a maze, some trenches full of water, and some not so bad, and what I saw of it was like a lot of rabbits running about with a ferret after them. We took up a line about a hundred yards back, which was a much better one, in fact the first line was untenable when we took it over, and had I had my old and trusted Captains, this would have been recognised at once in the dark, and we should have never tried to stop where we were. Meanwhile, poor Monty's Company No. 1 (Gilbert's old Company) did their best and were splendid, but the water hampered them and they had to give way to keep in line with the others. Alas, poor Monty was shot, also

Nevill and Goschen (reported missing, but feared dead). The last only joined a week and a nice boy – I believe the son of the Ambassador, but I must make sure before I write to him. At night we had eventually to dig a new part of the line, which took all night, as it was dug under constant sniping and rockets, and we had no time to finish it, so two platoons under a splendid young fellow, Buchanan (just out), had to remain in the water all that night and next day till after dark, when we all got away for forty-eight hours, after which we go back again. The whole business cost me about ninety casualties, and a lot of officers, three killed as I told you, Churchill badly wounded, Williams hit in the foot but still going, and I hope will be all right, Eyre, a little boy just out, has had to go sick.* I have fifty-five today suffering from frost-bite and two officers rather shaky from the same cause, but sticking to it. The second night it froze hard, and I was very anxious for the men in the water – who were cut off from the others by a ditch with water up to their middles, and who were up to their knees themselves – as to whether they would not be killed by cold – but they came out all right – stiff, cold and hungry, for they had very little for forty-eight hours (I couldn't get it to them) – but chattering and talking quite happily as they hobbled along, splendid fellows that they are. I had a hot meal ready for them afterwards and they will, I hope, be mostly right tomorrow, but my Battalion is not what it was three days ago, alas!, and it is the first time the Battalion has given up a trench to the Germans – which is very sad. . . .

Percy came today, and said everybody at Headquarters was very happy, and the general position excellent; that is good news and helps you when you are up to your knees in water!

I am sending home my Christmas card, and shall send my Christmas present from Princess Mary. Bless her – she has been a nuisance! !

The high hopes of August seem far away from this dismal year's end.

---

* The War Diary notes, 'Eyre, having had to swim to his trench, collapsed and has been sent home'.

Sunday, 27 December

Fine, frosty morning, but thaw set in in the afternoon. In reserve all day at Le Tournet. Raining and country once more very wet. Took over the same line in front of Rue des Cailloux at 7 p.m. Very wet and our new trench as bad as the old one.

Monday, 28 December

In the trenches. Very wet and mud awful. At night blew a gale and the cold awful, alternately raining and snowing.

Tuesday, 29 December

Trenches in dreadful state, crumbling in in many places, and mud and water everywhere over our knees. Sniping and a few shells caused a few casualties. Relieved 7 p.m. by 3rd Coldstream and back to same billets in Le Tournet.

Wednesday, 30 December

In reserve in Le Tournet. Cavan has decided that owing to the awful conditions no tour in the trenches is to be more than 48 hours.

Thursday, 31 December

Back in the same trenches, which fall in as fast as they are built up. Continual sniping by the enemy, who seem to do it to keep themselves warm! Neither side could attack in these conditions, as both are stuck in the mud. Little artillery fire, but a good deal from the *minenwerfer*. I went along the line in the evening and talked to some of the Officers, who were getting down on their luck. Told them they *must* keep cheerful and set an example that way. The men marvellously cheerful in the circumstances, especially Sergt. Leach, a first rate N.C.O. who was in my Company in 3rd Battalion. He was roaring with laughter and making jokes and keeping all his men cheerful. The rifles get rusted and choked with mud, and it is continual work to keep them clean.

Next day Wilfrid Smith wrote home

> I saw the New Year in last night in the most depressing way, wet, cold, slush and bullets and rockets. The Germans sung carols, so our men shot at them to make them keep quiet . . . . Never was warfare made more difficult.

It was a scenario that remained virtually unchanged until 1918.

No. 7. Coy. 5 Res/Batt. Grn. Gds.
Chelsea. Bks.
London. S.W.

Lady. Maria. Welby.

Madam —

I am so very sorry. I have been so slow in writing. But I have been so uncomfortable lately. I have lately found out about your son (Lieut. Welby) and he was very brave.

If any one was entitled to the Victoria Cross. Mr. Welby was. He was wounded first, and the Commanding officer to Mr Welby to go back. but he stuck with his Company, and cheered his men on, besides bringing back a wounded Officer, when he was wounded himself. All the men that knew Mr Welby honoured him, he was a fine Officer, and took care of his men.

I am quite well now, and expect I shall soon be off to the front again but I am in hopes of getting a short leave first. I hope you will excuse me bringing up about Mr. Welly. but it is a thing I could not help. now 'my Lady' I must close.

I remain
Yours Ever Grateful
W. G. Baker. Sergt

This letter from Sgt Baker to Lady Welby, written in early 1915, only came to light in January 2012. Lt Welby was killed on the Aisne on 17 September 1914 (see page 92).

Biographical Index

(Note: Army records were not always easily maintained in 1914 and unfortunately it has been impossible to identify some individuals.)

Abbreviations

AAG	Assistant Adjutant General
AA & QMG	Assistant Adjutant and Quartermaster General
BEF	British Expeditionary Force (France)
DAAG	Deputy Assistant Adjutant General
GSO 1	General Staff Officer 1st Grade
EEF	Egyptian Expeditionary Force
G. Gds	Grenadier Guards
C. Gds	Coldstream Guards
I. Gds	Irish Guards
W. Gds	Welsh Guards
k.i.a.	killed in action
d.o.w.	died of wounds

ALEXANDER, Harold Rupert Leofric George   1891–1969
Entered Army 1910; commissioned Irish Gds; Lieutenant 1 Batt. I. Gds BEF August 1914; Captain 2 Batt. I. Gds BEF March–October 1915; Second-in-command 1 Batt. I. Gds 10–31 December 1916; Major, Officers School July–September 1917; Lieutenant-Colonel 2 Batt. I. Gds October 1917–March 1918; Acting Brigadier-General 4 Gds Brigade 23–30 March 1918; commanded 2 Batt. I. Gds April–October 1918. Subsequently Field-Marshal 1944; Supreme Allied Commander, Mediterranean theatre; Minister of Defence 1952–54 and 1st Earl Alexander of Tunis, KG, PC, GCB, OM, GCMG, CSI, DSO, MC.   115

ARDEE, Reginald Le Normand Brabazon, Lord   1869–1949
Entered Army 1889; Commissioned G. Gds; served S. Africa 1900–2; Major 1906; Lieutenant-Colonel 1912; Lieutenant-Colonel 1 Batt. I. Gds 18 September–31 October 1914; employed under Ministry of Munitions 1916–17; Colonel I. Gds Regimental District February 1917–January 1918; Brigadier-General (temp.) 4 Gds Brigade BEF February–April 1918; succeeded father as 13th Earl of Meath 1929. CB, CBE.
97

BAILEY, Hon. Wilfred Russell   1891–1948
Entered Army 1911; commissioned G. Gds; Lieutenant 2 Batt. G. Gds BEF August 1914; Captain & Adjutant 2 Batt. G. Gds BEF 1915–16; Acting Major 1916; commanded 1 Batt. G. Gds October 1918; Acting Lieutenant-Colonel October 1918; retired 1924; rejoined 1939; commanded Training Batt. W. Gds; Colonel GHQ 1942; succeeded father as 3rd Baron Glanusk 1928. DSO   95, 130, 139, 151, 152, 162

BAKER-CARR, Christopher D'Arcy Bloomfield Saltern.   1878–1949
Entered Army 1898; commissioned Rifle Brigade; left Army 1906; volunteered for active service August 1914; attached GHQ BEF France 1914–15; Brigadier-General (temp.) 1 Tank Corps Brigade 1917–18. CMG, DSO.   157

BANBURY, Charles William ('Cakes')   1877–1914
Entered Army 1899; commissioned C. Gds; ADC to GOC 1 Division 1909–10; ADC to GOC-in-C Eastern Command 1912; Captain, staff

appointment August 1914; Captain 3 Batt. C. Gds August 1914; d.o.w.
September 1914. 56, 89, 92

BATTENBURG, H.H. Prince Alexander ('Drino') 1886–1960
Entered Army 1911 after service as a naval cadet and midshipman;
commissioned G. Gds; Lieutenant 2 Batt. G. Gds BEF August 1914;
invalided home November 1914; subsequently promoted Captain; retired 1919; assumed surname Mountbatten and created Marquess of
Carisbrooke 1917. GCVO. 27, 82, 90, 92, 93

BEAUMONT-NESBITT, Frederick George 1893–?
Entered Army 1912; commissioned G. Gds; second Lieutenant 2 Batt.
G. Gds BEF October 1914; Captain July 1915; ADC November 1915–
August 1916; GSO 3 May 1917–January 1918; Brigade Major January
1918–September 1918. MC. 95, 162

BINGHAM, Hon. Sir Cecil Edward ('Cis') 1861–1934
Entered Army 1882; commissioned 3rd Hussars; Lieutenant 2nd Life
Gds 1886; Captain 1st Life Gds 1892; S. Africa 1899–1902; Brigadier-
General (temp.) 2 Cavalry Brigade 1910–11; commanded 4 Cavalry
Brigade 1911–14; Brigade Commander BEF 1914–15; Major-General
1915. GCVO, KCMG, CB. 28, 29

BUCHANAN, John Nevile 1887–1969
Lawyer; G. Gds Special Reserve; Second Lieutenant 2 Batt. G. Gds BEF
December 1914–November 1918. DSO, MC. 158, 162

BULFIN, Edward Stanislaus 1862–1939
Entered Army 1884; commissioned Yorkshire Regiment; Brigadier-
General 2 Infantry Brigade 1913–14; Major-General 28 Division BEF
1914–15; 60 Division 1915–17; Lieutenant-General XXI Corps Palestine 1917–19; promoted Major-General and Lieutenant-General for
distinguished service in the field; General 1925; retired 1925. KCB, CVO.
125, 146

BURN, Hugh Henry 1895–1916
Entered Army 1914; commissioned C. Gds; Second Lieutenant C. Gds
1914–16; d.o.w. September 1916. MC. 162

BURTON, Stephen John 1882–1917
Entered Army 1902; commissioned C. Gds; employed with Egyptian
Army 1908–12; Captain 3 Batt. C. Gds BEF August 1914; Major;
k.i.a. July 1917. 54

CAPPER, Thompson ('Tommy') 1863–1915
Entered Army 1882; commissioned East Lancashire Regiment; Commandant Staff College, Quetta, India 1906–11; Brigadier-General 13
Infantry Brigade 1911–14; Major-General 7 Division BEF 1914–15;
k.i.a. September 1915; KCMG, CB, DSO. 125

CAVAN, Frederic Rudolph Lambart, 10th Earl of 1865–1946
Entered Army 1885; commissioned G. Gds; served S. Africa 1901; re-
tired Colonel Reserve of Officers 1913; Brigadier-General (temp.) 4 Gds
Brigade BEF September 1914–September 1915; Major-General Gds
Division BEF 1915–17; Lieutenant-General attached 10th Italian Army
Piave front 1918; commanded XIV Corps Italy 1918; C-in-C Aldershot
1920–22; General 1921; CIGS 1922–26; Field-Marshal 1932. GCB,
GCMG, GCVO, GBE. 14, 21, 95, 101, 102, 105,
122, 125, 126, 129–30, 144, 146, 148, 154, 161, 171

CAVENDISH, Ralph Henry Voltelin 1887–1968
Entered Army 1906; commissioned G. Gds; ADC to Governor of Madras

1912–14; Captain 2 Batt. G. Gds August 1914; Acting Major and Commanding Officer 3 Batt. G. Gds BEF. MVO.

10, 108, 142, 143, 162

CECIL, George Edward 1895–1914
Entered Army 1913; commissioned G. Gds; Lieutenant 2 Batt. G. Gds August 1914; k.i.a. September 1914. 5, 54, 59, 60, 61–8

CECIL, Hon. William Amherst 1886–1914
Entered Army 1906; commissioned G. Gds; Lieutenant (Machine Gun Officer) 2 Batt. G. Gds BEF August 1914; k.i.a. September 1914.

45, 92, 93

CHAMPION DE CRESPIGNY, Sir Claude Raul ('Crawly') 5th Baronet
1878–1941
Entered Army 1900; commissioned G. Gds; Captain 1908; Staff Captain 4 Infantry Brigade BEF October 1914; Captain and Major 2 Batt. G. Gds BEF 1915–16; Lieutenant-Colonel and OC 1 Batt. G. Gds BEF 1916–17; Brigadier-General (temp.) 1 Gds Brigade BEF 1917–18; succeeded his father as 5th Baronet 1935. CB, CMG, DSO.

108, 162

CHARRINGTON, Harold Vincent Spencer ('Rollie') 1886–1965
Entered Army 1905; commissioned 12th Lancers; Egyptian Army 1913–14; Lieutenant 12th Lancers BEF August 1914; Captain September 1914; Acting Major 1916; commanded 12th Lancers 1927–31; Brigadier 6th Midland Cavalry Brigade 1931; commanded 1 Armoured Brigade Middle East and Greece 1940–41; retired 1943. 168

CHETWODE, Philip Walhouse, 1st Baron Chetwode 1869–1950
Entered Army 1889; commissioned 19th Hussars; served Burma 1892–93; served S. Africa 1899–1902; Colonel 1912; Brigadier-General (temp.) 5 Cavalry Brigade BEF August 1914–May 1915; commanded 2 Cavalry Division BEF 1915–16; Major-General 1916; commanded Desert Corps Egypt 1916–17; commanded XX Corps Palestine 1917–18; distinguished military career; Field-Marshal 1933. GCB, OM, GCSI, KCMG, DSO, DCL. 45, 53

CHOLMELEY, Sir Montague Aubrey Rowley, 4th Baronet 1876–1914
Lieutenant 4 Batt. Lincolnshire Regiment; Captain (Reserve of Officers) G. Gds; Captain 2 Batt. G. Gds BEF August–December 1914; k.i.a. December 1914. 158, 159, 160, 162, 166, 167, 169–70

CHURCHILL, Edward George Spencer ('Mis') 1876–1964
Entered Army 1899; served Boer War; Captain G. Gds BEF December 1914. MC. 163, 167, 170

CLIVE, George Sidney 1874–1959
Entered Army 1893; commissioned G. Gds; Major 1909; GSO 2 London District 1914; Liaison Officer French GQG 1914–18; military Governor of Cologne; British Military Representative League of Nations 1920–22; Major-General 1924; Military Secretary to S. of S. for War 1930–34; Lieutenant-General; retired 1934. GCVO, KCB, CMG, DSO. 161

CLIVE, Percy Archer 1873–1918
Entered Army 1891; commissioned G. Gds; Captain 1899; South African War 1899–1901; left army; MP 1900–6; rejoined G. Gds August 1914; Captain 2 Batt. G. Gds BEF 1914; commanded 7 Batt. E. Yorks. Regiment May 1916–April 1918; k.i.a. April 1918. 158, 160

COLBY, Lawrence Robert Vaughan ('Beef') 1880–1914
Entered Army 1899; commissioned G. Gds; Captain 1905; Major 1 Batt. G. Gds BEF August–October 1914; k.i.a. October 1914. 128

COLSTON, Hon. Edward Murray   1880–1944
Entered Army 1900; commissioned G. Gds; Captain 2 Batt. G. Gds BEF August 1914–September 1914; Major March 1915; GSO 2 May–July 1916; Brigadier-General (temp.) Infantry Brigade EEF; Colonel 1924; retired 1932. Succeeded his father as 2nd Baron Roundway 1925. CMG, DSO, MVO.   10, 14, 30, 31, 42, 52, 100

CONGLETON, Henry Pugh Fortescue Parnell, 5th Baron   1890–1914
Entered Army 1911; commissioned G. Gds; Lieutenant 2 Batt. G. Gds BEF August 1914; k.i.a. November 1914.
                                        95, 130, 131, 134, 148, 149

CONWAY-GORDON, Gwynedd   1868–1936
Entered Army 1888; commissioned 1 Dragoon Gds; Lieutenant Army Service Corps 1892; served S. Africa 1900–1; Lieutenant-Colonel 1911; Assistant Director of Supplies and Transport, Scottish Command 1911–14; AA & QMG 2 Division BEF August 1914; Colonel 1916; Deputy Director of Supplies and Transport 1916. CBE.   58

CORKRAN, Charles Edward   1872–1939
Entered Army 1893; commissioned G. Gds; Major 1907; Brigade Major 1 Brigade BEF August–November 1914; GSO 2 1915; Brigadier-General (temp.) 1915–17; Commanded G. Gds 1919; Commandant Royal Military College 1923–27; GOC London District 1928–32. KCVO, CB, CMG.   136, 150, 151, 152

CORRY, Noel Armar Lowry ('Porky')   1867–1935
Entered Army 1887; commissioned G. Gds; Colonel 1914; commanded 2 Batt. G. Gds August 1914–September 1914; temporary command of 4 Brigade BEF September 1914; relieved of command of 2 Batt. G. Gds 9 September 1914 and sent home; commanding officer 3 Batt. G. Gds BEF September 1915–January 1916; hon. Brigadier-General 1920. DSO.
                14, 25, 30, 34, 35, 36, 42, 44, 51, 53, 54, 56,
                                        59, 60, 63, 71, 74, 75, 128

CRAIGIE, John Churchill   1890–?
Second Lieutenant G. Gds Special Reserve 1914; 2 Batt. G. Gds December 1914; Captain 3 Batt. G. Gds BEF March 1917–November 1918. MC.
                                        163

CRAWLEY, Eustace   1868–1914
Entered Army 1889; commissioned 12th Lancers; ADC to Lieutenant-General Ireland 1894–95; served S. Africa 1900–2; employed with W. Africa Frontier Force 1902–4; Major 1905; DAAG India 1909–13; Major 12th Lancers BEF August 1914; k.i.a. November 1914.   59

CRICHTON, Hon. Hubert Francis   1874–1914
Entered Army 1896; commissioned G. Gds; Captain I. Gds 1900; served in Egypt 1898; served S. Africa 1900–2; ADC to GOC I Army Corps Aldershot 1902–5; Major 1 Batt. I. Gds BEF August 1914; k.i.a. September 1914.   60, 66

CUNLIFFE, see Pickersgill-Cunliffe.

CUNLIFFE-OWEN, Charles   1863–1932
Entered Army 1883; commissioned Royal Artillery; Lieutenant-Colonel 1909; commanded 26 Brigade RFA BEF 1914; 2 Infantry Brigade November 1914; Brigadier-General RA ANZAC Corps 1915; Gallipoli; Brigadier-General RA Dardanelles Army 1915–16; Brigadier-General RA BEF France 1916–18; retired 1919.   139, 153

CUNNINGHAME, Alfred Keith Smith   1891–1916

Commissioned G. Gds from Special Reserve 1913; Second Lieutenant 2 Batt. G. Gds BEF August 1914; Captain May 1916; k.i.a. September 1916. 31, 100, 143, 144, 162, 168

DARELL, William Harry Verelst 1878–1954
Entered Army 1897; commissioned C. Gds; Captain 1903; Major 1913; DAAG Southampton 1914; DAQMG 7 Division BEF 1914; AA & QMG 3 Division 1915; AA & QMG Gds Division 1915–1916; DAA & QMG IV Corps 1916; Lieutenant-Colonel 1 Batt. C. Gds 1919; Deputy Director of Mobilisation and Recruiting War Office 1920; AAG War Office 1921; commanded I. Gds 1924–28; retired 1929. CB, CMG, DSO.
28

DAVIES, Henry Rodolph 1865–1950
Entered Army 1884; commissioned Oxfordshire Light Infantry; Lieutenant-Colonel 52 Light Infantry 1911–15; Brigadier-General (temp.) 3 Infantry Brigade 1915–16; Major-General (temp.) 1917; retired 1923. CB. 138, 148, 152

DAWNAY, Hon. Hugh 1875–1914
Entered Army 1895; commissioned 2 Life Gds; served S. Africa 1900–2; Major 2 Life Gds BEF August 1914; k.i.a. November 1914. DSO.
131

DAWSON, Richard Long 1878–1914
Entered Army 1898; commissioned C. Gds; served S. Africa 1899–1900; Captain 1907; resigned from Army; Captain Reserve of Officers August 1914; Captain C. Gds August–November 1914; k.i.a. November 1914.
155

DE TRAFFORD, Sir Humphrey Edmund, 4th Baronet 1891–1972
Entered Army 1911; commissioned C. Gds; Second Lieutenant 2 Batt. C. Gds BEF August 1914; Captain 2 Batt. C. Gds October 1915; Staff Captain 1917–19; retired 1925. MC. 162

DES VOEUX, Frederick William 1889–1914
Entered Army 1910; commissioned G. Gds; Lieutenant 2 Batt. G. Gds BEF August 1914; k.i.a. September 1914. 27, 89, 93

DOWLING, Charles Milne Cholmeley 1891–?
Entered Army 1911; commissioned G. Gds; Lieutenant 2 Batt. G. Gds August–November 1914; Captain 3 Batt. G. Gds. 117, 131, 141

DUFF, Sir Robert George Vivian, 2nd Baronet 1876–1914
Lieutenant, Reserve of Officers 2 Life Gds BEF August 1914; k.i.a. October 1914. 112

EDWARDS, Guy Janion ('George') 1881–1962
Entered Army 1904; commissioned C. Gds; Lieutenant and Adjutant 2 Batt. C. Gds 1910–13; Captain 1 Batt. C. Gds August 1914; commanded 1 Batt. C. Gds 7–21 November 1914; Adjutant 4 Pioneer Batt. C. Gds 1917–19; Major 1919; Brigade-Major, Brigade of Guards 1919–20; Lieutenant-Colonel 2 Batt. C. Gds 1922–26; Colonel 1926; AAG War Office 1927–30; retired 1930; re-employed as OC C. Gds Regiment and Regimental District September 1939–May 1941. DSO, MC. 141

EYRE, J. B. Dates unknown
Second-Lieutenant G. Gds Special Reserve 1914; 2 Batt. G. Gds BEF December 1914; wounded December 1914; Lieutenant Reserve Batt. G. Gds 1915–18. 170

FEILDING, Geoffrey Percy Thynne 1866–1932
Entered Army 1888; commissioned C. Gds; served S. Africa 1899–1902; Lieutenant-Colonel 1912; commanded 3 Batt. C. Gds BEF August–

September 1914; GOC 4 Gds Brigade 5–17 September 1914; commanded
3 Batt. C. Gds 18 September 1914–March 1915; Brigadier-General
(temp.) 149 Brigade 1915; commanded 4 Gds Brigade June–August
1915; commanded 1 Gds Brigade 1915–16; Major-General (temp.) Gds
Division BEF 1916–18; GOC London District 1918–20; retired 1927.
KCB, KCVO, CMG, DSO.   42, 60, 70, 71–2, 78, 90, 112, 162

FITZCLARENCE, Charles   1865–1914
  Entered Army 1886; commissioned Royal Fusiliers; transferred I. Gds
  1900; served S. African War 1899–1900; twice wounded, awarded VC;
  Lieutenant-Colonel I. Gds 1914; Brigadier-General (temp.) 1 Gds Brigade
  1914; k.i.a. Polygon Wood December 1914. VC.
                                                136, 137–8, 150, 151, 152

FLEMING, Rev. Herbert James   1873–?
  Entered Army 1902; Major 1913; RMA Woolwich 1914; attached BEF
  August 1914.   28, 102

FOLLETT, Gilbert Burrell Spencer ('Gillie')   1878–1918
  Entered Army 1899; commissioned C. Gds; served in S. Africa 1899–
  1900; Captain 2 Batt. C. Gds August 1914; Lieutenant-Colonel 2 Batt.
  C. Gds BEF March–July 1916; commanded 1 Batt. C. Gds BEF September–November 1916; commanded 2 Batt. C. Gds BEF November 1916
  and March 1917; Brigadier-General (temp.) 2 Gds Brigade BEF March–
  April 1918; commanded 3 Gds Brigade BEF April–September 1918;
  k.i.a. September 1918. MVO, DSO.   113

FOSTER, Arthur William   1884–?
  Entered Army 1907; commissioned RHG; Captain 1911; Adjutant
  RHG October 1914–May 1915; GSO 3 War Office May 1917–April
  1918; Major 1918; GSO 2 War Office April–November 1918. MC.
                                                                  121

FOULKES, Charles Howard   1875–1969
  Entered Army 1894; commissioned Royal Engineers; Major 1914;
  commanded Sapper Field Company BEF 1914; GSO 1 1915–16;
  Brigadier-General (temp.) 1917; Director of Gas Services 1917. CMG,
  DSO.   134

GATHORNE-HARDY, Hon. John Francis   1874–1949
  Entered Army 1894; commissioned G. Gds; Lieutenant-Colonel 1913;
  GSO 2 War Office 1913–14; GSO 2 II Corps BEF 1914–15; GSO 1 7
  Division BEF 1915–16; Brigadier-General General Staff XIV Corps 1916–
  18; Major-General General Staff, British Forces in Italy 1918–19; GOC-
  in-C Aldershot Command 1933–37; retired 1937. GCB, GCVO, CMG,
  DSO.   158

GORDON-IVES, Victor Maynard Gordon   1890–1914
  Entered Army 1910; commissioned C. Gds; Lieutenant 3 Batt. C. Gds
  BEF August 1914; d.o.w. September 1914.   82, 92

GORDON-LENNOX, Lord Bernard Charles   1878–1914
  Entered Army 1898; commissioned G. Gds; S. Africa 1900; China
  1904–6; Major 2 Batt. G. Gds BEF August–November 1914; k.i.a.
  November 1914.   1, 5, 9, 14, 22, 37, 46, 60, 76, 79, 80, 91, 93,
                                94–5, 98, 103, 104, 116–7, 117–8, 123,
                                124–5, 128–9, 133, 134, 135, 140, 149

GOSCHEN, George Gerard   1887–1953
  Honorary Attaché Berlin 1911–14; Second Lieutenant G. Gds Special
  Reserve; 2 Batt. G. Gds BEF December 1914; wounded and taken
  prisoner December 1914.   167, 170

Entered Army 1906; commissioned C. Gds; Lieutenant 3 Batt. C. Gds BEF August 1914; prisoner of war August 1914; Captain 1915; retired 1919.   45

MCDOUGALL, Iain ('Lunga') 1887–1914
Entered Army 1906; commissioned G. Gds; ADC to Governor and C-in-C New Zealand 1911–13; Lieutenant and Adjutant 2 Batt. G. Gds BEF August 1914; k.i.a. September 1914.   14, 59

MACEWEN, Douglas Lilburn 1867–1941
Entered Army 1889; commissioned Cameron Highlanders; Lieutenant-Colonel 1912; GSO 1 War Office (temp.) August–September 1914; Lieutenant-Colonel 1 Batt. Cameron Highlanders BEF September 1914; Temporary Commander 1 Gds Brigade 11 November 1914; Brigadier-General (temp.) 1916–18. CB, CMG.   138, 152

MACGREGOR, Philip Arthur 1877–1934
Entered Army 1897; commissioned C. Gds; served S. Africa 1899–1900; Major 2 Batt. C. Gds August 1914; Lieutenant-Colonel (temp.) 2 Batt. C. Gds BEF May 1915–March 1916; Commandant Scottish School of Infantry April 1916–February 1917; Commandant Officer Cadet School, Bedford February–July 1917; Commandant Officer Cadet School August–October 1917; commanded 87 Training Batt. 1917–19; retired 1919. DSO.   159, 162

MACKENZIE, Allan Keith ('Sloper') 1887–1916
Entered Army 1910; commissioned G. Gds; Lieutenant 2 Batt. G. Gds BEF August 1914; wounded September 1914; Captain 3 Batt. G. Gds BEF April 1916; d.o.w. September 1916.   72, 89

MAKGILL-CRICHTON-MAITLAND, M. E. 1882–1972
Entered Army 1901; commissioned G. Gds; served S. Africa 1901–2; Captain 2 Batt. G. Gds BEF October 1914; Major 1915; Lieutenant-Colonel (temp.) 1 Batt. G. Gds July 1916; Lieutenant-Colonel 1923; retired 1928; recalled to active service as Colonel G. Gds 1939. CVO, DSO.   108, 114

MANNERS, Hon. John Nevile 1892–1914
Entered Army 1912; commissioned G. Gds; Lieutenant 2 Batt. G. Gds BEF August 1914; k.i.a. September 1914.   54, 59, 60, 63

MATHESON, Sir Torquhil George, 5th Baronet of Lochalsh 1871–1963
Entered Army 1894; commissioned C. Gds; served in S. Africa 1899–1902; Captain and Regimental Adjutant 1903–5; Major 3 Batt. C. Gds BEF August–September 1914; commanded 3 Batt. C. Gds 1914–15; Brigadier-General (temp.) 46 Infantry Brigade BEF 1915–17; Major-General 20 Division BEF March–September 1917; commanded 4 Division BEF September 1917–September 1918; commanded Gds Division BEF September 1918–March 1919; GOC Waziristan Field Force 1920–24; commanded 54 Territorial Division 1927–30; GOC-in-C Western Command, India 1931–35; General 1934; retired 1935; MP 1938–45; raised and commanded D Company Ross-shire Batt. Home Guard 1940–42. KCB, CMG.   45, 78, 84, 85, 86, 87, 159

MILLER, Frederic William Joseph Macdonald ('Donald') 1891–1914
Entered Army 1912; commissioned G. Gds; Second Lieutenant G. Gds BEF August 1914; k.i.a. October 1914.   27, 95, 98, 114

MONCK, Hon. Charles Henry Stanley 1876–1914
Entered Army 1897; commissioned C. Gds; served in S. Africa 1899–1902; Captain 3 Batt. C. Gds BEF August 1914; k.i.a. October 1914.   40, 112

1 Batt. G. Gds 1927–29; AAG War Office 1929; retired 1933; Assistant Military Secretary GHQ BEF 1939; Sussex Home Guard Commander 1940–44. CBE, MC.

5, 10, 60, 83, 90, 91, 100, 101–2, 103, 123, 130, 132, 133–4, 136–7, 139, 140, 151

PITMAN, Thomas Tait 1868–1941

Entered Army 1889; commissioned 11th Hussars; served N.W. Frontier, India, and S. Africa 1897–1902; Lieutenant-Colonel 11th Hussars BEF 1914–15; Brigadier-General (temp.) 4 Cavalry Brigade BEF 1915–18; commanded 2 Cavalry Division 1918–19; retired 1930. CB, CMG.   98

PONSONBY, John 1866–1952

Entered Army 1887; commissioned C. Gds; served in Uganda, Matabeleland, S. Africa 1888–1900; Lieutenant-Colonel 1 Batt. C. Gds October 1913–September 1914, November 1914–January 1915 and March 1915–August 1915; Brigadier-General 2 Gds Brigade BEF August 1915 to November 1916; Brigade-Commander Home Forces November 1916–March 1917; Major-General 40 Division BEF August 1917–June 1918; Commanded 5 Division June 1918–April 1919; GOC Madras, India 1922–26; retired 1927. KCB, CMG, DSO.   31, 97

POWELL, Evelyn George Harcourt 1883–1961

Entered Army 1901; commissioned G. Gds; Captain 1908; 2 Batt. G. Gds BEF August 1914–November 1914; wounded November 1914; Captain 3 Batt. G. Gds September 1915; Acting Lieutenant-Colonel London Regiment September 1916–September 1918; retired 1927; MP 1931–35.

24, 27, 91, 123, 134, 148, 149

RAMSAY, Archibald Henry Maule 1894–1955

Entered Army 1913; commissioned C. Gds; Second Lieutenant 2 Batt. C. Gds BEF August 1914; Captain 2 Batt. C. Gds BEF 1915; severely wounded 1916; Staff duties War Office 1917–18; British War Mission in Paris 1918; retired invalided 1922; MP 1931–45; detained at Brixton Prison under Regulation 18B 1940–44.   162

RASCH, Sir Frederick Carne, 2nd Baronet 1880–1963

Entered Army 1901; commissioned Essex Regiment; Lieutenant 6th Dragoon Gds 1903; ADC August–September 1914; Major February 1915.   29

RIDLEY, Edward Davenport 1883–1934

Entered Army 1905; commissioned G. Gds; Captain 2 Batt. G. Gds BEF September 1914–March 1915; Captain 4 Batt. G. Gds BEF September 1915; Captain 3 Batt. G. Gds 1917; Second-in-Command Household Brigade Officer Cadet Batt. Home Forces 1918; Chief Instructor, Small Arms School 1925. MC.

10, 60, 91, 99, 100, 114, 115, 134, 135, 138, 152, 156, 157, 161, 162

ROSE, Ivor Sainte Croix 1881–1962

Entered Army 1900; commissioned King's Royal Rifle Corps; resigned 1907; Lieutenant Special Reserve G. Gds 1908; Lieutenant 2 Batt. G. Gds BEF October 1914; Captain November 1914; employed by Ministry of Munitions 1917; retired 1919. OBE.   108, 123, 124, 146

ROWLEY, George Richard Francis 1889–?

Entered Army 1910; commissioned C. Gds; Lieutenant 3 Batt. C. Gds August 1914; transferred to RHG November 1914.   45

RUGGLES-BRISE, Harold Goodeve 1864–1927

Entered Army 1885; commissioned G. Gds; Colonel 1911; Brigadier-General (temp.) 20 Infantry Brigade BEF August–November 1914; Briga-

dier-General General Staff 1915; Major-General 1917; Military Secretary
GHQ France 1918. KCMG, CB, MVO.   128

RUMBOLD, H. C. L.   Dates unknown
   Second Lieutenant Special Reserve G. Gds 1914; 2 Batt. G. Gds BEF
   December 1914–February 1915; Lieutenant Reserve Batt. G. Gds
   1915–18.   163

RUSSELL, Hon. Alexander Victor Frederick   1874–1966
   Entered Army 1894; commissioned G. Gds; Major 1910; Military
   Attaché, Berlin 1910–14; GSO 2 II Corps BEF France 1914–15; Military
   Attaché, Berne 1918–20; Special Military Mission to Chile 1921; retired
   1926. CMG, MVO.   158, 160

MONTAGU-DOUGLAS-SCOTT, Lord Francis George   1879–1952
   Entered Army 1899; commissioned G. Gds; served S. Africa 1900–2;
   ADC to Viceroy of India 1905–10; Captain 1908; attached 1 Batt. I.
   Gds BEF September 1914; Major November 1914; Lieutenant-Colonel
   (temp.) Service Batt. Royal Fusiliers September–November 1915; retired
   1920; rejoined Army 1941; Assistant Military Secretary to GOC East
   African Forces 1941; late Member of Executive and Legislative Council,
   Kenya. KCMG, DSO.   97

SCOTT-KERR, Robert   1859–1942
   Entered Army 1879; commissioned G. Gds 1879; Major 1896; S. Africa
   1900–2; Brigadier-General (temp.) 4 Gds Brigade BEF August 1914;
   wounded September 1914; Brigade Commander 1915–18. CB, DSO,
   MVO.   14, 18, 42, 47, 54

SKIDMORE, John Henry   1872–?
   Quartermaster and Hon. Lieutenant 2 Batt. G. Gds; retired August
   1915.   168

SMITH, Arthur Francis   b. 1890
   Entered Army 1910; commissioned C. Gds; Lieutenant 3 Batt. C. Gds
   BEF August 1914; Adjutant 3 Batt. C. Gds September 1914–November
   1915; GSO 3 Gds Division 1915–16; Staff Appointment 1917–18; distinguished career in the Army in peacetime and during World War II
   in the Middle East, India and Pakistan; retired 1948; Lieutenant of
   the Tower of London 1948–51. KCB, KBE, DSO, MC.   84

SMITH, Wilfrid Robert Abel   1870–1915
   Entered Army 1890; commissioned G. Gds; Nile Expedition 1898; S.
   African War 1900–2; Major 1906; Lieutenant-Colonel commanding 2
   Batt. G. Gds September 1914 to May 1915; d.o.w. May 1915. CMG.
             1, 10, 95–6, 100, 100–3, 106, 107, 108, 112, 118, 119, 122,
                123, 126, 127, 129, 130, 132, 134, 135, 136, 139, 140,
                   142, 143–5, 155, 158, 159, 161, 163, 167, 169–70, 172

STEPHEN, Albert Alexander Leslie   1879–1914
   Entered Army 1899; commissioned Scots Gds; served S. Africa, Mace-
   donia, Turkey 1900–11; Captain and Adjutant 1 Batt. Scots Gds BEF
   August 1914; d.o.w. September 1914.   50, 97

STEPHEN, Douglas Clinton Leslie ('Tich')   1876–1914
   Entered Army 1900; commissioned G. Gds; Lieutenant and Captain in
   service with Macedonian Gendarmerie 1906–9; Captain 2 Batt. G. Gds
   BEF August 1914; d.o.w. September 1914.   14, 57, 58, 71, 74, 75

STOCKS, Michael George   1892–1914
   Entered Army 1910; commissioned G. Gds; Lieutenant 1913; Lieutenant
   2 Batt. G. Gds BEF August–November 1914; k.i.a. November 1914.
                                                           134, 135, 149

BEF August 1914; Captain 2 Batt. C. Gds BEF 1915; Temporary command 2 Batt. C. Gds 17–26 July 1916; k.i.a. September 1916, MC.
162

VIVIAN, Valentine   1880–1948
Entered Army 1899; commissioned G. Gds; Captain 1913; GSO 3 August–September 1914; Brigade-Major 4 Gds Brigade BEF November 1914–April 1915; GSO 1915–16; Lieutenant-Colonel 1916; Assistant Military Attaché, Paris 1920–22; retired 1922. CMG, DSO, MVO.
164

PRINCE OF WALES, H.R.H. Edward Albert Christian.   1894–1972
Later King Edward VIII and Duke of Windsor. Cadet at Dartmouth 1909; commissioned G. Gds August 1914; Staff Appointment GHQ BEF November 1914; Staff Appointment HQ Gds Division 1915; HQ XIV Corps Italy 1917; ascended throne as King Edward VIII 1936; abdicated 1936.   158, 159, 160, 162, 163, 165, 166

WALKER, Cecil Francis Aleck   1885–?
Entered Army 1908; commissioned G. Gds; Lieutenant 2 Batt. G. Gds BEF August 1914; wounded September 1914; Captain 1915; 3 Batt. G. Gds BEF September 1915–September 1917; Major 4 Batt. G. Gds January 1918–July 1918; commanded 2 Batt. G. Gds October 1918–November 1918. MC.   89

WELBY, Richard William Gregory   1888–1914
Entered Army 1910; commissioned G. Gds; Lieutenant 2 Batt. G. Gds August–September 1914; k.i.a. September 1914.
10, 39, 79–80, 89, 92, 93

WELLESLEY, Lord Richard   1879–1914
Entered Army 1900; commissioned G. Gds; Captain 1908; Captain 1 Batt. G. Gds BEF August–October 1914; k.i.a. October 1914.   128

WESTMACOTT, Claude Berners   1865–1948
Entered Army 1888; commissioned Worcestershire Regiment; Colonel 1914; Acting Brigadier-General 5 Brigade BEF November 1914; Brigade-Commander 1915–18. CBE.   152

WHITBREAD, Robert   1876–?
Entered Army 1900; commissioned C. Gds; Captain 1910; employed with Egyptian Army 1910–14; Captain 3 Batt. C. Gds BEF August 1914; Major September 1915; Staff Duties January 1918–March 1919; retired 1920.   45

WICKHAM, William Joseph   1874–1914
Entered Army 1900; commissioned Scots Gds; Captain 1 Batt. Scots Gds BEF August 1914; k.i.a. September 1914.   50, 97

WILLIAMS, E. G.   ?–1915
Second Lieutenant G. Gds Special Reserve; 2 Batt. G. Gds BEF December 1914–August 1915; accidentally killed Trench Mortar School August 1915.   163

WILSON, Gordon Chesney   1865–1914
Entered Army 1885; commissioned RHG; served S. Africa 1900–2; Colonel RHG 1911; k.i.a. November 1914, MVO   121, 131

WYNDHAM, Percy Lyulph   1887–1914
Entered Army 1909; commissioned C. Gds; ADC to GOC 3 Division 1912–14; Lieutenant 3 Batt. C. Gds BEF August 1914; k.i.a. September 1914.   89